Seeing with New Eyes

Resources for Changing Lives
A series published in cooperation with
THE CHRISTIAN COUNSELING AND EDUCATIONAL FOUNDATION
Glenside, Pennsylvania
Susan Lutz, Series Editor

Available in the series:

SEEING WITH NEW EYES

Counseling and the Human Condition
through the Lens of Scripture

DAVID POWLISON

PUBLISHING
P.O. BOX 817 • PHILLIPSBURG • NEW JERSEY 08865-0817

Scripture quotations are from the NEW AMERICAN STANDARD BIBLE®. ©Copyright The Lockman Foundation 1960, 1962, 1963, 1968, 1971, 1972 1973, 1975, 1977, 1995. Used by permission.

Italics within Scripture quotations indicate emphasis added.

Printed in the United States of America

Library of Congress Cataloging-in-Publication Data

Powlison, David, 1949–
    Seeing with new eyes : counseling and the human condition through the lens of Scripture / David Powlison.
        p. cm.
    Includes bibliographical references and index.
    ISBN-10: 0-87552-608-X (pbk.)
    ISBN-13: 978-0-87552-608-9 (pbk.)
    1. Pastoral counseling. 2. Bible—Psychology. I. Title.

BV4012.2.P59 2003
253.5—dc22

                                                    2003059577

To Bob Kramer,
the man used by God to first open
my eyes to a shining new world

CONTENTS

I pray that the God of our Lord Jesus Christ, the Father of glory,
may give to you a spirit of wisdom and of revelation in the knowl-
edge of Him.
I pray that the eyes of your heart may be enlightened,
so that you will know what is the hope of His calling,
what are the riches of the glory of His inheritance in the saints,
and what is the surpassing greatness of His power toward us who
believe. Ephesians 1:17–19

That's an eye-opening request. "Unveil yourself, God of glory. Wake us up to know you, Savior-King. Enlighten the eyes of our hearts. Drive away the darkness that blinds, chokes, and shrinks us. Make us see."

This is the first of three books I plan to write about "counseling." But it's counseling with an unusual twist. Intentionally helpful conversations—that's all counseling is—look *different* when you look at them from the perspective of seeing God. You see people and their troubles in a different light. These books will talk about problems in living, about conversations that seek to be helpful, about how to think through the things people struggle with, about skillful pursuit of personal and interpersonal objectives. So these books will be about "counseling" kinds of things. But familiar objects will be cast in a *very* different light.

Have you ever had the experience of getting angry, upset, or worried about something—only later to discover some crucial fact you hadn't known? Or have you ever been delighted with something or someone, and later found out you'd been had? Something you had not taken into account explained *everything* in a different way. You had no reason at all to be upset—or happy. When you began to see more fully, everything changed. These books are about taking into account something that changes everything. Let me tell a story to capture this.

One day I noticed a disheveled stranger pacing through our neighborhood. He was chain-smoking, jerking his head to the side, and shouting out into the air, "OK! OK! OK!" He had a wild, disturbed look. After about fifteen minutes of erratically walking up and down the sidewalk, he started to trespass through back yards, continuing to carry on. Convinced that a madman was on the loose, I called 911.

A few minutes later the squad car pulled up. By now the man was standing on the sidewalk right in front of our house, still agitated, still shouting out "OK! OK!" The policeman cranked down his window, leaned out, and asked, "Can I help you, buddy?" (I could hear the conversation through an open window.) The man leapt over to him and effused, "Oh, officer, I'm so glad you're here. I'm visiting this neighborhood, and I've lost my little brown puppy. He's named José. I've been looking all over, calling his name over and over again. He doesn't know the area to find his way back to the house. Could you please keep your eyes out for him?"

The officer paused, and said, "Sure, buddy, I'll look around." He rolled up his window and started to drive off. I could see him slowly shaking his head, as if to say, "Oh brother, who's the madman in *this* neighborhood?!"

I had important facts that concerned me: a disheveled stranger, agitated, chain-smoking, repeatedly shouting a word that rhymed with oh-ay, trespassing. But once I *saw* in a different light, everything changed. Should I have felt threatened—or felt compassion? Should I have called 911—or gone looking for a lost puppy? When you see differently, you interpret differently. You react differently, intend differently, act differently.

GOD IN THE PICTURE

It's similar with those things, activities, persons, and processes that we identify with counseling. When you include God in the picture, it changes the way you think about "problem," "diagnosis," "strategy," "solution," "helpful," "cure," "change," "insight," and "counselor."

When the lights go on, you see God and know that God sees you. Not one of these "counseling" words can stay the same. The world is still populated with the same problems begging for help (in fact, seeing God, you see more problems!), but it's as different as José or OK, reality or fantasy.

My goal in these books is to help us see God in the counseling context. How can we see what he sees, hear what he says, and do what he does? As we grasp this, we will become more thoughtful in understanding people, and more skillful in curing souls. This involves developing the church's model for systematically biblical counseling. A comprehensive model has four components. A *conceptual framework* defines norms, problems, and solutions. A *methodology* engages in skillful, intentional conversation to remedy defined ills. A *social structure* delivers cure and care to people in need of help. An *apologetic* subjects other systems to criticism and defends one's model against competitors. Each of the various counseling models offers a version of these four components. Seen this way, all counseling models— whether secular or religious—are essentially differing systems of "pastoral care and cure."

Concepts

Concepts are the first and defining ingredient in any system of counseling. Every theory defines its version of human nature and the dynamics of human motivation. Every theory defines or assumes an ideal of human functioning by which problems are named and solutions prescribed: right and wrong, value and stigma, true and false, good and bad, sound and defective, healthy and pathological, solution and problem. The various personality theories and psychotherapies differ from each other—and from the Bible—in the ways they explain people and in the solutions they offer.

The Bible's truth competes head-to-head with other models. God speaks a truth that is intended to make sense of us and change us. It is not truth about how to find a job, or how genes transmit eye color, or how to fix a clogged drain. The truth that is in Jesus reveals and changes what we live for. He changes how we live. The Bible's "theory" for personal ministry mediates true Truth, claiming that other conceptual systems give expression to variants on "the lie." Other systems of thought systematically suppress awareness of our dependency on and accountability to God.

The biblical model is more than one more "model," conceptual system, or personality theory among many. Truth mediates a Person, a working Redeemer. To be human is to love a Savior, Father, Master, and Lord. Instead of "psychopathology" and "syndromes," we see "sins" against this Person, and we see sufferings that are "trials" revealing our need for a true Deliverer and refuge. Instead of proposing that some psychodynamic insight, met need, altered self-talk, or behavioral rehabituation will cure us, we receive God's actual mercies as our salvation. Instead of defining change as an intra-psychic, psychosocial, or biological process of "healing" or "growth," we define change as turning to a Person whom we trust, fear, obey, and seek to please. Instead of letting the goal of "health" cue our system to a medical metaphor, we set the goal of being transformed into the likeness of this Person with whom we live in relationship. The Bible's conceptual framework surely addresses "psychological," "behavioral," "emotional," and "interpersonal" phenomena. But Scripture is so radically about persons-vis-à-vis-a-Person that it utterly shatters and wholly reconfigures the culture's stock categories for thinking about personhood. Our system is aligned interpersonally, morally, and covenantally. Relationship with God pervades every feature of psychological and social existence.

METHODS

A counseling model also involves *methods* designed to facilitate a change process; it is counsel*ing*, as well as counsel. Wisdom, in the biblical sense, is practical knowledge; it is truth practiced, spoken, walked out, and applied. Ephesians 4:15 crystallizes two central actions: truth-speaking and loving. Of course, every other counseling methodology contains some analogy to or counterfeit of these. But Paul infuses loving conversation with its true contents and intentions: God-centered, Christ-centered, redemptive, and pastoral.

The wider context in Ephesians teaches and illustrates other ingredients in a comprehensive methodology of face-to-face ministry:

radical dependency on God (1:16–19; 3:14–21); core attitudes of kindness toward others' failings (4:2–3, 32); timeliness and appropriateness that arise from knowing people and their life-situations (4:29); appropriate self-disclosure (Ephesians 1 and 3); grasp of the change process as progressive, practical, and detailed, both inside and out (4:17–6:9); awareness of the other voices and instincts that tug at people (4:14, 17–22; 5:6); ability to communicate with constructive and compelling reasonableness (4:29; 6:19–20); and faithfulness to God's revelation as the definitive word on what is true, good, and transformative (throughout Ephesians!). The entire letter models Paul's approach to both public and private ministry. He knows who he is in Christ, and walks the same path to which he calls others. He loves those with whom he speaks. He knows them, what they face, and where they struggle. He addresses them candidly and constructively. He works them through what change looks like and does, right down to the everyday details. No counseling methods ever dreamed or practiced are superior to such a Live, Love, Know, Speak, and Do—the ingredients of pastoral methodology given us in shorthand for us to develop, make our own, and "improve."

INSTITUTIONS

Third, every counseling model entails a "delivery system," a social structure. Ideas and practices inhabit *institutions*. Concepts and methods comprise the knowledge and tools of professions and social systems. In modern America, the "mental health system" is a vast complex of higher education, hospitals, publishers, third-party insurers, drug companies, licensing boards, and private practice psychotherapists. But the loving truth and truthful love of Ephesians 4:15 come embedded in a different social system: the *ekklēsia* of the people of God.

The most magnificent institutional structure imaginable is a community living up to how Ephesians 4 weds pastoral leadership with every-member mutuality. Both the special gifts from God and the general call to all God's people traffic in the cure of souls, as each part does its part. Christ's change agenda, the transformation of fallen humanity, drives both public and personal ministry. Wisdom incarnates in both proclamatory and interactive communication. God's new society in Christ, come into its own and coming into its own, is *the* institution for counseling ministry.

The institutional structures within which wise counsel should flourish will take many forms, as biblical norms are applied and adapted. Local congregations will variously structure their care and counsel, based on God's allocation of gifts, the configuration of human needs and problems they face, contingencies of congregational and staff size, and demographics. The regional church will equip, organize, and oversee counsel and counseling, and will deliver experienced counsel as a backup to local churches. Para-church institutions will serve particular focused mission purposes: auxiliary preaching and counseling within prison ministries, crisis pregnancy centers, rescue missions, discipleship training programs, counseling ministries, chaplaincies, hospices, schools, church-planting mission agencies, and the like. Whether finding expression in local church, regional church, or para-church, God's new society is called to develop and provide radical alternatives to the current system of autonomous counseling professions licensed by the state, creedally committed to the secular psychologies, and funded on a for-profit, fee-for-service basis. God's wisdom has institutional implications.

APOLOGETICS

The fourth element in every counseling model is *apologetics*. A model gives a standpoint from which to interact with others. We make the case for what we believe is true and good. We subject competing models to systematic questioning. We defend our own model against critics. We develop our model under the stimulus of criticisms by others. We seek to win others. Each of the modern psychologies ministers its own distinctive "word"; each disciples its hearers into its particular ideal "image"; each criticizes other psychologies (and Christianity) for misconstruing the human condition. We also critique them from our standpoint.

Any psychology or psychotherapy that suppresses God cannot help but serve the varied desires and falsehoods congenial to the flesh. Most psychotherapies in their "high" form are morally austere, rather than nakedly self-indulgent. Classic psychotherapies—psychoanalytic, existential, cognitive, and moralistic—make strong demands on their subjects, appealing to the flesh's more refined lusts: pride, self-righteousness, self-trust, the acquisition of inner-circle knowledge. Psychotherapies in their "low" or "pop" forms pander to coarser desires of flesh and ego: cravings for acceptance, love, self-esteem, significance, power, success. But whether highbrow or lowbrow, the secular psychologies construct diagnoses of the human condition that suppress awareness of sin, and they offer cures that evade the necessity of Jesus Christ's redeeming work. Believers, practitioners, and clients of such systems can be won, even while we protect the faithful from their teachings.

This first book, *Seeing with New Eyes*, focuses on the *conceptual*. It unfolds Scripture's view of people and problems. It reinterprets common counseling phenomena through God's eyes, as revealed in Scripture. The second book will focus on the *methodological* and the *institutional* aspects of biblical counseling wisdom. And the third book will focus on the *apologetic* component, understanding our times and critiquing other models, while also attempting to further develop our own model as we listen to the critiques that others offer of us. My hope is that these books will do their part to assist the church in the care and cure of souls, and to encourage God's people, individually and corporately, to lay hold of the promises and calling that are ours in Christ.

Introduction:

The Gaze of God

I believe in Christianity as I believe that the sun has risen, not only because I see it, but because by it I see everything else.[1]

"By it I see everything else." This risen and rising sun—Light of the world, no less!—opens our eyes to see. We come to "see" a man we've never actually laid eyes on. In fact, we not only see him, but we love him, trust him, and delight in him (1 Peter 1:8). Along the way he teaches us to see everything else the world contains. We aren't talking about retinal images processed in the brain. This seeing, this gaze, means to wake us up from our fantasies, fictions, and nightmares to see things as they are in fact. God has the real take on things. And God teaches us his gaze.

We learn (slowly! in fits and starts!) to see how God sees. God, self, others, problems, circumstances, all now appear in the true mirror. Learning the gaze of God, we come to weigh life aright. We discern good and evil, fair and foul, lovely and degraded. Our Father enlightens the eyes of our hearts. We become able to pry apart true from false, instead of living in a murk of half-truths and flat lies.

All sorts of things start to look and to mean different when the lights come on: friendship, artistic abilities, Orion's belt brilliant on a winter night, bone cancer, a frustrating job search, money in the bank, the waste of our wraths and sorrows, forgiveness sought and granted, old hurts and fresh affronts, kind hearts and opportunities not to be missed, anorexia-bulimia, quiet desperation and joy inexpressibly full of glory, Day-Timer or Palm Pilot, the sounds and smells of tonight's dinner sizzling in the pan. The sins and sufferings of the human condition (the "stuff" of counseling) look different.

Consider this example. Both Caiaphas and Peter "saw" the same

9

retinal images of Jesus. (To widen the metaphor, we might add that both "heard" the same tympanic vibrations when Jesus spoke.) But the priest saw a threat and heard a charlatan. The friend saw the maker, judge, and savior of the world, and he heard words of eternal life. When you wake up to see the sun, and hear the waterfall, and smell the coffee, and touch the garment's hem, and taste that the Lord is good, it must change how you see everything.

To think Christianly is "to think God's thoughts after him." Of course, our thinking is both finite and distorted. We never see it all; and we often misconstrue what we do see. We see in a glass darkly, skewed reflections in a battered bronze mirror—but we do see. God, who sees all things directly in full daylight, enlightens the eyes of our hearts. We see surfaces, catching glimpses of interiors; God sees to the inky or radiant depth of every heart, all the way down to fundamental hate or fundamental love. Our glasses are sometimes rosy, sometimes jaundiced, sometimes bluesy, sometimes mirrored on the inside of the lens (so that all we can see are the turbulent contents of our own interiors). The madness in our hearts generates warped spectra. But God sees all things in bright, clear light—and this God is the straightener of crooked thoughts. He makes madmen sane.

Lest this sound overly cognitive, we also learn "to intend God's intentions after him." Christianity is both a way of seeing and a way of proceeding. Christ enters and engages the world he sees. He acts and reacts. The "mind of Christ" is no mental list of theoretical doctrines. His gaze brings with it ways of experiencing, patterns of appropriate reaction, and a game plan for engaging what he sees. So, we learn to pursue God's pursuits after him, to act God's acts, feel God's feelings, love God's loves, hate God's hates, desire God's desires. When the Word became flesh, Jesus lived all God's communicable attributes on the human scale. No, we will never be all-knowing, or all-powerful, or all-present. But yes, we will be wise and loving, true and joyous. We will weep with those who weep. We will lay down our lives for our friends, bear sufferings, love enemies, and say with all our heart, "Thank you."

A Look at Counseling

Does God have a take on counseling? Does his gaze have anything to say about the myriad issues counseling deals with? Has he communicated the way he thinks? Of course, yes, amen. This book aspires to listen well, to look closely, to think hard (however haltingly) within the patterns of God's gaze.

Seeing with New Eyes presents a collection of essays written over a period of almost twenty years. Most of them originally appeared in the *Journal of Biblical Counseling* between 1985 and 2003.[2] They have been edited to eliminate redundancies or irrelevancies, and to enhance the coherence of the whole. These articles are of many sorts: Bible exposition, topical essay, editorial, sermon. You will find a number of interlocking themes appearing again and again. Everywhere evident is God's gracious self-revelation in Jesus Christ and Scripture. The real needs and problems of real people—our sins and miseries, our need for the Father of mercies—are always in view. Our current social and cultural context—the modern psychologies and psychotherapies, these alternative theologies and alternative cures of soul—are continually engaged.

One evening many years ago, my wife Nan and I got into one of those memorable "What is your life about, really?" conversations. We each asked, "What should the epitaph be on your gravestone?" I knew instantly.

I had been a most unlikely candidate for Christian faith. (I suppose that made me an ideal candidate!) I was taken with the typical passions of the '60s and '70s: existentialism, Hindu mysticism, psychodynamic psychologies, literature, aesthetic experiences, personal pleasures, radical politics, finding Truth by an inward-looking journey, calling the shots about the meaning of life, changing the world, hating hypocrisy. Of course, I hated Christianity. Becoming a believer was not at the bottom of the possible options list; it was at the top of the "No way!" list.

But God arrested me with the love of Christ. My epitaph was obvious: "The God who said, 'Let light shine out of darkness,' has shone into our hearts to give the light of the knowledge of the glory of God in the face of Christ" (2 Cor. 4:6). He turned on the Light of the world in a benighted heart.

This book is unabashedly personal. It is about things that delight me. It is divided into two sections. First comes Scripture: God's voice speaks into real life to reveal the gaze and intentions of the Christ who pursues us. We will seek to let the light of Christ shine. The first section seeks to embrace, probe, and unravel *Scripture*. Second comes understanding people amid their real life struggles: the pursuit of wise truth. We will seek to interpret (and reinterpret) real life through God's eyes. The second section seeks to embrace, probe, and unravel the *problems of daily life.*

The vision that animates this book is close kin to some words of Dietrich Bonhoeffer. By all accounts, he was a man of faith, integrity, and courage. Because of Christ, he stood up to the cant, rant, and cruelty of Hitler and the Nazis, and he died for it. While he lived, he closely observed and thoughtfully reflected on what makes for a true and deep understanding of people. It's easy to skim or skip through long quotations (I confess my own tendency), and this is a long quotation. But do pause, and read it carefully. See what Bonhoeffer has seen.

> The most experienced psychologist or observer of human nature knows infinitely less of the human heart than the simplest Christian who lives beneath the Cross of Jesus. The greatest psychological insight, ability, and experience cannot grasp this one thing: what sin is. Worldly wisdom knows what distress and weakness and failure are, but it does not know the godlessness of man. And so it also does not know that man is destroyed only by his sin and can be healed only by forgiveness. Only the Christian knows this. In the presence of a psychiatrist I can only be a sick man; in the presence of a Christian brother I can dare to be a sinner. The psychiatrist must first search my heart and yet he never plumbs its ultimate depth. The Christian brother knows when I come to him: here is a sinner like myself, a godless man who wants to confess and yearns for God's forgiveness. The psychiatrist views me as if there were no God. The brother views me as I am before the judging and merciful God in the Cross of Jesus Christ.[3]

When our gaze awakens to the gaze of God, we have started to see. Seeing clearly, we can love well.

* * *

It is a pleasure to mention debts that express joys, not frets; obligations whose burden is gratitude, not disgruntlement! My difficulty comes in naming all those whom I owe in writing this book. Let me mention only those whose influence I feel most immediately and keenly.

Thank you, Augustine, Luther, Calvin, and Edwards, in whom I witnessed how truth catches fire into the real times, places, and persons that we call "history." Thank you, Cornelius Van Til and John Frame, from whom I learned to look at life with God in view. Thank you, Jay Adams and Jack Miller, in whom I saw how Jesus Christ continually reaches and teaches people through the Word of life. It is a privilege to work within such a tradition of practical theological reflection and action. It is no accident that I acknowledge my debt to pastor-apologist-theologians who make it their life's work to bring the Word to life. Simple faith goes to work through love, creatively redeeming the ever-mutating complexities of the human plight.

Thank you, colleagues at CCEF. Thank you, also, to the many men and women whom I've been privileged to know in various teaching, counseling, and preaching contexts. Every chapter bears the imprint of particular persons and interactions. This book is so deeply rooted in how you live, think, feel, question, act, struggle, change, and serve that I have a hard time knowing who might be responsible for what. The things I've sought to communicate are the product of a community at work.

Thank you, Jayne Clark, Sue Lutz, and Stephen Lutz for your work in conceptualizing this book and bringing it to completion.

Thank you, Nan, Peter, Gwenyth, and Hannah for your particular love to me, and the ways that every chapter bears the imprint of our lives together.

One final acknowledgment: I've always found a particular pleasure in singing those hymns of adoration and trust whose authorship God only knows. We don't know the writers' names for "Fairest Lord Jesus," "How firm a foundation," "All hail the power of Jesus' name," "O, come, all ye faithful," and "When morning gilds the skies." In an age of copyright, self-promotion, and property claims, it's refreshing when no person can get any obvious credit for honoring God. Anonymity provides an object lesson that reaches even to where acknowledgments can be made. We must acknowledge our debt to God alone for what proves enduring in truth, goodness, and beauty. I sincerely hope that strands in this book will prove worthy of contributing to the mind, heart, hands, and voice of the church of Christ. I am sure that certain strands will be found wanting, forgettable, or dubious. But I know with certainty that in whatever proves worthy, credit is due to the God and Father of our Lord Jesus Christ, in whom we exult with an unknown worshiper: "Glory and honor, praise, adoration, now and forevermore be Thine."

Part I Scripture Opens Blind Eyes

I suppose all of us who read Scripture find ourselves particularly gripped by certain parts. Three books most deeply delight me: Ephesians, Psalms, and Luke. Ephesians dwells in a high and holy place, and also with the humble and contrite in heart. Appearing on the same page, even in the same sentence, are God's highest glories and the gritty practicalities of how we are to live. The Psalms capture faith on the wing: alive, human, both blunt and thoughtful, whether needy or glad, caught in the act of communicating with God. Luke portrays the tenderly powerful Jesus, friend of the needy, upsetter of powers-that-be. The articles in this section sample these books.

We engage Ephesians at three different levels. Chapter 1, "Counsel Ephesians," stands back and asks, "How do we begin to understand this astonishing letter?" It's about the dynamic nature of Scripture. In technical terms, it's about *hermeneutics*, how we fairly interpret what God has given us.

Chapter 2 plunges into Ephesians, looking for the answer to one big question: "Who Is God?" In technical terms, it does *systematic theology*, taking one topic at a time and asking questions.

Chapter 3 unpacks in detail the passage on marriage, family, and work relationships. In technical terms, "Godly Roles and Relationships: Ephesians 5:21–6:9" does *exegesis* and *ethics*. It considers specific text in specific context. And because that text is about practical attitudes and behaviors, the chapter organizes and applies the ethical instructions.

Two chapters on the Psalms grapple with two aspects of evil that dog us throughout our lives: sin and suffering. Chapter 4, "Peace, Be

Still: Psalm 131" unfolds Psalm 131. This brief, quiet psalm takes dead aim at the restless pride of our grasping hearts, and works to calm us.

Chapter 5 brings Psalm 10 to people who have been used, mis-used, and abused by others. "Why Me?" captures the anguish of the needy and victimized, as well as the clear thinking and intelligent faith that sufferers need to face up to evils.

Finally, Chapter 6, "Don't Worry," is a sermon on a sermon that Jesus preached (Luke 12:22–34). Jesus pours on reasons not to worry—in the very areas we all too easily fret. Why a sermon in a book on counseling? Public ministry (the scripted, planned talk) inhabits the same truths as interpersonal ministry (improvised conversations).

I COUNSEL EPHESIANS

Newcomers to biblical counseling often experience a sharp-edged uncertainty reflected in questions like the following: "Where should I begin? I am keenly aware of my inability and incompetence, but I want to *help* people. I want to reflect and communicate Jesus Christ! But I know the Bible is vast and deep. The particulars of God's working can be unclear. At the same time, the problems and burdens people bring are perplexing and overwhelming. And I have my own sins and struggles. My understanding and ability are limited and compromised. I'll never begin to help other people grow in wisdom if I need to master the entire Bible *and* solve every variant of the human condition, including my own! Where do I start?" Experienced counselors—unless they've become dry and rote—also feel the sharp edge of similar questions, not about how to begin, but about how to continue on. When you step into the light of God and into the darkness of mankind, you step into unfathomables. Who is sufficient for such things? How will you master what exceeds your comprehension and ability?

You will not go wrong if you plunge into Paul's letter to the Ephesians. Master it. Be mastered by it. Work Ephesians into your thinking, your living, your prayers, and your conversation. The Bible is vast and deep, and human life is diverse and perplexing. But in a pinch you *could* do all counseling from Ephesians. It's all there: the big picture that organizes a myriad details. And Ephesians is not only "counsel," but also "counseling." It talks and walks method as well as content. Paul himself is a changed man. He lives out and teaches wise pastoral strategy. Ephesians aims to teach you how to live. That is a synonym for counseling biblically, for doing face-to-face ministry.

This essay is not a "commentary" on Ephesians. It attempts a different genre, being written for people involved in the face-to-face aspects of ministry, as shepherds of individual souls. Ephesians itself was written by a shepherd of souls. Yes, Paul was an exegete and a theologian, but he was first a man in Christ, and then always a pastor, to *all* of God's people (in other words, a preacher) and to *each one* of God's people (in other words, a counselor). Someone once described Jonathan Edwards this way: "His theology was all application, and his application was all theology." That's the sort of theology and application that Ephesians incarnates. It's also what is attempted here: to write practical theology from Ephesians.

Let me begin by addressing a crucial preliminary question. How do we interpret Ephesians? What is it we are dealing with? I have neither space nor wisdom to give a comprehensive hermeneutic philosophy and exegetical methodology as these bear on counseling. But let me make three points to orient us as we seek to think accurately about this book.

Ephesians Is Practical Theology

Ephesians is not just about practical theology, it *is* practical theology. The distinction between "biblical truth" and "practical application" is artificial. In the Bible, truth arrives in action. Paul teaches by applying biblical truth to himself and others. Ephesians is not a treatise, manual, or commentary. It is a letter. Ephesians *is* application, life lived out before our eyes. The very truth of God comes via the author's life in Christ, and via the contents of his letter. This truth embodies the faith and faithfulness that are its intended results in readers. "Practical theology" and "pastoral practice" speak and act personally: a *message*, from *me*, to *you*.

Ephesians is a letter. It is not about various theological or ethical "topics." It is not a collection of aphorisms or a treatise about God and human beings in general. It is not a story. Paul writes in the first and second person. You hear him talking with you as if he were saying: "God predestined *us* to adoption. *I* give thanks for *you*. *You* were dead in sins. *We* have received an inheritance. Pray for *me*." Ephesians expresses a three-sided encounter between God, Paul, and his hearers.

Practical theology takes place in the first and second persons: you, I, we. It only talks "about" something or someone when that best serves talking "to" someone. In Ephesians, ministry, life, and relationships are *happening*, so Paul's words come packaged as prayer, worship, self-disclosure, and direct address.

Let that grab you: Paul's words come as prayer, worship, self-disclosure, and direct address. This is very different from most books. It is different—sadly—from most sermons, teachings, and counseling sessions. It is different from the distance and presumed objectivity of most scholarly theological reflection, or the clinical mode of most counseling writing. When Paul discusses the glory of God's grace in Christ, he audibly exults in that grace (Eph. 1:1–14). When he teaches about the power of God in Christ and your deepest need, he lets you hear how he prays for you (1:15–23). When he gives his doctrines of sin and salvation, he directly addresses you: "You were dead. We were dead. By grace you have been saved. We are his workmanship" (see Eph. 2:1–22). When Paul expounds theology about how all nations are welcome in Christ, he tells his own story and breaks forth into another prayer: "Hear about the stewardship of God's grace which was given to me for you . . . I bow my knees before the Father that he would grant you . . ." (see Eph. 3:1–21). When Paul goes on to write extensively about ethics, relationships, and the dynamics of change, he speaks directly to you: "*I* beseech *you* to walk worthy of *your* calling . . ." (4:1–6:18). When he signs off, it is with a prayer request, some personal information, and a warm goodbye (6:19–24). Ephesians is practical, relational, and pastoral. Living faith itself happens in the first and second persons. Since faith in Christ is caught as well as taught, Paul pulls out the personal stops to make what he says infectious. Ephesians is practical theology. It is living faith. It is ministry in action. All this is tremendously significant for how you understand and use Ephesians today.

By definition, most thoughtful writing about Ephesians has been scholarly. As such, it runs the danger of misrepresenting Ephesians by failing to come back full circle to practical life and ministry. Good scholarship *can* serve ministry well, if we recognize what the Bible is, and what it intends to accomplish. Failure to recognize this sends scholarship over the cliff into either error or irrelevancy, and renders ministry misguided and impotent. Ephesians, like life and ministry, does not operate in the genres of most theological education. It is practical theology and pastoral practice, and aims to produce the same. It is neither exegesis, nor systematic theology, nor redemptive story.

Ephesians Is Not Exegetical Theology

It is not in the form of a Bible study or commentary. Though Paul quotes, paraphrases, or alludes to many Old Testament passages (and New Testament realities), he steers his background study and understanding toward a different present purpose. The Ten Commandments, Psalms, Isaiah, and Proverbs appear, but they appear in action, in the here and now, spoken and applied in new ways. His message is always old, arising from Bible study, and coherent with other Scripture. But his message is always new, reworked for ministry now. He *uses* older Scripture. He does not just "exposit," because he is not governed by exegetical interests. He constructs a *message*, governed by ministry-to-real-people interests. Likewise, our job is only begun, not done, when we have studied Ephesians in itself. We, too, must be governed by fresh ministry-to-real-people interests, or we will never really understand Ephesians or be able to use it for the well-being of others.

Exegesis probes the original audience, author, and message. We must exegete, but we must do more than exegete. We must move beyond the original.

Ephesians Is Not Systematic Theology

Yes, it is a primary source of answers to questions central to the system of biblical truth. For example, there is no clearer teaching anywhere about God's high sovereignty: his purpose, power, grace, and glory in Christ are so exalted that he who has ears to hear what the Spirit writes to the churches must become a heart-afire Calvinist. Here, too, you find unique insight into union with Jesus Christ, the nature of the church, the process of sanctification, our social relations, and spiritual warfare. But Paul's explicit purposes are not systematic. Rather, he is pastoral and personal. His teaching that we are in Christ comes in the course of worshiping, praying, and exhorting. Why? You also must worship, pray, exhort—and listen to Paul—so that you and others would *know* this Christ dwelling in your hearts through faith, and would *know* the love of this Christ that surpasses knowledge. Systematic theology organizes the whole of the Bible with a philosophical logic, but we must do more than catechize people with our doctrinal categories if we are to minister to them.

Ephesians Is Not Biblical Theology

It is not a recitation of the story of God's redeeming work throughout history. Yes, the Story is all here: God's eternal purposes to be carried out in Christ; predestining love; creation by the Maker of all things; the fall into all-absorbing sin and just wrath; deliverance through the Beloved's blood; the raising up of Christ and of us in Christ; his coronation upon the throne of all power; the present indwelling of the Holy Spirit in both church and heart; the expansion of the promise to include all peoples in promises originally for Jews only; the anticipated day of his return when the kingdom will be revealed in all its glory, perfection, and wrath. But the Story is scattered through Ephesians in snippets. While the pieces are capable of reassembly into a redemptive historical narrative, Paul is up to other purposes. Yes, every story is embedded in this Story. Everyone lives tucked between eternal purpose and eternal destiny, a story within the Story. But, note well, Paul did not write a narrative. He did not write a piece of biblical theology. He does not content himself with storytelling when he intercedes for you, pleads with you, sings high praises, promises, and commands. Biblical theology organizes the whole of the Bible with a historical and narrative logic, but we must do more than tell the Story if we are to minister to people.

Ephesians *is* fair game for the labors of exegetical, systematic, and biblical theology.[1] These auxiliary disciplines are crucial for understanding the Bible in and of itself. But never forget, Ephesians is and does practical theology, speaking from the Lord into people's lives. We only reach Paul's intended goal when we also *do* practical theology, speaking the truth in love to grow up together into Christ, our head. You must close the loop. Paul's walk and fresh message must lead to your own walk and fresh message. We must apply its present message to its present audience to truly understand it. Practical theology is the end in view. Ephesians sings and dances; it is not just a book containing lyrics, score, and choreographic diagrams. It is written to change you and make you an instrument of change in the lives of your brothers and sisters. Yes, bring the tools of Bible study and theological reflection to bear. But never allow the support disciplines to degenerate into ends in themselves. Explore the practical wisdom that is Ephesians's chief end, so that you, too, will live and do ministry the way Paul does.

Ephesians Is a Door to the Rest of Scripture

A second key for understanding and using Ephesians well is to see the "hot links" to the rest of Scripture and to see the particular way Paul uses other Scripture. Ephesians communicates a sense of the entirety of Scripture. It is dense with specific citations and allusions and uses other Scripture for present purposes. Scripture bleeds Scripture, and God's new message is constructed out of God's former messages. The new message is consistent in general to older messages, but it innovates in the specifics.

What is the hermeneutic principle by which Paul appropriates the rest of Scripture? Paul's method is quite striking, perhaps even disturbing to common views of Bible study. To be sure, Paul is *not* fanciful or arbitrary. He does not play fast and loose with Scripture, as if anything goes. He does not bend Scripture to his own fancy by proof-texting, by spinning fantastic allegories, by numerology, by word association, or by arbitrary spiritualizing of texts. He never does out-of-control things like taking Numbers 13:33 to mean "the spies in the land suffered low self-esteem because they saw themselves like grasshoppers." His logic is not the sort that says, "Nehemiah first inspected the damage to the walls of Jerusalem, therefore counselors must first explore the woundedness of those they counsel." But it is also noteworthy that Paul does not use the rest of Scripture in a grammatico-historical way either. In fact, he never exegetes and expounds the original meaning of the many passages he cites or alludes to. He comes close to proof-texting when he takes an old text in a different direction from its original: e.g., his use of "be angry but do not sin" (Ps. 4:4; Eph. 4:26). He comes close to allegory and spiritualizing when he extends and reconfigures the meaning and application of old texts: e.g., the victorious Lord's "ascending on high" (Ps. 68:18; Eph. 4:8–11) and a husband's "leaving and cleaving" (Gen. 2:24; Eph. 5:31f). In every case, Old Testament words and themes become bigger than they once were, showing spectacular new dimensions of meaning. Paul is extremely creative! Grammatico-historical interpretation of the originals does not lead to what Paul says and does.

We must ponder this carefully. What principles control Paul's use of older Scripture? A full answer lies well beyond the scope of this chapter, but the kernel of the answer can be stated in two principles. First, Jesus Christ super-fulfills the Old Testament. Second, there is a general thematic coherence rather than either contradiction or exact replication between new use and original meaning. Paul is creative, but not fantastic, contradictory, or disconnected. *Christ* creates both the difference and the coherence; the new purposes of ministry express both the difference and the coherence. Imagine that in 1905 God had promised your great-grandparents that someday he would give their descendants a Model T Ford, a radio communications system using Morse code, and a biplane. When he decided to deliver in 2003, he gave you a Dodge Viper, a satellite-linked cell phone, and an F–117A Stealth Fighter. The promise was fulfilled . . . in ways beyond imagination. You travel, do business, and fight in ways that show a thematic coherence with 1905—it is still recognizable as transportation, communication, and war—but the details have changed. Similarly, the prophecies, songs, commandments, and stories of the Old Testament become supercharged with the power and glory of the Holy Spirit by whom Jesus Christ indwells his people. They are tailored to the needs of a different people living in a different time, facing recognizable but different problems.

In opening doors to the entirety of Scripture, Ephesians "alters" previous Scripture. When Christ becomes the sacrificial offering (Eph. 5:2) and we become God's temple (2:21), we are invited to read Leviticus and 1 Kings differently—not with fanciful allegories, but as metaphors in blood and stone of a Christological dimension. When anger threatens the unity of Christ's people in the midst of their sanctification process (4:26), we are invited to read Psalm 4 differently, with entirely new implications. There are far-reaching differences between Paul's citations and the cited originals. It is as though the original were a solitary star seen by the naked eye. But seeing both Christ and contemporary need, Paul gazes at that star through a powerful telescope, and now he beholds the Andromeda Galaxy: billions upon billions of stars, a disk of radiant beauty 100,000 light years across, a vast spectacle of glory previously unimagined. The scope of application and the depth of implication multiply as Paul rereads the Old Testament and Gospels through the glory of the reigning Christ, and through his task of writing a practical charter for the church. Ephesians opens doors into other parts of the Bible, but it reworks the things it opens before us. Consider a half-dozen examples.

1. When Paul says, "Be filled with the Spirit, speaking to one another with psalms, hymns, and spiritual songs, singing and making melody with your heart to the Lord, always giving thanks for all things in the name of our Lord Jesus Christ to God the Father" (Eph. 5:18–20), he opens a direct link to all 150 psalms. But Paul's words also make all 150 psalms mean something more than they first meant. In the first place, David's meditations, cries, shouts, and songs are recharged in the light of the Lord Jesus Christ and God the Father. In the second place, the psalms are here presented not as merely objects of Bible memory or liturgical recitation. Rather, "psalms" provide a paradigm for a living, speaking faith in Christ.

   To be "filled with the Spirit" is to have your language alive to God, both your daily conversations with others and the inward conversation within your heart. Your cognitive stream-of-consciousness and your social interactions are meant to be psalm-like and psalm-informed. That includes the ability to quote a psalm in a timely and relevant way, but it is something much more. Paul calls you to a lifestyle of joyous dependence on Christ, to live in faith like the Psalms.

   A videotape of your outward speech and inward thoughts would look like a continuously updated and personalized psalm. The realities of a living relationship with Christ infuse the way you process the specifics of your daily life. You speak and think new-minted re-creations and applications of Scripture into the exigencies of the moment, updated at every point by Jesus Christ. Examples of the Spirit filling people for psalm-like and psalm-informed words appear in Elizabeth, Mary, and Zechariah (Luke 1); in the teachings and prayers of Jesus (Luke 6; 11); in the speeches of Peter (Acts 2; 4); in the praying of believers (Acts 4); in the praises, prayers, and exhortations of Paul's entire letter to the Ephesians; in the times you speak the Word of God with boldness, clarity, and faith; in the times you bless the Lord with all that is within you. Paul has pointed you to Psalms with a radical new application: go and live like the psalms do, seeing the Lord Jesus Christ.

2. Not only does Paul point to the Psalter as a whole, but he specifically quotes three psalms. Each case gives the Old Testament a fresh application and a Christ-enriched focus. When God "puts all things in subjection under his feet" (Ps. 8:6; Eph. 1:22), a passage originally about the creation glory of mankind comes to picture the redemption glory of the unique Son of Man, in whom we also are raised and enthroned as the new humanity. Psalm 8 is recognizable, and not contradicted. But radio-transmitted Morse code has become a satellite-linked cell phone.

In Ephesians 4:8–11 Paul amplifies, and even alters Psalm 68:18: "When he ascended on high, he led captive a host of captives, and he gave gifts to men." The original proclaimed the Lord's victorious ascendancy at Mount Sinai, in an undefined future when all nations would bow. That future has now been defined, in Christ, and everything changes. A psalm about "ascending" is now taken to be pregnant with the prior "descending" of the Lord (incarnation, suffering, death). The place ascended is not Sinai, but the throne of the universe. The victory parade is reworked to tell of the Lord's "giving" gifted people to lead his church, actually inverting the original that had the Lord "receiving" gifts in homage.

When Paul writes, "Be angry, and yet do not sin" (Ps. 4:4; Eph. 4:26), he again shifts the direction of application in addressing a very different context. The original appeared as part of an extended meditation on stilling your heart into peace and trust, so that you would not sin when you are upset at the wrongdoing of God's enemies. The fresh restatement develops the necessity of dealing quickly with anger, primarily in the context of the remnant sins that can irritate and provoke those in Christ. It develops the devilish dimension, how unresolved anger plays into the divisive agenda of the accuser of the brethren. It sets our dealing with anger in the larger context of "learning Christ" (Eph. 4:20), one piece of the transformation of our lives. Psalm 4:4 has been adapted to a larger vision. The quotation sparkles with new meanings, not contradictions.

3. Ephesians opens a door into Proverbs. When Paul discusses walking in wisdom instead of folly (Eph. 5:15–18a), he creates a live connection to the whole book of Proverbs (and the wider wisdom tradition) that details this theme. He caps things off with a direct quote from the Greek translation of Proverbs 23:31, itself a loose paraphrase and amplification of the original Hebrew. This quotation does not function as an exegesis of Solomon's vivid discussion of drunkenness in Proverbs 23. It serves as a "for instance" of foolish pleasure that contrasts with the solid pleasures of being filled with the Holy Spirit and knowing the Lord. Several clauses later, the "fear of Christ" (5:21) makes a Christ-enriched allusion to the first principle of all the wisdom literature, the fear of the Lord.

4. Paul's radical Christifying of the Old Testament gets pushed to the extreme when he cites the call to "leave and cleave" (Gen. 2:24; Eph. 5:31–33). The principles of marriage—and Paul is still teaching on marriage—get pressed to serve radical Christ-and-church conclusions. Actual marriage becomes a secondary application of a text explicitly about marriage! The love of Christ for his wife and the submission of the church to her husband are a wellspring of truth about marriage. Genesis 2:24 remains thoroughly true in itself, but relatively narrow in meaning compared to what Paul now sees: the Andromeda Galaxy. Such a metaphorical use—we could call it "allegorizing" if that word retained any positive connotations—is not arbitrary, however. It is thematically consistent with the exegesis of Genesis 2.

5. Even the Ten Commandments are reworked and enriched in Christ and by present purposes. For example, Paul directly cites the fifth commandment (Ex. 20:12; Eph. 6:2–3), calling children to be subject to parents. Here he comes closest to replicating the original text, but, still, in at least three ways this fresh application is more than simple citation. First, he does

not lead with the Scripture citation, but with his own Christ-loaded words—"Children, obey your parents in the Lord." The Bible passage is then brought forward as a supporting text, not the primary point. Second, he editorializes in the middle of the quotation, inserting his comment about "the first commandment with a promise," before finishing off the quote. Third, though the words are identical, "live long on the earth" in Ephesians means something decidedly different than "live long in the land" in Exodus. Israel has become all nations; the Lord has been revealed as Jesus Christ; the promise of real estate has been swallowed up in the promise of Christ.[2]

6. The source of one quotation in Ephesians remains a mystery: "For this reason it says, 'Awake, sleeper, and arise from the dead, and Christ will shine on you' " (5:14). Previously, when Paul wrote, "Therefore, it says . . ." (4:8), he meant, "The *Bible* says," and anyone could go look up Psalm 68:18. But here we do not know the "it" that says what follows. It is not the Bible, at least not directly. The best guess is that Paul cited the words of a well-known, first-century Christian hymn, rather as if he had quoted from "Amazing Grace" or "When Peace, Like a River."

That analogy serves us well. Such hymns speak truth that is quotable in ministry: new, Christified psalms. Just as John Newton and Horatio Spafford had meditated on the Word of God, and that Word mapped onto their personal stories (a fact that both hymns vividly reflect), so Ephesians 5:14 was biblical even before it became Bible.

One can easily imagine a brother or sister who had received a wake-up call from God out of the dark torpors of sinfulness, and who now lived with a keen, urgent sense of the light of Christ. The language arises very naturally out of a conflation of Isaiah 26:19, 51:17, 52:1, and 60:1, but Isaiah's language has been Christified and personalized to a somewhat different purpose. Isaiah never quite said what some first-century believer said in applying Isaiah's words, which Paul then quoted for all time. So a contemporary paraphrase and adaptation of the Old Testament, reworked in the light of

Christ, became part of the Scriptures with which we now
work and live.

Does Paul's way of using Scripture make you nervous? It will, if
you expect him to be doing exegetical theology, not practical theology. Should his way of using Scripture unsettle us, who stake our faith
and practice on the authority, sufficiency, and clarity of God's self-
revelation? Not at all. Paul's use of other Scripture does not contradict
the original sense—biplane and Stealth Fighter remain analogous—
though he never seeks to replicate the original sense. Exegetical theology has been respected, though pastoral usage flexibly adapts in
order to make new points for new listeners in a new time.

Paul's *modus operandi* is actually quite familiar to biblical theologians and systematic theologians. They seek to answer *our* questions,
just like practical theology does. Good biblical theology is comfortable with looking backwards at earlier things and seeing richer meanings: types, foreshadowings, prophetic words, pregnant events that
only in retrospect reveal super-fulfillment as Christ enriches and alters previous revelation. Similarly, Paul's teachings are consistent with
how good systematic theology proceeds to use the Bible. It uses the
Bible to answer new questions of doctrine and ethics. And systematics
often takes biblical words and defines them with either a broader or a
narrower semantic field than they have in the Bible itself. Done faithfully, this does not pervert Scripture or exegesis, but it answers questions that need answering in a true and biblical manner.

Scripture itself uses language this same, normal, flexible way:
"faith" has a different scope in Hebrews than in Romans; "justification" has a different slant in James than in Galatians. Paul's pastoral
practice—like biblical theology, systematic theology, and wise living—manages to remain coherent with the content of specific texts,
and yet it adapts texts to new purposes. Paul addresses new questions,
and crafts a fresh message to contemporary hearers in a way that looks
surprisingly freewheeling at first glance. What a remarkable, provoca-
tive, and unusual door Ephesians opens into the rest of the Bible! The
light of the Lord Jesus Christ and current ministry needs lead Paul to
rework Scripture and put Scripture to work.

What does all this mean? We see Paul opening doors into the rest
of the Bible, yet we see him doing something quite different and more

complicated than just quoting or exegeting Bible texts. He is a man *transformed in Christ*. He is *doing ministry*. He is *living psalmically and proverbially*. His faith speaks afresh to God and man in the exigencies of his particular life situation as apostle to the nations; he lives new-minted wisdom in that situation.

Here is the million dollar question: *May we do something like what Paul did, even with Ephesians?* Or was he exercising an apostolic prerogative when he Christified, paraphrased, recontextualized, and reworked Scripture? I will clarify what I mean and do not mean in the next paragraphs, but let me first state the answer bluntly. Not only *may* you do something like what Paul does, you *must* do so—and you *already* do so, every day.

Life and ministry that are faithful to God's Word and relevant to the varied conditions of humankind use Scripture in creative and personalizing ways. Honest, relevant, extemporaneous prayers pull together snippets and paraphrases of Scripture, interweaving the Bible with the current needs of people. Sermons quote and exegete Scripture, but they also cite Scripture out of context, play with language in fresh ways, tell new stories, and apply in creative ways. Heart to heart conversations quote or allude to passages and phrases from the Bible, all of it colored, reworked and personalized by the details of our lives. Good hymns work off of one particular passage or a collage of passages, elaborating them, pouring in Christ, weaving in human experience, developing analogous metaphors: "Christ the Lord is Risen Today," "How Firm a Foundation," "Amazing Grace," "What a Friend We have in Jesus."

Make no mistake, you are not writing or receiving the inscripturated Word of God. Your praying, preaching, counseling, singing, and living the Word embody a derivative authority only. You are not a mouthpiece of Scriptural revelation any more than John Newton or Horatio Spafford was. But if you live your life and do your job faithfully, you are praying the Word, preaching the Word, counseling the Word, singing the Word, and living the Word. In a way analogous to Paul, though not identical in authority, you will use Scripture with that multitude of adaptations, personalizations, paraphrases, and story-tellings that are part of the normal Christian life. We must do something *like* what Paul did, as well as stay faithful and subordinate to what Paul said. Faithful does not mean rote. Faithful does not mean you keep your nose in a book, even The Book, because The Book models something different.

I am *not* arguing for relativism. I am *not* arguing that revelation is ongoing and progressive. I am *not* arguing that parts of the Bible are passé and discardable. I am *not* arguing for "every man does what is right in his own eyes" when it comes to Bible interpretation. I am *not* arguing for departing from or modifying Scripture. I am *not* arguing that all meaning is in the eye of the beholder, as in postmodern, deconstructionist interpretation. I am *not* arguing for adding to the Bible, supplanting the Bible, or going beyond the Bible. I am *not* arguing for subjectivism. The Bible is absolute, eternal, infallible, authoritative, sufficient, perspicuous, unchanging, reliable truth, the Word of the living God. But I *am* arguing that good living, preaching, praying, counseling, conversing, teaching, meditating, and singing all *do something* with Scripture. Only in this way are we truly faithful to Scripture. "Wisdom" and "living faith" necessarily embody creative adaptations, applications, and personalizations.

The Bible models how truth is used, and such usage involves a flexibility and adaptability that may seem shocking, dangerous, and unfamiliar. But the alternatives to such an insightful and creative pastoral practice would have seemed shocking, dangerous, and unfamiliar to the apostle Paul. He was not wooden, "biblicistic," or superstitious about Scripture. I will say again, you *must* do something like what Paul did in the way he used Scripture. You already do something like it every time you pray, ponder, preach, or counsel wisely. Becoming more conscious of what you do and should do will help you live and minister better.

EPHESIANS IS HARD TO UNDERSTAND SOMETIMES

Peter once commented that the letters of "our beloved brother Paul" contain "some things hard to understand, which the untaught and unstable distort, as they also do the rest of the Scriptures, to their own destruction" (2 Peter 3:15–16). If even a fellow apostle could find Paul hard to grasp, how much more will we find ourselves perplexed on occasion! Did Peter have Ephesians specifically in mind when he said Paul could be perplexing? We don't know, but the shoe fits. And our ignorance and instability can lead us to distort the obvious as well as the difficult. We may not be those who utterly twist Paul's words to our destruction. But beware, the *defining* characteristics of evildoers are always the *remnant* tendencies and temptations of those who believe.

In our ignorance, we tend to blunder into foolish interpretations. In our instability, we tend to get sidetracked. The net effect is always a headstrong, desire-driven life that evades the central thrust of God's message. Instead, let us be thoroughly and consistently taught to know the Lord, to build stable lives of growing faith and growing love. We do well to ask God, "Give us more wisdom. Enable us to listen well." Our ability to understand is greatly affected by the clarity or confusion of our faith and by the obedience or disobedience of our practice. Here are three ways Ephesians can be hard to understand.

Incomprehensible without the Spirit

First, Paul himself acknowledges that Ephesians discusses matters that are incomprehensible unless the Holy Spirit opens our minds and hearts. God must give us a "spirit of wisdom and of revelation . . . that the eyes of our heart may be enlightened" to understand the very things printed on the page in front of us! God must enable us to "know the love of Christ that surpasses knowledge," or we remain in a stupor. This difficulty does not arise because Ephesians is particularly obscure. It is not full of dark sayings, odd imagery, and allusions to long-lost cultures. The book of Judges has places that are obscure to us, but Ephesians tends to be beyond us. Its meaning eludes us for reasons akin to what the old hymn says, "Immortal, invisible, God only wise, in light inaccessible, hid from our eyes . . . O help us to see 'tis only the splendor of light hideth Thee." Ephesians expresses the divine glory. We get bedazzled and blinded by the available light. The easily understandable things in Ephesians are islands of light in a sea of light brighter than the sun, not islands of light in a sea of darkness. By definition, we need God's help to understand Ephesians.

Divisive Debate vs. Unity

Second, a great deal of theological debate and ecclesiastical-interpersonal conflict has swirled around Ephesians, the book of unity. Such debate can have two immediate negative effects. Sometimes our attitudes become discolored by controversy itself. Sometimes our opinions are marked by particular errors. In either case (and often both happen together), we will have a hard time hearing what Ephesians really says. Controversy, even for good causes, tends to create tunnel vision and to breed ungodly attitudes. We make one mountain into the whole mountain range, or one molehill into a mountain. What we see, or think we see, consumes our minds. We lose sight of the mountain range, the context in which both mountain and molehill can be seen and weighed for what they are. We may be exactly right about our particular issue, but narrowed truth becomes unbalanced truth. It loses the ability to listen and be corrected. Narrowed truth becomes half-truth, and broadly false. Narrowed truth loses love and the redemptive modus operandi. As it does so, it becomes reactive error. It becomes increasingly distorted. It becomes a vehicle for interpersonal conflict and self-righteousness.

But Ephesians speaks a truth that calls us to live "with all humility and gentleness, with patience, forbearing one another in love . . . speaking the truth in love." That does not leave much room for the sour and suspicious attitudes that fester in controversy. Controversy tends to make us forget Christ, causing us to become angry, messianic, despairing, or fearful. Ephesians presses us about such attitudes and the words they produce. Whether our words are spoken or written, they must never be rotten or harmful. They must always be grace-filled and constructive. They must always be tailor-made to time, place, person, and circumstance.

Particular false views will also markedly affect our ability to hear Ephesians for ourselves and use it well for others. For example, every professing Christian believes both in God's grace and in human responsibility. But when it comes to determining whether God's grace or human decision has priority in conversion, controversy often reigns. Nevertheless, every point of view must reckon with Ephesians. I find Ephesians 1:3–2:10 incontrovertible regarding the priority of grace. Our standing in Jesus Christ comes about because "God chose us in Christ before the foundation of the world" to fulfill "his purpose, who works all things after the counsel of his will" (Eph. 1:4, 11). Yes, at every point, we choose: we believe or stray, we repent or harden, we obey or rebel, we love or hate. But, the "glory of his grace" is so glorious, and the "deadness in trespasses and sins" is so dead, that any notion of dead men initiating or sustaining life-giving faith toward God without being made alive by God seems absurd to me.

In addition, God's hand in my own conversion was so strikingly invasive and intervening—so Ephesianic—that I have never doubted the utter sovereignty of grace to rescue the utterly perverted. But many Christians, of sincere faith and of more godly character than I, some of whom I know as friends and brothers, teach a more sanguine view of human ability and a less exalted view of God's grace. We disagree with each other. I think their view shallow regarding both God and man, and liable to disconcert faith's maturing and enduring joy. They think my view dreary about God and man, and liable to demotivate people. One of us is wrong about the logic of grace and responsibility. Wherever the error lies, it will certainly hinder our understanding of Paul, and will have a significant effect on how we minister to others.

Controversies of many other sorts also fight out battles in the sentences of Ephesians: church government, the nature of worship, charismatic gifts, male-female roles, the mode of spiritual warfare, the permissibility of anger, and so forth. Being wrong will make Ephesians hard to understand, and will harm both the church and the individual.[3]

Our Heart's Agenda

Third, the biggest hindrance to understanding arises within our own hearts. Both the intrinsic difficulty of Ephesians and specific theological controversies intersect with *us!* Our ability to understand Ephesians correlates with our ability to live Ephesians. Clearer faith and obedience directly enables greater understanding. Greater understanding directly fuels more energetic obedience and faith. Ephesians makes clear that two kinds of hearts operate. One basic nature is dark, hard, ignorant, self-serving, and blind: "you were formerly darkness." The other basic nature is light, tender, knowing, loving, and seeing: "now you are light in the Lord; walk as children of light" (Eph. 5:8). Paul warns against the former. He prays for and exhorts us unto the latter. And so we must warn, pray, and exhort. When you read Ephesians, believe. Ask for help. Walk it out. Encourage others. Your understanding and effectiveness will grow.

Let me make a final comment about the difficulties of understanding Ephesians and then writing about it. As an author, I am not satisfied with what I have written here. Paul wrote only a short letter. Did it take him even one day to dictate it to his secretary? From the rough syntax of 3:1–2, it looks like he nailed it on the first take. Paul's mere 2,400 words would occupy only four pages in this book. Yet the ink spilled here does not come close to doing justice to the glory of God's grace. This outline on Ephesians is rather like a park ranger's commentary at the foot of a majestic mountain. The summit stands far, far above us still, in air too rare and light too bright. I hope that you will profit from what you read, that you will think, live, and practice for the better. And where you find missteps or gaps, take up the burden, so that God's people may together attain to the unity of the faith and the knowledge of the Son of God.

2   WHO IS GOD?

Who is God? More particularly, who is God in *Ephesians?* And what relevance does God have for the content and practice of personal ministry?

Imagine yourself as a naive, first-time reader of Ephesians. You've just opened the envelope—or unrolled the scroll—and begun to read. The letter talks straight to you from God, via a messenger who identifies with you: Grace to *you* and peace from God *our* Father and the Lord Jesus Christ. You read on through a long, tumbling, soaring sentence (Eph. 1:3–14), and find that God chose and anointed you—us—to be caught up into the glory of his Beloved Son. You find that the Lord Jesus Christ wraps your life—our lives—into his own. You find that the Holy Spirit binds you—binds us—into Christ as God's personal property.

This is no letter to the editor pontificating about human beings or human nature in general. This is a letter to you about us and God. The point is clear: God has put us in Christ. You know this already; but you don't know. This is Christian Faith 101; yet this is knowledge that surpasses knowing, far beyond anything we can ask or even imagine.

Even to proceed further, we need to pray and ask for help, as Paul himself does throughout this letter: *Our heavenly Father, you have spoken such wonderful things. They are true, but we stumble in the dark. Overcome our hearing-impaired, sight-impaired, mind-impaired, heart-impaired natures. Our God, you let us glimpse what is true and right, holy and perfect, what is worthy of adoration. You give us a glimpse of Christ himself. Paul blazed with light in Christ, and we want to blaze with light also. Make us know you better. Help us, our Father, we pray in the name of your Son, Jesus, who has brought us into life. Amen.*

This letter crams God, Christ, you, and us into every square inch. *Christ* comes at *you* and at *us*. Of course it is an artifice to slice a mere 2400-word letter into six chapters and then to dice it into 155 verses. It is a convenience to help us find our way. And of course, counting the frequency of words is the crudest of ways to access meaning. But that said, consider that in these mere 155 verses there are some 120 direct references to Jesus Christ, eighty references to God the Father, and fifteen references to the Holy Spirit. In addition, Paul talks to "you" over eighty times, and about "us" forty-five times. So God appears about one and a half times per verse, and you are talked to almost once per verse![1] Paul is compelled to mention Christ and you in almost every sentence. It's not hard to get what *this* letter is about.

A PERSONAL ENCOUNTER

Ephesians ought to produce an intensely personal encounter with the Lord. It ought to take you into some very sober reflection on what you're really like by nature. It ought to lift you up into joyful praise, and give your life purpose and resolve. But we all know that the greatest challenge of ministry is to make people come alive to the message and the message come alive to people. The Holy Spirit needs to enlighten and awaken us. We must lean hard on God. At the same time we must think hard about whether we "use" Ephesians the way God intends it to be used. Too often both our understanding of Ephesians and our way of using it in teaching, preaching, counseling, and conversation slides into abstractions. Ephesians becomes truths about God in the third person impersonal, not God grabbing you, me, us. Consider the practical difference between the following two statements, both of which are equally "true."

#1: The doctrine of election says that God chose a people to belong to himself. Ephesians 1:7 teaches that sins are forgiven by the atoning work of Jesus Christ. Those who have trusted the good things promised in the indicative should then live out the implications of the imperative.

#2: "God chose you to be his. In Christ we have redemption through his blood, the forgiveness of our trespasses, by the riches of his grace that he lavished on us. I plead with you, live worthy of your calling."

The first statement *says that* certain things are true: a propositional truth, a Bible verse, and a generalization. It needs no quotation marks, because there is no conversation. But the second statement *says*. Someone talks to you. God claims you, presses wonders upon you, and pleads with you through his personal representative. If both our knowledge and communication of Ephesians remain in the first mode, we give thin gruel to those we teach and counsel. We fail to communicate the immediacy of the living Christ.

Let me illustrate the difference with an extended metaphor. Ephesians talks about being storm-tossed and driven by waves and wind (Eph. 4:14), an experience all too familiar to Paul (2 Cor. 11:25–27). But what is a *wave?* The answer might seem obvious, but it's not. Both Oceanography 101 and a book of sailing adventures talk about waves. Here is what a wave is in oceanography class:

$$C = \sqrt{\frac{g^1}{2\pi}\left(\tanh\frac{2\pi d}{1}\right)}$$

A wave is nothing more than a disturbance that moves from place to place in some medium, carrying energy with it. The common waves of the ocean, as well as the greater ones occurring during storms, are oscillations of the sea caused by the frictional drag of the wind on its surface. For such waves, a general equation is c= where C is the velocity of the waveform, l is the wavelength, tanh means the hyperbolic tangent, d is the depth, and g is the gravitational constant.

The paragraph is true, but the form, scope, and implications of truth are shriveled. The em*pha*sis is on the wrong syl*lab*le. Is a wave "nothing more than . . ."?

Compare that definition of waves with this description of what a Royal Navy frigate faced while rounding Cape Horn in the early 1800s, and we will see that true oceanographic information bears little dynamic relationship to actually facing a stormy sea.

At the beginning of the graveyard watch, the southwest wind came in with a shriek. The shriek rarely lessened in the days and weeks that followed. . . . [The sailors] suffered cruelly from the ice on deck, ice on the rigging, ice on the yards, the sail cloth board-hard with frozen flying spray. . . . The enormous rollers sweeping east-wards grew more monstrous still, their white, wind-torn crests a quarter of a mile apart with a deep grey-green valley between. . . . The scale of the rollers was so vast that the frigate, opposing them, behaved more like a skiff. . . . [One] evening, in a lull between two storms of sleet that came driving horizontally with the force of bird-shot, . . . the lines parted. . . . The maintopsail [was] shaking so fu-riously that the masthead must have gone had not Mowett, the bosun, Bonden, Warley the captain of the maintop, and three of his men gone aloft, laid out on the ice-coated yard and cut the sail away. Warley was on the lee yardarm when the footrope gave way under him and he fell, plunging far clear of the side and instantly vanishing in the terrible sea. . . . Striving harder one would have said than it was possible for men to strive, . . . they succeeded in the end, and then they began knotting and splicing the damaged rig-ging: they also carried their hurt shipmates below. Captain Aubrey came down into the sick-bay when the ship was reasonably snug. "How is Jenkins?" he asked. "I doubt he can live," said the doctor. "The whole rib-cage is . . . And Rogers will probably lose his arm. What is that?"—pointing to the Captain's hand, wrapped in a hand-kerchief. "It is only some nails torn out. I did not notice it at the time."[2]

So, a wave is nothing more than a moving disturbance caused by the frictional drag of wind on the ocean's surface? Tell that to a man snuffed out, or dying, or dismembered, or to a man who passed through such extreme crisis of activity that he did not notice his fin-gernails being torn out! Ephesians is for storm-tossed people (Eph. 2:1–3; 4:14–22; 5:6). The people to whom you minister—even the oceanographers!—do not live, move, and have their being in Oceanography 101. They sail wooden ships in places where the wind shrieks and the scale of the rollers is vast, where a decrease in the value of the hyperbolic tangent means shipwreck, and where some-one can walk on water and still storms.

There is nothing wrong *per se* with oceanography. I've read and profited from some excellent "oceanographic" commentaries on Ephesians. They perform a useful service, enlightening us in our ignorance of original speaker, audience, and context. But they do not capture the pastoral heart of Ephesians as God reveals himself. Let's start with application, as Paul does, and, by the grace of God, let's continue with application all the way through, as Paul does.

Who is God? Everything we will say about him is intended to change your faith, the way you talk to people, and the way you approach change. Let's look at those three things in turn.

God and Your Faith

First, he is the person on whom you rely. You talk directly to him. You think about him as in his presence. You talk about him as a present reality. As you ask the question, Who is God?, and as you hear the answers, live the Psalms (Eph. 5:18–20). Believe, trust, think, and cry out to the One whom the answers describe. We could well say that Ephesians is a New Testament psalm, because it sparkles and crackles with Paul's own faith, excitement, and drive. His teaching easily slides into worship and prayer, because the Lord of whom Paul speaks is right there and right here. What does this mean in counseling? Living and vital faith is mandatory for the counselor. Without it, God may still use what you say and do, but he will use your words and care despite you, not because of you.

Some practitioners of "biblical" counseling wrongly attempt to expunge the human ingredient, as if "you" interfered with the purity of the Word that needs to be presented to people. They try to reduce biblical counseling to Bible verses and formulas. How different from the Bible and all lively ministry! The attempt to expunge *sinful* human ingredients—messianic expectations, superiority, fear of man, sheer force of personality, manipulation, morbid curiosity, self-indulgent sharing, and the like—is admirable. But if you expunge the human ingredient itself you actually interfere with how the Living Word uses both his Word and his servants. Faith, hope, and love are contagious, just as grumbling, anxiety, and contempt are contagious. Biblical counseling is not formulaic.[3] Paul begins Ephesians with joy in the Lord and fiercely intelligent concern for his hearers. You, like him, enter into personal worlds where the weather report is often "storms of sleet and high seas." How will you not become discouraged, anxious, blasé, or self-confident? You must bring your own gladness and fierce love into the situation, confident in your Lord.

If your faith lives, you will pray *intelligent* prayers that braid together the real God and the real person in the real life situation. If you are alert to both the Redeemer and the real needs of the needy, you won't ever pray *pro forma* prayers. You also won't pray about truth in general and people in general. You won't just pray for situations to go well—for health, success, a spouse, or children. You'll pray for the person God is working in. Your prayers will be warmly personal, inclusive, and caring. Those you counsel will know that you intercede for *them* before the God who is here and on whom we learn to depend. Your prayers will be concrete and immediate.

During the first dozen years of my Christian life, my pastor's way of praying for people had a profound effect on me. He would never close a conversation by saying, "I'll be praying for you about this." Instead, he would say, "Let's ask God right now to help you." That made a huge impression. His faith in Christ was contagious; he nourished my faith. Yes, he also prayed later on, and he might subsequently ask how things were going. But in the moment, those specific and relevant prayers communicated that God is here, and that he cares about you and is up to something in your life. From this, I learned who God is, and I learned about God's call in my life. Notice how Paul prays and seeks prayer, and do likewise: "I pray that the Father would open your eyes wide to know him. Pray for me to have the right words to say and to speak boldly of Christ" (author's paraphrase). Live like David and Paul lived, thoughtful and talkative before the face of God.

God and the Way You Talk to People

Second, knowing God teaches you to speak directly into people's lives. Speak of him and from him, representing him to others. We are to speak the truth in love to each and all. Don't just point toward truth. Paul points truth toward you and points you toward truth. All along he leaves you with the liveliest impression that all this is for us all. He never lectures or moralizes or nags. The truth is always for the speaker as much as for us who hear. Paul does not give a catalog of divine information in a book of scholastic theology. He does not say, "Predestination means that God chooses some people, not others."

Not that it's wrong to say that, but said that way, a warm and personal love sounds chilly and capricious, and people tend to react needlessly. They ask, Is God fair? How does it all work? Is it determinism? Our minds fill with distracted questions—or dogmatic defensiveness, equally distracted from the pastoral point of the original.

But Paul says instead, "He chose us [in Christ] before the foundation of the world that we would be holy and blameless before him. In love he predestined us to adoption as sons through Jesus Christ" (Eph. 1:4–5). Hearing this, we respond with delight. We might still say that God is "not fair," but accusation has turned into adoration: "You are so spectacularly unfair, because you do not treat us as our sins deserve! Thank you, thank you, thank you!" (cf. Ps. 103:10). Instead of dwelling on picky little questions, we persevere in faith's joy and hope.

I remember the very first time I grasped something of God's call to speak directly into people's lives, rather than being general and theoretical. I was talking with a Christian man who was bothered by his indulgence in sexual fantasies. He was discouraged, oppressed by a low-grade sense of guilt. But he was not very motivated to grapple with the perversity of his thought life. With a shrug he said, "Of course, what can I expect? I'm in the flesh." I responded, "But you aren't in the flesh, you're in the Spirit!" He rocked back and his eyes opened wide, and he started to think hard. He got very serious. From that moment, the terrain on which his battles were being fought was redefined. I could easily have forgotten the truth myself, and vaguely sympathized, "Yeah, everyone struggles, but. . . ." Or I could even have voiced the same truth one step removed toward abstraction, "It says in Romans 8:9 that 'you are not in the flesh but in the Spirit, if indeed the Spirit of God dwells in you.'" Or I could have said, "Do a Bible study of Romans 8 and Galatians 5:14–6:10 on the battle between the flesh and the Spirit." In fact, we did talk about those passages a few minutes later. But both the citation and the homework had been set up by the personal directness of challenge and encouragement.

I once talked with a woman who was picking through the rubble of her marriage. Her husband had treated her very badly, rejecting and betraying her. But she had also contributed to the demolition of love. She had lived a lifestyle of fear, passivity, and what we came to call her "I'll-wait-and-*see*-how-he'll-treat-*me*" attitude. Over the years she had drifted and nursed her self-pity, rather than wrestling with herself in order to love her husband and fighting to save her marriage. She now faced yet another fork in the road: either continue in the old lifestyle driven by fear of man or forge a new lifestyle driven by faith in Christ. She would have many opportunities to interact with him as the divorce proceedings played out.

While all this is going on, Christ calls her to deal with God about the log in her own eye. He calls her to bring grace and forgiveness into the rubble. He calls her to speak candid, constructive words to her husband. He calls her to a bold humility, not a cowardly self-absorption.

She was struggling with all this, but starting to light up. I could finally say to her, "It is a hard row to hoe, isn't it? But you know that the worst thing that could happen is that you'll be rejected again. He might spurn your wisdom. So what? If you embrace what God is doing in setting you free of the crippling I'll wait-and-*see*-how-he'll-treat-*me* attitude, then the minimum good is that Christ is *alive* in you, and you *know* him and his love, and *you* change. And the best that can happen is that you can be an agent of the glory of God in this man's life, as well as with your kids, who observe every tone of voice and facial expression. God alone knows, but it is possible for this marriage to be restored. Your sins and his sins are the only two things making it incinerate. As you deal with yours and find grace, then you'll have grace to give. The rest is between your husband and the Lord." Biblical counseling speaks relevant truth directly and personally.

Direct address is riveting. In your counseling, speak the truth the way Paul does. The Scriptures evidence a buoyant confidence about truth, because the writers model buoyant faith in the Lord of truth. When I was a new Christian, friends gave me Philippians 1:6 as an encouragement to my assurance of faith: "He who began a good work in you will bring it to completion." But it was only years later that I saw that this passage is also about the confidence of the speaker who says it to others: "For *I* am confident of this very thing, that He who began a good work in *you* will perfect it until the day of Christ Jesus." I can rest in the steadfast love of the Lord for you . . . and can say so.

Why use indirect speech when direct speech makes both faith and love so much more lively?[4] And why point to the truth with a layer of

Bible citations in between, when you can say the truth? Most often, follow Paul's example, and put the citations in the parentheses or end notes of the conversation, jotted down for later reference and reflection. The ministry the Bible models spends little time giving the references, and much time kneading the truth into lives. God comes at people directly and wants you to do the same.

God and Your Approach to Change

Third, where the Lord calls for change, connect those specific changes to what *God* is doing. Whenever you need to change, put the Redeemer in the center of the picture. Whenever others need to change, remember that the Light enlightens and the Holy One sanctifies. God is primarily interested in making us *know* him. Don't ever degenerate into giving advice unconnected to the good news of Jesus crucified, alive, present, at work, and returning.[5] Ephesians gives us no *Reader's Digest* list of "six principles for successful marital conversation" or "four keys to getting your life organized." Such advice is often reasonably OK, though rather pale and powerless. It often expresses a superficial analogy to biblical wisdom, in the same way that the moral codes of false religions often grope in the right direction.

But looked at more deeply, such things are only crude imitations of biblical truth. Paul never slips into giving pointers for life, because he has much bigger goals in view. He pleads with God that he would open our hearts to know Christ in the power of the Holy Spirit. So we don't dare read the communication discussion at the end of Ephesians 4 and *only* say, "Paul teaches four key principles. (1) Tell the truth, rather than lying. (2) Keep short accounts and deal with your anger daily. (3) Speak constructive rather than destructive words. (4) Forgive others, rather than becoming argumentative, or gossipy." Now those are terrific principles! But they are gutted of the knowledge of Jesus Christ, which is the point of human life and the power and reason to obey in truth.

Instead, Paul says to tell the truth rather than lying "because we are members of one another" in Christ. He says to keep short accounts "so the devil gets no foothold" to cause interpersonal conflict to fester into division. Speak constructively so you "don't grieve the Holy Spirit in whom you were sealed for the day of redemption." Forgive others "as God in Christ forgave you." The motive is not self-reformation or success in interpersonal relations. The motive is to know the Lord. Good principles gutted of the Lord—"deChristified," to put it clumsily but precisely—can only function as self-serving. But Ephesians portrays how the Spirit of the Lord is at work in the people of the Lord.

Never forget that you have *someone* to bring to the people you counsel. He animates the proceedings, because he is up to something in the lives of counselor and counseled alike. Our counsel becomes lively, attractive, and compelling when we express living faith in Christ, when we directly address people, and when we catch people up in who God is and what he is doing.

WHO IS GOD?

What is it about God that fuels the applications that we have just made? Many of the people we counsel live inside a black hole of self-will, misery, and confusion. They need God to break in on their shadowland from which sin has erased the light of the personal and living God. Often without realizing it, people live as practical atheists, worshiping themselves, their own will and opinions. They "see" God from within the black hole, and he appears remote, irrelevant, and distorted.

When people think about God by instinct, not by revelation, they ask many of the wrong questions. Will he meet my felt needs? Will he be co-pilot in my life? Can I get him to make my day, my spouse, my kids, my health, and my finances work out? Is he like a rabbit's foot? If I do my bit for God, will he do his bit for me? Is God capricious? Is it tough to figure out what he's up to, or what he wants? Is it possible he might disappoint me? Might he even betray my trust? Is he "the man upstairs" to whom I pay my respects and dues? Is he sour-tempered and displeased, a hard-edged taskmaster? Is he my true inner self? My higher power? Is he the theoretical uncaused cause and prime mover? Is God a happy feeling or an intense emotion? Is he an inhabitant of religiously toned activities? Does he/she/it even exist?

In the letter to the Ephesians God tells us who he is and what he is like. Unmistakable. Radically different from our instinctive opinions. He tells us many different things. From this many-splendored wisdom I've picked eight truths to summarize. These are the basis for the applications we've been looking at so far. These are not minor points or asides. In each case the Lord piles on the truth, making the same point over and over from different angles so we can't miss it and won't forget it.

God Makes Himself **Known** *to Us in Christ*
Paul starts this letter by calling himself "an apostle" of Jesus. An apostle is only a messenger, an errand boy, an ambassador. God gave him this message to deliver with one purpose: so that you will know God. The letter floods us with this reality: *making known* and *enlightening* us to the *message* of the *wisdom* of the *insight* of the *revelation* of the *knowledge* of the *word* of his *truth*! How many more ways can Paul say it? God opens the eyes of our hearts to know him, his ways, and his will.

What would God have you know? Himself. His glory. Nothing less than the Lord who is the centerpiece of the universe and history, Jesus Christ. Reconciliation between yourself and God, so he hears your voice of reliance, need, and adoration, just as you hear his voice of revelation. The breakout of his light into every nation: the mystery now revealed, how the only true God comes to be known by all peoples. Our participation in his mission to invade darkness. Reconciliation between peoples as outcasts are welcomed into the community of promise. How to live in the way of peace and wisdom in all relationships. All this and more. You come to know wonder upon wonder, and all true.

This letter teaches us to know God as Trinitarian: the Father who thought, and the Son who bought, and the Spirit who wrought, as the preachers used to say. And you who are caught up into the radiance and life of this Trinitarian God. Ephesians tears the doors off mysteries. The love of Christ beyond knowing, now known. The unfathomable riches of Christ, now fathomed. Things exceedingly far beyond all you can ask or imagine, now revealed in front of your eyes.

As the letter unfolds, Paul is concerned that God would continue to make himself known and deepen our knowing. Of course, there are many things you can pray for. But other people, like you, *need* one thing more than anything: to know Him-who-is. Don't ever forget the best and deepest: to know the Lord. Pray Ephesians 1 and 3 prayers for everyone you teach, counsel, live with, and love. "O God, let this woman, my sister, know you. Amid everything else, do not let this man, my brother, miss the best: to know Christ. Lord, open our eyes. Show us, teach us, unveil who you are to all of us. Don't let us gloss over this. Don't let us content ourselves with knowing a bit *about* you. Don't let us busy ourselves with other things, throwing our lives away."

What Paul asks God to do, he tells us to do, for our calling always correlates to God's working. Know the mystery now revealed: "Learn Christ . . . if indeed you have heard Him and been taught in Him, just as truth is in Jesus" (Eph. 4:20–22). Know the power and presence of the Holy Spirit, Christ in your hearts. Know the church as the body of the living Christ. Come, to know Christ.

Other parts of Scripture reveal the multiplicity of gifts God gives to people: helps, administration, and the rest. But Ephesians emphasizes the gifts Christ has given in order to make God explicitly and verbally known: messengers who laid the foundation, bringers of good news who induct us into Christ, shepherds who make us grow (Eph. 4:11). At the heart of Ephesians is a revelation of who God is and what he is about. This is a speech-driven little letter, and it teaches us to speak the truth in love that we might grow up into this Christ. All the "armor" or "weaponry" of God (6:10–20) is forged of God's making himself known. Each piece is his self-revelation as the invading Redeemer and our refuge from counterattack. The armor and strength *is* God, and *is* the light, and *is* Christ. You are equipped and clothed with the Person you've come to know.

God Accomplishes His **Purposes** *toward Us in Christ*

As God reveals himself, what do we come to know? The letter opens by relentlessly pressing on us that God is in control. Things happen by his will (Eph. 1:1, 5, 9, 11). Paul piles up words to tell us that God *chooses* and *predestines* by the *good pleasure* of the *will* of the *purpose* of the *counsel* of the *plan* of his *calling* that he *prepared beforehand!* The universe works according to God's plan to glorify himself in Christ and in all true believers who incorruptibly love Jesus.

Listen to Ephesians, and you will know that life is not a sloppy, confusing mess. Perhaps you've heard the metaphor that we look at life from the tangled, knotty side of the tapestry, and later we'll see the beautiful, coherent pattern on the top side. That's a useful metaphor, but Ephesians lets us see the top side of the tapestry now. God says, in effect, "People of God, it all makes sense. It's all working out accord-ing to a definite plan. A hand is on the controls of history and of your life, with the power to perform what he chooses."

When Paul says that you have the hope of glory because you were "predestined according to His purpose who works all things after the counsel of His will," he's not trying to stir up debate about esoteric doctrines and philosophical riddles. He's not picturing an icy fate to make us fatalistic. From within the illogic of the shadowlands, *we* think that one must emphasize either God's sovereign will or the free-dom and responsibility of human choices. But standing out in the daylight of God's logic, one needn't err in either direction. God is ut-terly in control. Any other view would be absurd—this God spins galaxies and holds atoms together, after all. This God raised spiritual corpses to new life in Christ. Salvation is warm and bright because God planned it. He had your name in mind in Christ. He holds us in his hand, bringing about his purposes. And we choose at every point.

Human life is absolutely significant; every fleeting thought, every choice, and every experience matter. This God calls you to faith, obe-dience, and responsibility. Because his purposes will not be thwarted, you can leap to the call, learning to be courageous, optimistic, perse-vering in love through troubles. His purposes sustain you through it all. His rule establishes the significance of our choices. Any other view would be absurd—human life counts, God's will controls. His will of control (Eph. 1:11) is to be trusted as the frame of reference behind every experience; his will of command (5:17; 6:6)) is to be obeyed with all our heart.

The supremacy of God's purposes is not a debating point. It is the foundation of indestructible confidence and ravishing delight. God is in control, and you can bend all your energies to your calling, trust-ing that God's plans are working out.

Other parts of the Bible tell different parts of the same story. There are books dedicated to the tangled knots on the underside of the tapestry (though even these books turn the tapestry over periodi-cally and finally). In the book of Job, pain, misery, confusion, and heartache are front and center. But it is crystal clear who is in control, and who is glorified in the end. In Ecclesiastes, futility is front and center, and "madness is in their hearts." But sanity has the final say: the purpose of life is found in fearing God and keeping his commandments. Ephesians alludes to the dark side—the dangers of deception, division, and degeneration into the ways of darkness—but God's chief purpose is to take us up to the highest lookout point. We are in the hands of a Man with a plan.

God Lavishes **Grace** upon Us in Christ

If God reveals himself as up to something, what's the plan? He works for our spectacular well-being, completely contrary to what we deserve. Again, Paul goes to the thesaurus and every synonym he can find tumbles forth. God *gives* and *lavishes* and *abounds* with the *riches* of the *grace* of the *mercy* of the *love* of the *kindness* of the *forgiveness* of his *redemption!* This letter is bracketed with inexpressible Gift: grace and peace given to those who believe in Jesus (Eph. 1:2); peace, love, faith, and grace given to those who love Jesus (6:23–24).

Those you counsel must know that God is gracious. They must receive and depend on real grace. No one can truly change who does not know and rely on gifts from the hand of the Lord. Since Christ is both Giver and Gift, attempts to change without grace are barren of the very purpose, power, and Person that change is about. Self-manufactured changes do not dislodge almighty me from the center of my tiny self-manufactured universe. Still in the futility of my mind and the hardness of my heart, I only act a bit different. Successful living without grace describes mere self-reformation: get your act together, save your marriage, get off your duff and get a job. Failure in living describes failed self-efforts: when you can't get a grip, you despair. Christless, grace-less attempts at change conclude either with the praise of your own glory or with your shame.

But in mercy, God purposes to give us himself. Ephesians 1 marvels at the glory of the grace that gives us glory in Christ. Ephesians 2 marvels at the sheer goodness of God and God's grace, what a friend of mine calls "God's thermonuclear goodness." His goodness is of an all-consuming intensity, like the nuclear furnace of the sun. In his presence, we, the dead in sin, children of just wrath, would be incinerated by goodness. But Christ's incalculable grace multiplies goodness times forgiveness times kindness times mercy. Christ carries us into the center of the fiery sun of the living God. Ephesians 3 marvels that the light has called all nations into grace, and pleads with God that we would understand such a love as this.

Left to ourselves, we think we are either too good to need grace or too bad to receive it. Are you too good to need a major redemption? Do you counsel someone or live with someone who is "above" needing Christ? Do you work with someone who lives for his or her desires: superiority to others, greedy cravings for more and better stuff, the insect of sexual lust, well-nursed grievances, chasing pipe dreams of success and happiness? Grace pesters and pursues us—it is grace, after all, that makes me even aware that sin is my deepest problem.

Are you a wife who has contempt for your husband? A husband who has written off your wife as a hopeless case? A teenager who feels justified in feeding dark thoughts? A parent who frets or seethes at your children? A single whose life is stained by disgruntlement because you've been shafted by life? Grace wakes you up to your need for grace. You were dead and dark (Eph. 2:1–3; 5:8). God made you alive (2:4–10). Don't go back into darkness (4:17–19). Walk in light (5:9–20).

Perhaps you have been sinned against terribly. Perhaps your own selfishness and sense of entitlement make you magnify minor offenses into capital crimes. Perhaps your own sins provoked others to retaliate sinfully, reaping what you sow. Whatever the case, the riches of mercy for you can make you merciful to others. Grace turns you upside down: the self-righteous and destructive become the grateful and constructive.

Are you too bad to receive grace? Grace woos and comforts us when we think we are too far gone to be rescued. How could you be too bad to receive what is for the bad? Perhaps you are tempted to despair about yourself. Perhaps someone you counsel is tempted to give up: "God could not possibly love me or help me. My failures are too frequent, too deep. My sins are incurable. I'm stuck and will never change. God is as disgusted with me as I am disgusted with myself." Is there anyone whose badness exceeds God's diagnosis? Consider,

> You were dead in your trespasses and sins, in which you formerly walked according to the course of this world, according to the prince of the power of the air, of the spirit that is now working in the sons of disobedience. Among them we too all formerly lived in the lusts of our flesh, indulging the desires of the flesh and of the mind, and were by nature children of wrath, even as the rest. (Eph. 2:1–3)

If the diagnostic shoe fits, wear it. But then look at the wonderful, specific cure! Is there anyone whose badness exceeds the scope and power of the cure? "But God, being rich in mercy, because of His great love with which He loved us, even when we were dead in our transgressions, made us alive together with Christ—by grace you have been saved" (Eph. 2:4–5).

God lavishes grace on us in Christ.

God's **Power** Works in Us as He Worked in Christ

Does grace consist only in good intentions toward us? Does God feel a benign, tolerant acceptance of people? Is his kindness powerless to really do anything but accept? No way! His mercy comes with the power to bring about what he wills. Here again, Paul raids the thesaurus. All the words, in fact, are piled up in Ephesians 1:19: God does things by the "surpassing greatness of his *power* toward us who believe . . . in accordance with the *working* of the *strength* of His *might*." It is then no surprise that we are later encouraged to be *"empowered* in the Lord and in the *strength* of His *might"* (Eph. 6:10, author's translation). His power put us in Christ to make us alive; now living in Christ, we put on his power as we know and trust him.

God's self-disclosure is not merely a religious theory. His will is not merely a wish. His kindness is not merely an attitude. Power makes the difference. This power made everything that exists (Eph. 3:9). This power raised Jesus from the dead (1:20), and also raised us (2:6) and remade us as his workmanship (2:10). This power works within us (3:20). God is able to do what he wants to do.

When we look at the flow of this letter from beginning to end, we see a movement toward greater and greater intimacy of power. God's power works first in Jesus Christ's own life and at the cosmic level: raising Christ to rule the universe and the powers-that-be in the spiritual realm. He delivers spiritual blessings to you: chosen, adopted, set apart, forgiven, raised, seated in and with Christ. The power of God awakens faith, and makes real to us things we do not see or touch. The intangible, transcendent blessings are the roots of tangible, immediate blessings. The power of God indwells us, and gives us intimacy with Christ and the Holy Spirit. We are "strengthened with power through His Spirit in the inner man" (Eph. 3:16). God's power works in us, individually and together.

The fruits of intimate power become evident. God's children learn humility and patience, becoming less and less headstrong and opinionated as we walk in the light. We are given people with gifts of love and truth to shepherd and teach us, visible and audible demonstrations of God's power. We learn more and more to love, and less and less to be embittered, angry people. We learn to live with sexual and financial purity, less and less driven by sordid self-interest. We learn wise speech, becoming more and more able to strengthen others with a timely word. We learn to give money to meet others' needs, and we experience the generosity of others to us. In all this and more, the power of the living God who raised Christ now infuses the people of Christ.

The Lord Jesus Christ **Invades** *History to Make Peace*

Is power a mysterious spiritual energy? No, power acts personally and in real-time history, events, and peoples. When Paul speaks about being "in Christ," he is referring to a real man who did things. Jesus is the lead actor on the stage of history, and the whole supporting cast acts with respect to the lead, playing roles either as children of light or as sons of disobedience. Jesus' story reveals God and God's will to bring grace with power.

The story line of Christ's life is presented a bit abstractly in Ephesians. This is not the gospel of John, where God becomes a man, lives a life of love, dies a death of love, and is raised to indestructible life. This is not Luke, where we see the tenderness of Jesus touching the poor, the bereaved, the troubled; where we hear Jesus' very words and emotions. While Ephesians demonstrates Paul's directness in relating to God and God's children, it is like *Cliffs Notes* regarding the life of Jesus. No "he said, she said"; no blood, sweat, and tears; no miraculous feedings, healings, and storm-stillings. But the story is all here in Ephesians, though in outline form. You see the big picture, the *meaning* of Jesus' invasion. He came for all nations, not just a bereaved widow, some fishermen from the Sea of Galilee, and some random Gentiles who strayed into his path.

The plan unfolding in Christ had been made before the foundation of the world (Eph. 1:4). The whole Old Testament is captured in the contrast between the one people who knew covenants of promise and the many peoples who were formerly separate from God and the promised

Messiah (2:11–3:9). What was hidden to earlier generations broke into the open when the Christ came down, the Lord made flesh (4:9–10).

This real man, both Lord and Christ, was named "Jesus" (twenty times in this letter, scattered from 1:1 to 6:24). Jesus preached both to the people and to the peoples, laying the foundation for one new people (2:13–22). He was killed as a sacrificial substitute to forgive us, reconcile us, and make us holy (1:7; 2:16; 4:32; 5:2; 5:25–27). So the love of God is an action in real time by this person: He loved us and gave himself for us.

Reading Paul's summary, we don't wince at the crown of thorns or delight at the thief's candid, humble faith, but we do get the bigger meaning that threads through all the details. This Christ was raised from death to imperishable life and glory (1:20). He did not just become alive again, but was raised high, and "seated" as Lord and King over the entire visible and invisible universe (1:20–23).

We pause again to pray: *Jesus, open our hearts. We barely comprehend these things. We hear the sound of familiar words, but we sleep on. Make the all-too-familiar so unfamiliar and astonishing that we are compelled to sit up in awe, and to bow in joyous worship. Make us see you, so that we love you with indestructible and fervent love.*

This Lord Jesus Christ—it is hard to call him merely "Jesus" at this point—continues to work. We, too, are made alive, raised, and seated with him (Eph. 2:5). He mediates our direct and bold access to God the Father (2:18; 3:12), not as someone we can dial on a long distance call, but as someone who personally lives in us and with us, each and all together (2:21–22; 3:16–21). From the seat of power, he gives the long-promised Holy Spirit, who seals us into Christ, and works his presence and will into us (a dozen references, from 1:13 on). Christ continues to work through all time and in every place to wash us, nourish us, and change our lives. He teaches the wife with whom he is one flesh to do the same things he does, as we grow up together into his likeness (4:1–16; 5:1–2; 5:26–27). Finally, this story has a future. Christ and his people will be fully revealed together in glory. We will be revealed as one with him, and one with each other. All our darkness will be swallowed up in his light (see Eph. 5:6–14).

God Will Bring **Wrath** on Those Outside

Human history is about the rightful King and his allies invading a dark Reich. Everyone chooses sides. The pretense of neutrality and agnosticism is only a cover for darkness. The living God and his Christ are not optional. The choice is this: live or die, know him or else. Be forgiven by the wonder of what Christ did for you, or receive what you've done fair and square on your own head.

What if people really don't care about Jesus? They don't like "religious" people or "organized religion." They've served their own gods, pursued their own ends, and formed their own opinions. Perhaps life is even sort of working out for them. They're wrapped up in raising the kids, making a name for themselves, feeling loved, or making the world a better place. All these words about God and Jesus are just so much spilled ink and waste of paper.

Ephesians does not say a lot to such people. It's primarily written to you who are on the inside of the love of God. To God's children the Holy Spirit speaks of wrath to give us a vigorous warning: Don't go back. You used to want those things and to believe those ideas. You used to be part of disobedience and destruction. Remember which way is up and which way is down. Just often enough, God reminds you who you were by nature before grace intervened and changed you.

If you are still doing what comes naturally, however, the warnings come as a major wakeup call. If you turn away from the Man who is the centerpiece of history, you are in big, big trouble. Outside of Christ, life takes place in the black hole of sin and misery. It's dangerous—damnable—to live outside the grace of God. If you are in your sins, not in Christ, you are dead (Eph. 2:1). Though the devil doesn't make you do it, he's got you dancing to his tune (2:2). You only think you're free. Furthermore, if you do or think what comes naturally, then you live as one of the children of wrath like the rest of humankind (2:3).

Everybody, by nature, is on the outs with God. Without Christ, you have no hope and are without God in this world (2:12). That phrase "without God" is interesting: *atheos*. We usually think of an atheist as someone who asserts, "I don't believe in God." But this passage turns the tables. God, in effect, says to some people, "I don't know you. You are without me. You are in living death." Just being yourself means you are excluded from the life of God (4:18). Outside of Christ, you are darkness, and the wrath of God will come on you (5:6–8).

It can't be stated more bluntly. The things you hope in will turn to gravel in your mouth if you do not hope in the right thing. I once sat with an elderly man on his deathbed. He was trying to make sense of his life, to find something to hold onto in the approaching disintegration of his existence. Everything he held up in front of his eyes — accomplishments, family, people he had helped, possessions, experiences, travels — turned to ashes before his eyes even as he talked. He finally began to weep in bitter desolation. That experience helped propel me to Christ five years later, because it taught me to ask of my own life experience, "What lasts?"

Another time I spoke with an aging woman who had relied on herself, not Christ, her entire life. She did not like how demanding and imperious Jesus was: "How could anyone say or believe that 'No one comes to the Father but by me'? I think that God is different from all that picky theology that small-minded people believe. I think that God is an all-tolerant cosmic energy in which we all participate. There are many ways to God, and God is only as you understood him, or it, or her. As long as you have faith in something, that's what matters." I thought I could detect a note of nervousness behind the cheery bravado. But she didn't buy my faith. She was convinced that a fantasy theology was the only attractive alternative to a picky theology. Maybe she was more serene than I thought, but whether the *emotional* state is serene or desperate, the *natural* state of human existence is "under wrath."

Mercy and life happen in the company of the Invader of normality, in that most unnatural state called grace. If you are in grace, never, never forget it.

God **Indwells** Us in Christ through the Holy Spirit

All this is not mere words or theories that Christians happen to hold arbitrarily. These are the facts. Paul gets flooded with what it means to be in Christ and to have Christ in us. You are part of one kingdom, one household, one divine temple and palace dwelling, wedded in one flesh with your husband, one body, one church. That you are "in Christ" appears some ten times in Ephesians 1:3–14. That Christ is powerfully "in you" dominates 3:16–21. You are in Christ. He is in you. Christ in us fills us up to the fullness of God. We in Christ are the fullness of him who fills all in all.

This is too good to be anything but true. No one could make it up. It is too astonishing. And though the church often appears disheveled, and though our lives often become dilapidated, bank on it that Christ is both in you and in us together. You will witness Christ's glory in individual lives and in the church!

Anyone who looks at present experience compared with Ephesians 1:3–23 and 3:14–5:2 can't help but see a staggering gap. Some people conclude that the Bible sounds nice in theory, but that Paul was a bit of a dreamer. They become skeptical. But they do not see what is really going down. Yes, the gap is all too real. In fact, 3:14–5:2 is *about* the gap between achievement and destination, and about what to do to press in the right direction.

But Paul saw a reality better than you could ever ask or dream, and he teaches us how to close the gap. Christ lives in us, and we live out our lives in him. He will not fail. Let that seize you. Then do what Paul did and what he tells you to do. Pour your life into bridging that gap, in reliance on the immediate grace of God. I guarantee that you will see and taste glory. Sufferings? Yes. Defeats and defections? It happens. Disappointments? Sure. But you will also witness marvels: lives changed, loving and merciful acts, courage, spectacular humility, reconciliations, the powerful presence of God.

Are things bad? Is Christ's wife in filth and rags, ripped apart by pride and factions? Is your life seedy? Do what Daniel did in Daniel 9. Do what Nehemiah did in Nehemiah 1 and 9. Own the problem. Seek the Christ who lives in us. "Though the wrong seems oft so strong," become part of the solution. Do the constructive thing, however small. We *are* in Christ.

The skeptics don't take Christ seriously enough for themselves, let alone for others. They stand at arm's length from life in Christ, as if they stood outside the problem of evil and the process of redemption. Skeptics act as if the failings they witness in others, experience in themselves, and read in the news confer a superior knowledge and the right to criticize.

But plunge into the problem of sin and redemption the way Jesus did, the way Paul did. Live as if Christ is in you and in us, as if you are in Christ and we are in Christ. You will see great things. Christ's body does grow; his wife does change; we are being perfected. The particular beauties you are privileged to witness may never be chronicled by historians and reporters. But you will witness things that heaven chronicles as evidence that Christ lives in and works in his people. Live as you see the indwelling Person you love, and set about the process of speaking the truth in love. You will row your oar in the right direction, however much the sleet stings like bird-shot and the vast rollers make the boat pitch and roll.

God and His Children Will **Inherit** Each Other in Christ

In the last section, we drank in the reality that Christ is present in his people now. Now let yourself drink the reality that Christ will be present with us forever. Everything that is now semi-conscious, tainted, and half-baked will then be clear-minded, holy, and utterly fulfilled. We and God will inherit each other, will possess each other, will share together in his glory. We live in this hope.

In the fullness of time all shall be well and all manner of things shall be well. The Holy Spirit who rivets Christ into your heart now is the down payment of every good inheritance then and forever (Eph. 1:13–14). We are heirs of the promise (3:6). You will have God, and God will have you. We will be holy and blameless before him, a spotless church in all her glory. Everything will be summed up in Christ. We will have grown up together to the unity of faith and knowledge, complete in the maturity of the fullness of Christ.

All the storm and stress of human history, of church history, and of your individual life history will be seen as *about* the glory of Christ and the glory of the body of Christ, the fullness of him who fills all in all. The hope of our calling will be realized in indestructible glory and torrential joy, to the praise of the glory of his grace. So praise that glory. Live to the praise of the glory of his grace.

Who is God? Everything we have considered about him makes a difference. Remember that we began by saying, "Live out a faith like the Psalms yourself"? The 150 psalms sing, plead, meditate, command, and worship each of the eight truths we have considered. These are the ingredients that play out in a direct relationship with God. Paul's letter only rehearses garden-variety glories that appear wherever faith speaks to our Lord.

1. God makes us know him: "O continue Your lovingkindness to those who know You" (Ps. 36:10).

2. God acts according to his purposes: "Whatever the Lord pleases, He does" (Ps. 35:6).

3. God gives grace: "Surely goodness and lovingkindness will follow me all the days of my life" (Ps. 23:6).

4. God demonstrates power: "Once God has spoken; Twice I have heard this: that power belongs to God" (Ps. 62:11).

5. Christ invades to make peace between God and all nations: "My God, my God, why have You forsaken me?" (Ps. 22:1); "Praise the Lord, all nations; Laud Him, all peoples!" (Ps. 117:1).

6. God's wrath will fall on enemies: "Do homage to the Son, that He not become angry, and you perish in the way, For His wrath may soon be kindled" (Ps. 2:12).

7. God indwells his people and we indwell him: "The children of men take refuge in the shadow of Your wings. They drink their fill of the abundance of Your house: and You give them to drink of the river of Your delights. For with You is the fountain of life; in Your light we see light" (Ps. 36:7–9).

8. God inherits us and we inherit him: "You are my Lord; I have no good besides You. . . . The Lord is the portion of my inheritance" (Ps. 16:2, 5).

Paul's final call is that you live this way, with all prayer, at all times in the Spirit, on the alert with all perseverance, for all the saints (Eph. 6:18).

Remember that we also began by saying, "Speak the truth of God directly into people's lives." Paul's final request is for himself, and it is something you and I also need: speak boldly, as you ought to speak (Eph. 6:20). Even the most wonderful truths are not bold when stated impersonally. If I tell you theoretical truths, I don't demand your attention and I don't bid for your heart. It is all too easy to communicate just a nodding acquaintance with glories. Bold speech operates confidently and persuasively in the first and second person, both singular and plural. Paul was bold by grace. Do likewise.

Finally, remember that we began by saying, "Connect change in people's lives to what God is doing in Christ." Paul's final blessing does just this. He gives us something. Or, rather, God the Father and the Lord Jesus Christ give us something. Peace to the brothers, and love, with faith! Grace be with everyone who loves our Lord Jesus Christ with an indestructible and incorruptible love (Eph. 6:23–24). This is the supreme agenda: Trust and love Jesus, that through grace you might grow in peace both with God and with each other.

Ask and answer "Who is God?" rightly. You will learn to live and do these things that are nothing less than your humanity coming into its own.

3   GODLY ROLES AND RELATION-
SHIPS: EPHESIANS 5:21–6:9

How should we understand and structure the primary human relationships? Marriage, family, and workplace — the "domestic" issues that Ephesians 5:21–6:9 addresses — are hot topics. Should a wife submit to her husband, or is that a throwback to primitive patriarchy? Is a husband "the boss," whose home is the castle where he calls the shots? Must a teenager get parental permission regarding birth control or abortion? What does "family" mean in a society of divorce, remarriage, cohabitation, homosexuality, prolonged singleness, and out-of-wedlock births, where the "nuclear family" is no longer typical? Can a mother spank her child in the supermarket for throwing a tantrum? Is the chief purpose of schools to discipline and instruct children *in loco parentis,* or is their core mandate to foster self-expression, while medicating those who get out of hand? Can one party in the parent-child relationship "divorce" the other? Can an employer fire an employee for shoddy work? Both the legal system and popular opinion are perplexed by such questions. Rights, responsibilities, and authority are all up for grabs. While the believing church is not dancing on the ragged edge of such issues, Christian people are still deeply affected by the climate of uncertainty. We are too often confused and divided.

Ephesians offers sanity and wisdom to enable the people of God to grow up into oneness and maturity. But its answers might surprise you, whether you tend to be "traditionalist" or "egalitarian" about role relationships. Most of those who assert that Christ's grace *establishes* proper authority and role distinctions cite Ephesians 5:21–6:9 — end of discussion. They say that the commands are clear and consistent with the rest of Scripture. But a closer look at this particular passage

And be subject to one another in the fear of Christ. Wives, be subject to your own husbands, as to the Lord. For the husband is the head of the wife, as Christ also is the head of the church, He Himself being the Savior of the body. But as the church is subject to Christ, so also the wives ought to be to their husbands in everything. Husbands, love your wives, just as Christ also loved the church and gave Himself up for her, so that He might sanctify her, having cleansed her by the washing of water with the word, that He might present to Himself the church in all her glory, having no spot or wrinkle or any such thing; but that she would be holy and blameless. So husbands ought also to love their own wives as their own bodies. He who loves his own wife loves himself; for no one ever hated his own flesh, but nourishes and cherishes it, just as Christ also does the church, because we are members of His body. FOR THIS REASON A MAN SHALL LEAVE HIS FATHER AND MOTHER AND SHALL BE JOINED TO HIS WIFE, AND THE TWO SHALL BECOME ONE FLESH. This mystery is great; but I am speaking with reference to Christ and the church. Nevertheless, each individual among you

and its context puts a radical spin on submission and authority, pressing us with complementary truths that are often overlooked.

Meanwhile, most of those who assert that Christ's grace *eliminates* authority and role distinctions use other parts of the Bible to trump Ephesians 5:21–6:9. For example, both Galatians 3:28 ("there is neither slave nor free man, there is neither male nor female; for you are all one in Christ Jesus") and the prominence of "one anothering" commands (in Eph. 4, and elsewhere in Scripture) override the embarrassingly hierarchical language of Ephesians 5–6. But an honest look at this passage shows how the message of role differences is inextricable from the message of mutuality.

This chapter will look at three interlocking truths that make us wise. First, we all have a common call from God, defining us as peers with each other. Second, we each have a particular focus within our primary relationships, as servant-leaders and servant-submitters. Third, most of us wear multiple hats, sometimes called to lead and other times called to submit. If we hold these three things together—

also is to love his own wife even as himself, and the wife must see to it that she respects her husband. Children, obey your parents in the Lord, for this is right. HONOR YOUR FATHER AND MOTHER (which is the first commandment with a promise), SO THAT IT MAY BE WELL WITH YOU, AND THAT YOU MAY LIVE LONG ON THE EARTH. Fathers, do not provoke your children to anger, but bring them up in the discipline and instruction of the Lord. Slaves, be obedient to those who are your masters according to the flesh, with fear and trembling, in the sincerity of your heart, as to Christ; not by way of eyeservice, as men-pleasers, but as slaves of Christ, doing the will of God from the heart. With good will render service, as to the Lord, and not to men, knowing that whatever good thing each one does, this he will receive back from the Lord, whether slave or free. And masters, do the same things to them, and give up threatening, knowing that both their Master and yours is in heaven, and there is no partiality with Him.

—Ephesians 5:21–6:9

teaching ourselves and others to live them—we will live our life together with clarity, grace, and confidence, to the glory of God.

Our Common Calling

You have a common calling in all relationships to walk worthy of your identity as the Wife, Child, and Slave of the Lord. The Lord calls you to please him by humility, forbearance, candor, generosity, and tender-heartedness to all others. This common calling operates irrespective of the social roles you fill. It establishes a core attitude of mutuality that threads through every single relationship. We are one with each other and we are equals, leveled before God, whether apostle or new-hatched convert, four-star general or buck private, CEO or custodian. We live as peers before him who is no respecter of persons. Differences of competence, power, wealth, intelligence, achievement, opportunity, sex, age, and ethnic background vanish. All of

Ephesians 1:1–5:20 and 6:10–24 applies always, to every Christian, in every relationship.

You have been given God's grace, and commanded by your Lord Jesus to give grace to all others. Whether married or single, male or female, child or parent, employee or boss, you live within a mutuality: one church, members of one body, brothers and sisters to one another.[1] You are a *we*. You are called to be patient and constructive in every relationship. A husband and wife, or a parent and child, ought to communicate openly, drawing on each other for help and perspective, seeking to understand and encourage each other, repenting of the sins that interfere. No superiority, no double standards. If kids should not backtalk parents, then parents should not yell at kids. If wives should not be shrewish and domineering, then husbands should not be brooding and domineering. The common call applies equally to all.

More pointedly, when you think about the core of your identity, you are first and foremost *Wife*. You are one part of the body of Christ in union with her one Husband (Eph. 5:25–32).[2] Whether you are male or female, married or single, you are Wife to Jesus Christ, called to fear Christ and live subject to him. Similarly, at the core of who you are, you are essentially *Child*, beloved of the one Father (1:2; 1:5; 5:1). Whether you are a parent or a child, you are Child to God, called to obey and honor him. Furthermore, you are essentially *Slave* to the Lord (5:8–10; 6:5–9). Whether you are in authority or under authority in your workplace, you are Slave to Christ, called to obey and fear him. You may be a man, but you *are* a Wife. You may have kids, but you *are* a Child. You may have people answering to you, but you *are* a Slave. Each of us in our core identity is meant to live as a subordinate.

We all receive the love, provision, attention, mercy, protection, and upbuilding grace of our Husband, Father, and Lord. Christ is head, leader, master, and dominant partner. He is our "superior" and we are his "inferiors," in the good, old sense of the words. We are subjects, followers, and dependents. We stand under him. This subordinate relationship with the God who rules us and cares for us must color every aspect of our lives.

Growth in Christ, then, has a striking double thrust. First, maturity deepens submission. You increasingly learn to serve Christ, to please him (Eph. 5:8–10). But, second, this maturity makes you a leader. Submission heightens your likeness to him (4:32–5:2), and you increasingly picture the essence of leadership. You say No to self-will and self-serving. You say No to the world and the devil. You say Yes to a purposeful life for God that embodies clarity, conviction, integrity, wise counsel, forgiveness, generosity, patience, and self-giving love. So as any Christian submits to Christ's leadership, he or she becomes more of a leader in the best sense of the word. Good subjects grow masterly. Whatever the particulars of your calling as a husband-wife, parent-child, or boss-worker, they never override your core identity and common call as Wife, Child, and Slave. The common call conditions every detail.

Your Particular Focus

Your calling to "walk worthy" has a particular focus within each primary relationship in marriage, family, workplace. The Lord calls you to please him by emphasizing either submission or love within the spheres of your particular domestic relationships. The particular focus operates within "your own" domestic circles: with your own husband or wife, your own children or parents, and your own boss or workers. Within the various roles you fill, Christ says, "Pay particular attention to *this*." Your particular foci and the common calling do not override and cancel each other.[3] We might liken this to an orchestra and choir, assembled to perform a symphony in praise of the glory of God's grace. The common calling defines the key, rhythm, melodic themes, and lyrics which all performers and instruments hold in common as they submit to the conductor. The particular focus defines the distinctive parts performed by each instrument and voice, the timbre and harmony of bassoon and violin, of soprano and baritone.

The Particular Focus of Subordination

Are you a Wife, Child, and Servant of Christ who is also a *wife, child, or servant* to other human beings? You must particularly aim to submit, fear, respect, obey, honor, and serve. In doing so, not only do you do good to your own husband, your parents, and the persons over you in the workplace,[4] but you particularly serve Christ by standing under those God has placed over you. Your interactions with those persons should be continually shaped by a series of life-centering questions. "How can I consistently demonstrate—with my words, actions, and attitudes—the respect, honor, and submission due the person God has placed over me? How am I disrespectful, contrary, headstrong, lazy, or manipulative?" Ephesians takes hold of you: if you would fear Christ, fear your husband; if you would obey the Lord, obey your parents; if you would serve the Lord, serve your master.[5]

In these self-assertive times it is not popular to speak the language of subordination. But the Bible is consistent in the way it speaks of obedience, submission, and fear. First, we do all such things to God, but God never does them back to us. The common call presses all of us to obey, fear, and submit to the Lord. The only alternative? Serve the world's agenda, your own sinful flesh, and the devil. Second, the particular focus consistently presses wives, children, slaves, citizens, and the flock to serve those over them. But husbands, parents, masters, rulers, and pastors do not do the same back; they are to serve the welfare of those in their care. Both parties repent of self-will, but in different ways. Will you be headstrong and rebellious, or will you be consciously subject? Will you be headstrong and rebellious, or will you consciously love? (See also Col. 3–4; 1 Peter 2–3; Titus 2; Rom. 13; Hebrews 13; and 1 Tim. 6.)

The anarchistic, liberationist point of view contradicts what the Lord says about these things.[6] It must dismiss or twist the words Jesus has spoken through his messenger. The grain of truth—our common humanity—turns perverse when one asserts one's own will against God's will to submit. Many who would defend the Lord's clear words also weaken their force. Some, in effect, only pay lip service to God's will. They give so much attention to the *exceptions* to the rule that they fail to establish the relevance, beauty, and authority of the rule. "Yes, God calls a wife to submit, but of course if a husband is harsh, or asks her to sin, or does not consider her point of view, or won't lead spiritually, or is irresponsible financially, or. . . ." But Ephesians lists no exceptions. Paul camps out on the rule only, because the rule of submission so directly challenges our instinctive craving to get our own way.

Others weaken the force of the Lord's words by making the Bible sound as if it demeans and squelches humanity. They view submission and obedience as slavishness. They forget the common calling, and misunderstand the particular focus. They make submission look like "put up and shut up." They don't see how obedience leads to freedom from sin, and to freedom for love, courage, and purposeful living. The rule of submission, rightly understood and rightly lived, makes beauty, freedom, joy, and the glory of God shine forth.

There are, of course, exceptions. In every situation where you are called to stand under another, you must always "obey God rather than men" (Acts 5:29). Because of this overarching common call, a wife may need to admonish her husband for his attitude, a daughter challenge her mother's tone of voice, an employee dispute the boss's unfairness. In each case, the attitude of submission both to God and the person lends persuasiveness to the confrontation. There may be a time to call in the elders or even the police. There may be a time when a wife, child, or employee must say, "I want to honor you, but in conscience I can't participate in that because it's wrong." The particular focus never calls you to sin in violation of the common call to serve Christ.

But consider the immense quantity of gossip, sniping, covert and overt rebellion, stubbornness, disrespect, nagging, laziness, rolling of eyes, manipulating, grumbling, and domineering done by wives, children, and employees. These things are *never* right. That long and ugly list of contrariness does not need the occasion of someone else's wrongdoings—such things happen regardless. But even when a husband, parent, or boss is doing something terribly wrong, *never* pay back evil for evil to *anyone* (Rom. 12:17). Even when a person who ought to look out for your welfare is looking out only for his or her self-interest, let *no* rotten word come out of your mouth, but *only* what is good for edification according to the need of the moment (Eph. 4:29). The sin of another never cancels out either the general call or the particular focus. When godliness must challenge or resist human authority, it does so in a godly way, respecting both the human being and the office, even while opposing the sin of the human being who holds the office.

Is Christ's will difficult? Yes. Is it utterly contrary to the way the world acts and reacts by nature and habit? Yes. Is it contrary to the way you act and react by nature and habit? Yes. Is it contrary to what we most often hear and think? Yes. But is it right? Yes. And will Jesus Christ himself help you? Yes and amen! If you aim for submission when Christ calls you to submission, your life will thrive.

The Particular Focus of Nurture

Christ calls other people to particularly develop nurturing intentions and actions. A Wife, Child, and Servant who is also a *husband, father, or master* particularly aims to love, provide, care for, value, bless, bring mercy, give grace, purify, build up, teach, and treat fairly. In doing so, you do good to your own wife, your children, and the persons under you in the workplace. You particularly image Christ by looking out for the well-being of those God has placed within your care.[7] Leaders are to model themselves on Christ's way of leading: "Christ loved and gave himself up for us" (Eph. 5:2; 5:25).

It is striking that the common call tells each of us to follow his example (5:2), pursuing a merciful and redemptive agenda toward all others. His same example of self-giving is then particularly pressed upon husbands (5:25) and, by implication, upon parents and supervisors. Your interactions with your wife, children, and workers should continually be shaped by crucial questions. "How can I—by my words, actions, and attitudes—nourish, protect, care, and treat fairly the person God has placed under my care? How am I unfair, self-serving, harsh, neglectful, irritating, discouraging, or domineering?" Ephesians takes hold of you: if Christ loves you, love your wife; if your Father nourishes you, nourish your children; if your Master does you good, do good to those who serve you.

The chauvinistic, authoritarian point of view contradicts what the self-giving Lord says here.[8] The grain of truth—the necessity and propriety of authority relations—turns perverse when one asserts one's own will against God's will to give love. The submission of others to one's imperial will becomes the goal. This tendency weakens Christ's words by emphasizing the *rights* of an authority and the *responsibilities* of subordinates, rather than the responsibilities of those in authority. "I am the principal of this school, and I've learned to win by intimidation in my dealings with students, parents, teachers, and staff." "I am the parent, and what I say goes. Try me, and you'll regret it." "I've had a hard day at work, and when I get home I expect to kick back with the TV remote in my hand." But Ephesians does not list rights. Paul camps out on the rule only, because the rule of love so directly challenges the instinctive craving to get our own way.

Christ makes a devastating indictment of the normal habits of leaders, and he lived out a dramatic alternative. Yes, "the Son of Man did not come to be served, but to serve, and to give his life a ransom for many" (Mark 10:45). He served our best interest, but he did not serve our will, just as he did not come to indulge himself. Where we are called to lead others, we do so on his pattern. Husbands, parents, and managers, repent from self-will and from serving the other's will, so that you can serve the other's *well-being* before God. Paul is only reiterating Jesus' teaching: "Those who are recognized as rulers of the Gentiles lord it over them; and their great men exercise authority over them. But it is not this way among you, but whoever wishes to become great among you shall be your servant; and whoever wishes to be first among you shall be slave of all" (Mark 10:42–44). Look out for those whom God has placed under you. The rule of love, rightly understood and rightly lived, makes beauty, freedom, joy, and the glory of God shine forth. Husband, pursue your wife's well-being. Parents, nurture your children. Bosses, be fair and do good to those who work for you.[9]

There are, of course, rights. In every situation where you are called to look out for another's welfare, you must always lead. You cannot let your own desires rule. But you also cannot reverse roles, so that the desires of wife, child, and employee rule. There is a time to call someone on the carpet, to put an employee on probation, to discipline a child. There is a time when a husband, parent, or boss must say, "I love you and I want your best, but this is what we are going to do even if you don't like it." There is a time to take charge of a situation and frankly assert authority. The particular focus of showing tender consideration does not allow you to sin by shirking the responsibilities of leadership. The sins of others never justify ducking the particular focus on pursuing others' well-being, or forgetting the common call.

Consider the immense quantity of hostility, inconsiderateness, laziness, violence, self-serving, ingratitude, sheer neglect, favoritism, capriciousness, and bull-headed domineering done by husbands, parents, and bosses. These things are *never* right. That long and ugly list of self-serving tyranny does not need the occasion of someone else's wrongdoings—such things happen regardless. But even when a wife, child, or employee is doing something terribly wrong, *never* pay back evil for evil to *anyone* (Rom. 12:17). Even when a person under you acts out in rebellion, let *no* rotten word come out of your mouth, but *only* what is good for edification according to the need of the moment (Eph. 4:29). The sin of another never cancels out either the general call or the particular focus. When godliness must challenge another's wrong, it does so in a godly way, communicating the grace of God in word, deed, and attitude. It respects both the human being and the obligations of patient, redemptive authority, even while opposing the sin of the human being who is opposing authority.

Is Christ's will difficult? Utterly contrary to the way the world acts and reacts? Contrary to the way you act and react? Yes. But is it right? Yes. And will Christ himself help you? Yes and amen! If you aim for nurturing love when Christ calls you to nurturing love, your life will thrive.

Notice that in each case, you stand under or look after "your own." This is very important to keep straight. If you are a wife, you have a particular responsibility to submit to "your own" husband (Eph. 5:22; cf. Titus 2:5; 1 Peter 3:1), not to all other husbands, or males in general. If you are a husband, you are responsible to pursue the particular welfare of "your own" wife (5:28), not of every wife or females in general. As an employee, you owe obedience and service to "your own" master (Titus 2:9), not to all masters. The same pattern applies between parents and children, and to bosses with their workers.

A SYMPHONIC CALLING

The common call and the particular focus do not override each other. They work in symphony. This is crucial to timely and appropriate counseling ministry. For example, the mutuality between beloved children called for by Ephesians 4:1–16 and 4:25–5:2 *always* applies between husband-wife, parent-child, and master-slave. Many counseling problems are resolved when both parties tackle the common call to mercy, forgiveness, speaking the truth in love, and so forth, before their particular foci are even on the table. When a couple exchanges angry words or harbors bitter attitudes, the solution naturally begins with the common call to both.

Communication problems and conflict resolution usually have a certain temporal and logical priority: "How will each of you repent of bitterness and hostility, and of the demands and expectations that drive you? How will you learn Jesus, and so learn mercy, humility, and generosity? How can you communicate constructively?" Similarly, each person's knowledge of Christ and vital faith (3:14–21), each person's call to a lifestyle of change (4:17–24), and each person's walk of either folly or wisdom (5:3–20) will come on the table early and often. Two saints growing up out of their sins can learn to communicate with grace, as each party heeds the common call.

Ministry naturally proceeds to the particular focus of each person, to basic role failings that breed trouble. As husband and wife, they sin, and they can learn either to look after the other or to stand under the other, respectively. Many counseling problems are resolved as each party individually focuses on either the requisite submission or the requisite love. When counseling a wife, always explore, "How are you respectful toward your husband? How will you learn to actively pursue honoring your husband, rather than nagging him, ignoring him, resentfully going along with him, or despising him?" When counseling a husband, always consider, "How are you self-sacrificing, constructive, initiating, and constant in love toward your wife? How will you learn to actively pursue her well-being, rather than neglecting her, being preoccupied, or getting irritated?" Analogous questions operate in family and workplace conflicts.

Grasp the common call and the particular focus and you will be able to counter both liberationist and authoritarian tendencies. Each seizes onto one good thing and misses balancing truths. Liberationists are alert to grievous sins of tyranny and abuse, to inequities of power, and to unfairness. They aspire to maximize mutuality and humility, and to protect the weak. But they lose sight of the importance our Husband, Father, and Lord places on submission to husbands, parents, and masters, and his reproof of insubordination as a primal sin (see also 2 Peter 2:10).

Meanwhile, authoritarians are alert to grievous sins of anarchy and disrespect, to headstrong individualism, and to disorder. They aspire to respect duly constituted authority, and to protect the order within which human life thrives. But they lose sight of the importance Christ places on patient love for wives, children, and workers, and his reproof of authoritarianism as a primal sin (see also Mark 10:42–45). The Bible presses God's people to a third way, alert to the gamut of sins and aspiring to the gamut of righteousness.

YOUR MULTIPLE ROLES

Because you inhabit multiple roles, most of you will hear yourself addressed by Ephesians multiple times, from different angles. The common call addresses every one of us. But the particular focus addresses us in our unique situation, "your own" domestic relationships. As many as five of the six particular emphases might come with your name attached. If your parents are alive, and you are married with children, and you answer to a supervisor and have others answer to you in the workplace, then you are both boss and worker, both parent and child, and either husband or wife. A few people—for example, a retired, single person without children or parents—are only addressed by the general call. Ephesians 5:21–6:9 will not speak directly to their situation. Of course, the general principles that drive the passage do apply: we are Wife, Child, and Servant. Such persons still have plenty to occupy them, as the *rest* of Ephesians works into their heart and works out into their lifestyle! They will always be embedded somewhere in church and state, the two sets of submission-love relationships that Paul does not treat in Ephesians.

Single adults sometimes wonder, "Why does Paul leave me out of Ephesians? He only focuses on marrieds." But unmarried people are not left out by this single adult, Paul, who was sent on a mission by another single adult, Jesus. If you are single, you are directly addressed by Ephesians 1:1–5:20 and 6:10–24: the one flesh relationship between Jesus and his body. And much of 5:21–6:9 may apply. You are Wife. Though you do not have a calling as husband or wife, the background truths and specific exhortations will enrich your common call. You are Child. If you have living parents, you are addressed by 6:1–3; if you are a single parent, then 6:4 has your name on it. You are Slave. If you are an employee, you are addressed by 6:5–8 regarding your supervisor; if you are the boss, or have other leadership responsibilities, then 6:9 applies.

FIVE ILLUSTRATIONS

The net effect is that all of us are called to major on submission within some relationships and to major on initiating love within others. Imagine the following situation. Five members of your church work for a company that manufactures electronic equipment: a salesman, the sales manager, a secretary, the president, and a custodian. All five are called to live out the attitudes and actions of the common call. These will saturate their lives inside and outside work: how they treat each other, how they treat customers, how they reconcile conflicts, and so forth. But each of them also has a unique configuration of responsibilities to submit or to nurture.

The *salesman* is a single, twenty-eight-year-old man who lives with his parents. Ephesians 5:21–6:9 particularly addresses him three times. He is a child, servant, and master. He is called (1) to honor his parents, (2) to respect and serve his sales manager, and (3) to show kindness and consideration to his secretary. He naturally has no particular responsibilities to a wife or children. Notice how his submission to Christ gets channeled into submission to authority in some relationships and loving headship in others.

The *sales manager* is a married, forty-eight-year-old woman, with three college-age children and an elderly mother. Paul addresses her no less than five times, as a wife, child, parent, servant, and master. She is called (1) to respect and submit to her husband, (2) to honor her mother, (3) to nourish and lead her children, (4) to serve the higher-level management of the company, and (5) to treat the salesman and secretary with kindness and fairness as she leads them. She is challenged in two places to learn how to lead others, and in three places to learn how to respect others.

The *secretary* is a fifty-eight-year-old woman, never married, without children, whose parents have passed away. Paul's letter addresses her only twice, as servant and as master. She is called (1) to respect and serve the president, the sales manager, and the salesman, and (2) to show a master's kindness to the clerk and the custodian who answer to her. She has no particular responsibilities to a husband, children, or parents. But, like all of us, God has placed her in a situation where she must learn both how to stand under others and how to look out for others.

The *president*, a thirty-five-year-old married man with two elementary school children, inherited the company when his parents died. The Lord addresses him three times with the call to exercise leadership responsibly and constructively. As husband, father, and master, he is (1) to love and provide for his wife, (2) to nurture his children, and (3) to treat his employees in ways that do them good. Learning to live as Christ's Wife, Child, and Servant places him entirely in the leadership role in his domestic relations. He will learn submission elsewhere—in relation to his church elders, and in relation to the government authorities with whom he interacts regarding occupational safety, taxes, and legal disputes.

Finally, the *custodian* is a newly married, childless, twenty-two-year-old woman, whose parents are alive. She is addressed three times. She pours her energies into the roles of wife, child, and servant. She is (1) to submit to her husband, (2) to honor her parents, and (3) to serve all the others in her workplace. For her, submission to Christ places her entirely in the helper and subordinate role in domestic relations. She learns to image the loving authority of Christ only as part of the common call to build up brothers and sisters in Christ.

It is worth noting that all five persons are embedded in two other spheres. The exact same pattern described above holds for relationships within the church and with government authorities. First, in the church we are all Sheep of the great Shepherd. Those Sheep who are also *undershepherds* have a particular responsibility to shepherd the other Sheep in their charge. The Sheep who are also *sheep* in a local congregation have a particular responsibility to serve, honor, and submit to their undershepherds. In our example, all five persons are sheep called to submit to their elders.

We are also all Subjects of the great King. Those Subjects who are also *kings* or *other rulers* have a particular responsibility to provide, protect, and maintain justice for their subjects. Subjects of God who are also *subjects* have a particular responsibility to submit to those who govern them: pay taxes, obey laws, treat with respect. In our example, all five persons are called to stand under local, regional, and national government.

Changing Roles and Responsibilities

Notice that a person's roles usually change over time. Leaving one's parents to cleave to one's spouse changes the forms of honor shown to parents. The death of a husband or parents cancels obligations of submission. Abandonment by a wife or the marriage of a child cancels or greatly alters obligations for loving provision and guidance. In our example, if the custodian becomes a mother, she will gain a new role. If she gets involved helping with the church's youth ministry, she will gain two new obligations: to love and lead the teenagers, and to submit to the youth pastor.

Responsibilities also modulate as circumstances change. The sales manager treats her college-age children in a different way than the president treats his elementary school children. Both remain parents, but the appropriate kind of nurture evolves. Similarly, the salesman now expresses honor to his parents with "less" obedience than when he was a young child, and with "more" obedience than if he were to marry and move out. His parents no longer tell him when to take a shower, but he lives by the rules of the house, rather than setting his own.

Sometimes roles do not evolve: if one of the sales manager's children is mentally handicapped, she will exert a great deal of control as long as they both live. On the other hand, sometimes roles almost completely reverse. If the sales manager's aging mother suffers from dementia, the daughter will have to take charge of her affairs, imposing decisions on the mother who nursed her, led her to faith, and set her curfew. The call to honor her mother will remain until death as a core attitude affecting her manner and emotions, though in much of the business of life she must now act as a loving authority.

Finally, it is important to note that God is "no respecter of persons" (Eph. 6:9; KJV). Some people tend to favor persons in authority. They tend to look down on "little" people. They see sins of rebellion more clearly than they see sins of control and domineering.

Other people tend to favor persons who are in traditionally subordinate roles, and tend to despise authority in subtle or overt ways. They are soured toward "big" people. They see sins of domineering more clearly than they see sins of rebellion and self-will. But God shows no favoritism. Paul tells both *masters* (Eph. 6:9) and *slaves* (Col. 3:25) that there is "no partiality" with God. God does not play favorites. Don't think you can drift, wriggle, or run away from his revealed will for you.

This short letter to the Ephesians, along with the rest of Scripture, gives us the wisdom to find our way amid life's many variables. Trying to learn what is pleasing to the Lord, we learn the "fruit of the light" that consists in all goodness, righteousness, and truth (Eph. 5:9). God's pattern for relationships is exquisite and consistent.

Learn and live these three truths: First, we must all obey the general call to treat one another with redemptive love. Let it saturate every relationship at all times. Treat everyone the same.

Second, every person in a subordinate role must focus on standing under those placed over him or her. Every person in an authority role must focus on looking out for the welfare of those placed under him or her. Treat people differently.

Third, life is so arranged that all of us must submit to Christ by standing under some people, and almost all of us (barring only the severely disabled) must image Christ by looking after other people. "Must" in all three of these truths is not a given, of course, but the agenda of the light.

Those who do not submit to Christ follow the desires of body and mind instead, and they walk in darkness. Wherever they are called to whole-hearted submission, they will either usurp or play doormat. Wherever they are called to persevering nurture, they will either tyrannize or abdicate. They are blind to the radiant, wise lifestyle taught by the fear of Christ. But those who follow the Messiah Jesus, in whom the nations find both hope and God, will live in this light.

4

PEACE, BE STILL:
PSALM 131

God speaks to us in many different ways. When you hear, "Now it came to pass," settle down for a good story. When God asserts, "I Am," trust his self-revelation. When he promises, "I will," bank on it. When he tells you, "You shall . . . you shall not," do what he says. Psalm 131 is in yet a different vein. Most of it is holy eavesdropping. You have intimate access to the inner life of someone who has learned composure, and invites you to the same. Psalm 131 is show-and-tell for how to become peaceful inside. Listen in.

> LORD,
>   my heart is not proud,
>   and my eyes are not haughty,
>   and I do not go after things too great
>   and too difficult for me.
> Surely I have composed and quieted my soul,
>   like a weaned child on his mother,
>   like a weaned child on me is my soul.
>   Israel, hope in the LORD now and forever.
>   (Author's translation)

This person is quiet on the inside because he has learned the only true and lasting composure. He describes what the peace that passes understanding is like (Phil. 4:7).

Amazingly, this man isn't noisy inside. He isn't busy-busy-busy. Not obsessed or on edge. Pressures to achieve don't consume him. Failure and despair don't haunt him. Anxiety isn't spinning him into free fall. Regrets don't corrode his inner experience. He's not stumbling through the minefield of blind longings and fears.

He's quiet.

Are you quiet inside? Is Psalm 131 your experience, too? If your answer is No, what is the "noise" going on inside you? Where does it come from? How do you get busy and preoccupied? Why do you lose your composure? When do you get worried, irritable, wearied, or hopeless? How can you regain composure?

We'll get to these questions, because they are what Psalm 131 answers. But let's dip our toes in the water before taking the plunge.

ABOUT THE PSALM

First, think about who is talking to us in Psalm 131. We are listening to the inner conversation of someone whom God called "a man after his own heart" (1 Sam. 13:14). In other words, this man processes life the way we're meant to. That makes him worth listening to.

David wrote the original words 3000 years ago. The psalm bears the heading, *A Song of Ascents, of David*. Like others of David's most memorable psalms—16, 23, 31, 32, 103, 139—Psalm 131 captures the quintessence of one piece of human experience. We know many things about David, but two characteristics stand out. First, the Lord chose David, anointed him, loved him, and blessed him. God was *with* David. Second, David knew this Lord. He referred his life to God; he walked *with* God. Such a man lets you into his stream of consciousness.

A millennium later, someone else lived this psalm even more fully. Update the heading: *A Song of Ascents, of Jesus*. Psalm 131 expresses Jesus' life experience, the inner workings of his consciousness. Think about that. The Father's chosen, anointed, loved, and blessed Son lets you listen in. In Psalm 131, God who became a man thinks out loud for you. This isn't just an exhortation about how to think with the mind of Christ. Jesus' own internal peacemaking happens in front of your eyes.

Second, get a clear picture of what Psalm 131 is *not*. It does not portray unruffled detachment or stoic indifference. It's not about having an easygoing personality or low expectations. It's not retreat from the troubles of life or retirement to a life of ease. It's not the quieting of inner noise that a glass of wine or a daily dose of Prozac produces. After all, Jesus and David were both kingdom-builders who expected—and achieved—huge things in the midst of commotion and trouble. They experienced pressure, joy, heartache, outrage, affection, and courage. So Psalm 131's inner quiet comes in the midst of actions, relationships, and problems.

Third, understand rightly what Psalm 131 describes. *This composure is learned, and it is learned in relationship.* Such purposeful quiet is achieved, not spontaneous. It is conscious, alert, and chosen. It is a form of self-mastery by the grace of God: "Surely I have composed and quieted my soul." And it happens in living relationship with Someone Else. You are "discipled" into such composure. Listen and watch carefully. You'll come to understand a form of self-mastery that arises only in relationship. Can *you* get to this quieted place, here and now, in your actual life? Yes. This psalm is from a man who leads you by the hand. The last sentence of the psalm stops talking with God and talks to you. Psalm 131 aims to become your words as a chosen and blessed child. We'll look closely at the dynamic. Psalm 131 contains big things in a very tiny package, divided into three parts.

Deliverance from Noise

LORD,
> my heart is not proud,
> and my eyes are not haughty,
> and I do not go after things too great
> > and too difficult for me. (Ps. 131:1)

Faith delivers you from your biggest problem, a proud self-will. David says to the Lord, "I am *not* self-trusting, opinionated, and headstrong. I am *not* superior to others. I am *not* attempting the impossible." The process through which he was tamed is still implicit (until v. 2). The reason for such astonishing composure and humility is still implicit (until v. 3). We see the results first, and are intrigued. David is quiet. He has consciously distanced himself from everything that rattles inside us. To be able to say, "I am *not* something," you must learn to identify the thing you are not.

A pool of water in the stillness of dawn is highly sensitive to vibration. Watch the surface and you can detect the approach of the slightest breeze or a slight tremor in the ground. You locate the wriggling of a fish you cannot see or a tiny water bug skating over the surface. In the same way, this quiet psalm can make you highly sensitive to "noise." It is an instrument with which to detect gusts, tremors, or thrashing in the soul. What makes us so noisy inside? Turn the psalm into its opposite, the anti-psalm:

> Self,
>> my heart is proud (I'm absorbed in myself),
>> and my eyes are haughty (I look down on other people),
>> and I chase after things too great and too difficult for me.
> So of course I'm noisy and restless inside; it comes naturally,
>> like a hungry infant fussing on his mother's lap,
>> like a hungry infant, I'm restless with my demands and
>>> worries.
> I scatter my hopes onto anything and everybody all the time.

Noisiness makes perfect sense. You can identify exactly where the rattling noises come from.

Do you remember *Alice in Wonderland*, how Alice was either too big or too small? Because she was never quite the right size, she was continually disoriented. We all have that problem. We are the wrong size. We imagine ourselves to be independent and autonomous: *proud hearts*. We become engrossed in monstrous trivialities of our own devising. We pursue grandiosities and glories. One of the symptoms of the disease is that we become noisy inside.[1] Seventeenth-century English had a great word for stirring up much ado about nothing: *vainglory*. Or, in Macbeth's bitter words: "Life's but a walking shadow, a poor player, that struts and frets his hour upon the stage, and then is heard no more; it is a tale told by an idiot, full of sound and fury, signifying nothing" (V:5).

Of course, this doesn't seem like much of a problem while we busily telemarket our pride to ourselves and others. "I just want a little respect and appreciation. Of course I want the home appliances to work and the car mechanic to be honest. That's pretty normal. I want approval and understanding. Is that too much to ask? I want the church to thrive and my sermon to go well. It's for God, after all. I want satisfaction and compensation for the ways others did me wrong. I don't want much. If only I had better health, a little more money, a more meaningful job, nicer clothes, and a restful vacation, then I'd be satisfied. I want a measure of success—just a bit of recognition—as an athlete, a beauty, an intellectual, a musician, a leader, a mother. I want control. Who doesn't? I want to feel good. Doesn't God want me to feel good? I want to have more self-confidence, to believe in myself. I want . . . well, I want MY WAY. I WANT THE GOODIES. I WANT GLORY. I WANT GOD TO DO MY WILL. I WANT TO BE GOD . . . Doesn't everybody?"

Our slavery to the corruption that is in the world by lust (2 Peter 1:4) seems so plausible. Our restless disorientation seems so natural, so desirable. But it's noisy. The noise tips us off to what's going on. The static of anxiety, irritation, despondency, or ambition makes sense from within the logic of a proud heart. If you are *not* proud, then quietness and composure make sense.

It also goes with the territory that we are opinionated, routinely judging and belittling others: *haughty eyes*. Pride is not just about ME. It's also about you. I must look down on you in some way. Our absorption in judgmental opinions runs very deep. Pride says, "I'm right in myself." Haughty eyes say, "I'm right compared to you." Have you noticed that even people who feel lousy about themselves are judgmental toward others? When you feel inferior to others, you don't respect them or treat them with mercy. Instead, you envy, hate, grumble, and criticize. Even self-belittling tendencies—"low self-esteem," self-pity, self-hatred, timidity, fears of failure and rejection—fundamentally express *pride* failing, *pride* intimidated, and *pride* despairing. Such pride, even when much battered, still finds someone else to look down on.

A friend of mine once vividly described this problem. She said that she had almost no true peers, people with whom she related eye-to-eye. Her relationships were not characterized by generosity, candor, or trust. There were a few "pedestal people" in her life, people she thought could do no wrong. There were many, many "pit people" in her life, people she looked down on for one reason or another. The two categories were connected only by an elevator shaft! A person could fall off the pedestal and end up in the pit. She had a long history of disappointment in every relationship. Unsurprisingly, she was a woman with a lot of inner noise: fretful, self-absorbed, easily offended, depressed, competitive. But as she grew in Christ, she grew in composure. As she learned to live in the way of peace, lo and behold, she began to discover peers and to build friendships.

Another way of putting this is to say that she stopped *pursuing impossibilities*. That's the third phrase in Psalm 131:1: not going after things that are beyond you, "things too great and too wonderful" (author's translation). Even the small, everyday things that everyone races after are, in fact, "beyond us." From your daily bread to your abilities and opportunities, these are gifts from God that you don't control. What happens when you attempt to control another person's attitudes and choices? You set yourself up for despair or rage, anxiety or short-lived euphoria, suspicion or manipulation. What happens when you attempt to ensure that you will not get sick and die? You become obsessed with diet and exercise, or litigious toward doctors, or plagued with fear that any nagging pain might be the one that finally gets you. What happens when you are obsessed with getting people to like you? You become flirtatious or artificial, a coward or a deceiver, a chameleon or a recluse. What happens when you live for success in sports, career, or your physical appearance? You get injured. You retire. Someone comes along who is better than you. You get old and wrinkled. You die.

How different things are when you pursue what you are called to pursue! You've discovered what you're made for. You have composure. Paul put it this way, "Flee from youthful lusts and pursue righteousness, faith, love and peace, with those who call on the Lord from a pure heart" (2 Tim. 2:22). When you go after the right things, you'll find what you're looking for.

THE PROCESS OF PEACE

Surely I have composed and quieted my soul,
like a weaned child on his mother,
like a weaned child on me is my soul. (Ps. 131:2)

Having seen the result, we now see the process. Quiet your noisy self to know the peace that passes understanding. To gain composure is to go through a weaning process. Something that once meant everything comes to mean nothing. What is this composing, this quieting, this weaning?

Notice that you are definitively different at the end of the process. You aren't "sort of composed, sort of quiet, sort of weaned." You once were noisy, and now you've learned quiet. We always learn through a process, but in principle there are not gradations. You either know how to quiet yourself or you stay noisy. You're either a nursing infant or a weaned child. In the first word in Psalm 131:2, translated as *Surely*, David comes close to taking an oath: "If I don't . . . If this isn't so, then . . . I swear that . . . !" David means it. He is bound and determined to wrestle down his unruly soul.

Dying to your restless, fretful, and irritable ways does not come easily. There is no automatic formula or pat answer. To *compose* your soul means literally to level it. Bulldoze the building site. Get a grip. When Jesus said, "Peace, be still" to the stormy lake, he smoothed the turbulence. To *quiet* your soul means to silence the noise and tumult. "Sssshhh" to your desires, fears, opinions, anxieties, agendas, and irritabilities. We looked in detail at the assertions David made about himself in the first verse. Now we see that David had gone about unplugging the noise machines and knocking down the ladders. This sort of composure and quietness is not apathy, but alertness. It is conscious, not unconscious. It is self-mastery by grace, not sleepy ease.

How do you purify your heart? How does a proud heart become humble? Not by doing penance. Not by beating on yourself or resolving to mend your ways. You can do all those things and still be proud. You cannot destroy the tumult of self-will by sheer will: "I will stop being irritable. I will stop being fretful. I will stop imposing my will on the universe." Can the leopard change its spots? You are not strong enough; you are too strong. The only way you can wrestle yourself down is by the promises of God. You need help the way a drowning man needs help from outside himself to rescue him.

Only one thing is strong enough to overpower a stormy life: what God promises to do in and through Jesus Christ. It is by great and precious promises that we escape the corruption that is in the world by lust (2 Peter 1:4). From God's side, we escape ourselves by being loved by Jesus Christ through the powerful presence of the Holy Spirit. From our side, we escape ourselves by learning a lifestyle of intelligent repentance, genuine faith, and specific obedience.

In the 1700s, Katarina von Schlegel wrote a hymn about wrestling to compose and quiet her soul. It is an extended personalization of Psalm 131:2, presumably written in the context of some great loss.

> Be still, my soul: the Lord is on thy side;
> bear patiently the cross of grief or pain;
> leave to thy God to order and provide;
> in every change, he faithful will remain.
> Be still, my soul: thy best, thy heavenly Friend
> through thorny ways leads to a joyful end.

Think about that, and still yourself. Remember the Lord's favor, control, fidelity, and friendship. Remain patient in your sufferings.

> Be still, my soul: thy God doth undertake
> to guide the future as he has the past.
> Thy hope, thy confidence let nothing shake;
> all now mysterious shall be bright at last.
> Be still, my soul: the waves and winds still know
> his voice who ruled them while he dwelt below.

Why does she have to keep reminding herself, "Be still, my soul"? We need to be stilled. Who is strong enough to rule the things that wail, rattle, or shout within us? Only God, who is purposively active in his children. He will have the final say. Christ ruled the storms, rules them still, and will rule them. You can trust Someone Else amid your present uncertainties.

> Be still, my soul: when dearest friends depart,
> and all is darkened in the vale of tears,
> then shalt thou better know his love, his heart,
> who comes to soothe thy sorrow and thy fears.
> Be still, my soul: thy Jesus can repay
> from his own fullness all he takes away.

Perhaps irreparable loss is the hardest thing to face. A loved one dies, and will never again walk through the door to greet you. You retire, and can never again return to the work into which you poured your talent, time, and concern. You will never again be young. No second chance to do your college years or that failed marriage over again. Such things devastate us. Can you quiet yourself? Jesus gives you himself.

> Be still, my soul: the hour is hast'ning on
> when we shall be forever with the Lord,
> when disappointment, grief, and fear are gone,
> sorrow forgot, love's purest joys restored.
> Be still, my soul: when change and tears are past,
> all safe and blessed we shall meet at last.

Katarina von Schlegel was the ultimate realist. Most of the noise in our souls is generated by our attempts to control the uncontrollable. We grasp after the wind. We rage, fear, and finally despair. But this wise sister focused on an enduring hope. Be still, my soul. All that is hard now will be forgotten amid love's purest joys. This slight, momentary affliction is preparing for us an eternal weight of glory beyond all comparison (2 Cor. 4:17). Psalm 131 faith lives with eyes open.

David drives this home with a wonderful metaphor: *like a weaned child on his mother, like a weaned child, my soul rests on me*. The original sentence emphasizes the parallelism and does not even contain the verb "rests": "Like a weaned child on his mother, like a weaned child on me my soul." Most of us have seen a nursing child before the weaning process begins. For those of you who are mothers, this image is particularly evocative. When a hungry child is placed on his mother's lap, he is agitated. He roots around, squirming anxiously. If he doesn't get immediate satisfaction, he frets and fusses. Mother's milk means life, health, satisfaction, joy. If mother doesn't deliver right now, he'll thrash about. His emotions range over the whole spectrum of noisy, negative emotion, the childish versions of things that destroy adults: anxiety, depression, anger, jealousy, discontent, and confusion. We've all seen that.

But have you ever seen that same child when he is successfully weaned? A dramatic change has taken place. Now the child rests upon his mother, quiet and at peace (assuming she's spooning in the solid food!). The child has *changed*. Envision your own soul as a small child sitting on your lap. You used to be noisy, squirmy, and demanding. Now you sit still. That's the picture of learning peace.

T HE R EASON FOR P EACE

Israel, hope in the L ORD now and forever. (Ps. 131:3)

We looked first at the result, and then at the process. This last line gives the reason. The Lord, Jesus Christ, is your hope. Pride dies as the humility of faith lives. Haughtiness lowers its eyes as the dependency of hope lifts up its eyes. You stop pursuing impossibilities when you start pursuing certainties. This simple sentence distills wonders. Consider the command and invitation you are now receiving.

First, you are called by name. *Israel* originally named an insignificant family of nomads. Later it identified a mildly significant buffer state in the ancient Near East. But now the scope of Psalm 131:3 extends to every nation, tribe, tongue, and people. That includes you. We are all called to set our hope in the Lord now and forever. Sometimes Jesus applies the old name to his new people: "the Israel of God" (Gal. 6:16), or the Jew inwardly, with a circumcised heart (Rom. 2:29). But now we are more commonly called by other names:

> Beloved
> chosen
> holy ones (set apart to the Holy One; "saints")
> sons and daughters
> brothers and sisters
> slaves
> called out ones ("church")
> disciples

Disciple is the name most commonly used to describe you. You intentionally learn and change as you live with your teacher-for-life, Jesus Christ.[2]

Second, you are called to *hope in the* LORD. Who is this person who topples all the ladders to nowhere and gives you something better? He is the true God, the only Redeemer from the idols we construct. Your hope is in "I AM," who becomes known simply as "the Lord." Eventually, he more immediately and personally names himself: Jesus Christ is Lord.

What exactly are you to hope for? Psalm 131 is very condensed, stating the general principle without any specifics beyond the Person. You are free to particularize the content of hope with promises from throughout the Bible. But it would probably be wisest to start in the immediate vicinity. Psalm 131 is intentionally paired with Psalm 130, which gives details about what exactly we are to hope in (in italics).

> Out of the depths I have cried to *You*, O LORD.
> Lord, *hear my voice!*
> Let *Your ears be attentive*
> To the voice of my supplications.
> If *You*, LORD, should mark iniquities,
> O LORD, who could stand?
> But *there is forgiveness with You*,
> That You may be feared.
> I wait *for the* LORD, my soul does wait,
> And *in His word* do I hope.
> My soul waits *for the Lord*
> More than the watchmen for the morning;
> Indeed, more than the watchmen for the morning.
> O Israel, hope *in the* LORD,
> For *with the* LORD *there is lovingkindness*,
> And *with Him is abundant redemption*.
> And *He will redeem Israel*
> *From all his iniquities*.

The things in italics invite your hope. You will not go wrong if you fulfill Psalm 131:3 by living out Psalm 130. The sense of need, the eager anticipation, and the inner tension of waiting effectively illustrate what Psalm 131's composure is like. We are racehorses, not milk cows, called to equine alertness and focus, not bovine placidity and apathy!

Third, you are called to such hopes *now and forever*. David speaks in a generality, literally, "from now until forever." That pretty much covers the territory! But the time frame of our hope is even more clearly defined than David could have known. We hope fully on the grace to be given at the revelation of Jesus Christ (1 Peter 1:13). Both *now* and *forever* shine with newer, brighter meanings for us who read Psalm 131 in the light of Christ. Transpose this last line to include Christ as you personalize the psalm, for in him we have more details to inform intelligent faith.

PERSONALIZING PSALM 131

Your biggest problem is proud self-will. That's the noise machine inside you. And there is a way to gain composure through the Lord. What should you do now so you can honestly say, "My heart is not proud"? How can you make this psalm your own? How do you quiet yourself?

First, identify the ladders to nowhere that pride erects.

- Where do you raise up ladders of *achievement?* How do you go for victory, for grades, for promotion, for the big church, for the idealized devotional life?
- Where do you clamber up ladders of *acquisition?* Where do you say "if only"? Where do you seek the goodies, the security, the recognition?
- Where do you race up ladders of *appetite?* Where do you gratify your need for ease or control? Where do you gratify hunger or lust or superiority?
- Where do you scuttle up ladders of *avoidance?* Where do you get away from poverty, rejection, suffering, and people?

Pride sets up these ladders and climbs on high. The inner static reveals where your pride is located. You feel nervously happy when you climb up a few rungs. You feel bitter and despairing when you land in a heap at the bottom. Haughty eyes look down on anyone below you on the ladders you most cherish. You freely criticize others about some things, but not everything. Those particular ladders from which you gaze down in disdain are *your* precious and proud aspirations. You feel envy or despair when anyone else rises (or threatens to rise) above you in some things, but not everything. You chase after impossibilities, matters too great and too wonderful. No wonder you are noisy inside. Stairs of sand look so good. They promise to take you someplace, but they collapse beneath the weight of your life.[3]

Second, come to know Jesus. He never climbed the ladders to nowhere. He's the iconoclast, the ladder-toppler, the idol-breaker, the lie-piercer, the pride-smasher. He gives life, makes peace, gives joy, and makes you over. Seek Jesus, carrying your sins in your hands. Psalm 131 is his consciousness: quieted but not placid, composed but not detached. His composure is a communicable attribute, something he willingly teaches and gives away. Psalm 131 embodies a radical dynamic. It goes against everything we innately cherish, yet it gives us something worth cherishing forever. You need Jesus to liberate your heart in a coup-d'état. Psalm 131 overthrows the powers-that-be to establish the reign of Him-who-is.

This is a quiet little psalm, but it contains a revolutionary dynamic. Marx, Nietzsche, and Freud have been well described as "masters of suspicion." They rip veils off civilized, self-righteous complacency. They rattle the cage with counter-cultural analyses of the human condition. *Calvin and Hobbes, The Far Side,* and *Non Sequitur* give suspicion a touch of whimsy. Beats, hippies, existentialists, punks, and Goths try giving suspicion a viable lifestyle. They see something of what's wrong, and aim for something truer. But how can you criticize pride in others without being immolated in your own? When it comes to suspicion, only one person really pulls it off.

Jesus is the Master of masters of suspicion. And he's master of the lifestyle alternative, too. The Psalm 131 person engages in self-suspicion and social suspicion, toppling vainglory at every turn. But such a person ends in mirth and frolic, not cynicism and hypocrisy. Jesus gives you his own joy. His counterculture refreshes itself over the long haul. It has a principle of self-renewal: the demolition of pride, the creation of peace, humility, composure. "This is eternal life, that they may know you, the only true God, and Jesus Christ whom you have sent" (John 17:3). Jesus unveils our inner worlds and floods our hearts with light. He exposes both the self-righteously complacent and the self-righteously suspicious. He turns all the inner worlds upside down. He disassembles the noise machines. He saves you from yourself. He teaches you quiet. He gives you himself.

Third, live the mindset of Psalm 131. When you set your hope in the right place, you become the right size. No pride, no looking down from on high, no hot pursuit of pipe dreams. The soul-storms meet their Master: "'Be quiet. Be still.' What is this? He commands even the demons, and they obey him! Who is this, that wind and sea obey him?" (see Mark 1:25–27; 4:39–41).

Psalms are meant to be read and quoted verbatim. Read Psalm 131 again. Read it slowly and take in each sentence.

> LORD,
>   my heart is not proud,
>   and my eyes are not haughty,
>   and I do not go after things too great and too difficult for me.
> Surely I have composed and quieted my soul,
>   like a weaned child on his mother,
>   like a weaned child on me is my soul.
> Israel, hope in the LORD now and forever.

Memorize these words. It will take you only a few minutes to make them your own. Then turn these words over in your mind before drifting to sleep. Before counseling someone else. As you drive in your car. When you approach God to talk. When you get noisy inside for whatever reason. Read these words together in public worship. Preach or teach this psalm. Get the music, and sing this psalm with your brothers and sisters.

Psalms learned verbatim teach you to play "classical music," compositions practiced from the score, memorized, and played note-perfect. Psalms also intend to teach you how to play "jazz." Psalm 131 is a model as you improvise within your life experience. Most of life you make up as you go along. You'll probably say thousands of words out loud today. And that's nothing compared to the audio and video streaming continuously within your soul. Most of daily life is extemporaneous speech, not read from a manuscript. Few scenes in life are scripted, rehearsed, and recited. Psalm 131 is for jazz as well as classical. It gives a "for instance" for the rest of your thinking, sketching the general contours of a God-related life of dependent faith. You color in the living details, playing out personal variations on the Bible's theme. Create such inner conversations moment by moment. "Rejoice always, pray without ceasing, give thanks in all circumstances, because this is God's will for you in Christ Jesus" (1 Thess. 5:16–18). The Holy Spirit forms in you a psalm-generating heart and lifestyle. As you live in Christ in all circumstances, Jesus teaches you to think the way he does.

5 WHY ME? COMFORT FROM PSALM 10

Helen had been betrayed by her husband. He had played the part of the dutiful, churchgoing husband, father, and provider for many years. But unbeknownst to Helen, he had maintained mistresses in three cities. Helen had trusted him with all the family finances, including a half million dollars she had inherited. He siphoned off all her money into his name. He spent much of it and ran up debts besides, financing a lifestyle of gambling and immorality. Helen had been ignorant of this, but she was not unaware of other evils. For many years, she had been forced to commit sexual acts she found repellent. In public her husband's demeanor was good-natured, but in private he would berate her and threaten to beat her. He routinely called her names and blamed her for every problem.

Helen suffered in silence until bankruptcy broke his secret life into the open. Helen was a believer who had sought God as her refuge amid the sexual and verbal abuse. But when everything exploded, she felt unprotected and insecure. All along, genuine faith in God had intertwined with her tendencies toward keeping up appearances: "Put up with it, pretend it's not really happening, and everything's okay." Now she couldn't pretend. She was in trouble.

What should she say? How should she think? What should she do? Where is God amid such devastation? God knows our hearts; he anticipates these questions in a time of storm. And his word speaks hope, power, and comfort to those in such situations. Psalm 10, for example, was written for those who have been victimized by others. It was written for Helen. It is a message of anguish and refuge. It is *not* about pretending, but about facing reality and truth.

Why do You stand afar off, O LORD?
Why do You hide in times of trouble?
In pride the wicked burn, pursuing the afflicted.
They are caught in the plots which they have devised.
For the wicked boasts of his heart's desire.
The greedy man curses and spurns the LORD.
The wicked, in the haughtiness of his countenance, does not
     seek Him.
All his thoughts are, "There is no God."
His ways prosper at all times.
Your judgments are on high, out of his sight.
As for all his adversaries, he snorts at them.
He says to himself, "I will not be moved;
throughout all generations I will not be in adversity."
His mouth is full of curses and deceit and oppression;
under his tongue is trouble and wickedness.
He sits in the lurking places of the villages.
In the hiding places he kills the innocent.
His eyes stealthily watch for the unfortunate.
He lurks in a hiding place as a lion in his lair.
He lurks to catch the afflicted.
He catches the afflicted when he draws him into his net.

Helen must pick up many pieces. She needs the daily comfort of pastor and friends. She needs the church to play grace-giving hardball with her husband about his sins. (He skipped town two weeks later, moved in with one of the mistresses, and was excommunicated for his impenitence.) Helen needs legal advice, immediate financial help, and financial counsel about what to do next. She needs to find out if she has a sexually transmitted disease. She needs to praise God, to hear the Word of life, to participate in the Lord's Supper, to pray with others. She needs counsel to console her and to nourish good fruits already present: faith, buds of forgiveness, and love. She needs counsel to deal with bitterness, fear, and unbelief. Most of all, Helen needs to know that God is present, powerful, listening, just, caring, and understanding. She needs God to do something.

> He crouches, he bows down,
> and the unfortunate fall by his mighty ones.
> He says to himself, "God has forgotten.
> He has hidden His face. He will never see it."
> Arise, O LORD. O God, lift up Your hand.
> Do not forget the afflicted.
> Why has the wicked spurned God?
> He has said to himself, "You will not require it."
> You have seen it, for You have beheld trouble and vexation to
>   take it into Your hand.
> The unfortunate commits himself to You.
> You have been the helper of the orphan.
> Break the arm of the wicked and the evildoer.
> Seek out his wickedness until You find none.
> The LORD is King forever and ever.
> Nations have perished from His land.
> O LORD, You have heard the desire of the afflicted.
> You will strengthen their heart.
> You will incline Your ear to vindicate the orphan and the op-
>   pressed,
> so that man who is of the earth will no longer cause terror.
>
>   Psalm 10

Psalm 10 is for Helen. It is also for the family in Sri Lanka that wonders where the next terrorist bombing might occur. It is for the young man who was molested in boarding school. It is for the pastor facing church members who are out to get him. It is for the factory worker being persecuted for her faith, and the college student whose professor has an ax to grind against God. It is for the family that lives in a high crime neighborhood, and the widow cheated by a home-repair scam. It is for anyone under assault in a world where many people wish to use us and harm us.

Psalm 10 guides a person into knowing God in the midst of being violated. How can Helen—and you—make these words and experiences your own? Think of a psalm as a "four-part harmony" and savor the layers of significance and reservoirs of power that fill the

Word of God. Join the four-part chorus; don't think that you sing or pray alone.

THE PSALM'S FOUR VOICES

The first voice in the psalm calls out the experience of the writer. Psalm 10 was written about 3,000 years ago by a sufferer who called on the Lord. Yes, the truths are universal, part of God's Word for all ages and people. But first they were *personal*, written by a man who felt abandoned, overwhelmed, and outraged in the face of evils. Yet he knew God, so he worked through his experience in relationship to him. This psalm's ideas about evil, hurt, and God's love and power arise in heartfelt conversation with that good and powerful Person. Helen can listen in on someone else's heart, someone else's conversation with God.

A second voice sounds the experience of God's people through all ages. Israel and the church have *suffered together* in this fallen world. Your individual experience is part of a larger whole, God's new society. The Lord—Yahweh, Jesus—is the hope of all the afflicted and needy, all the poor in spirit. Countless others have made this psalm their own. You are part of a choir, and sometimes others can carry the tune while you catch your breath.

The third voice registers Jesus' experience. He expressed these sentiments as a man of sorrows, acquainted with grief. Your individual experience is the subset of his experience, if you are *in Christ*. Imagine! You can love the Jesus who felt, thought, and said these things. Psalm 10 expresses the inner life and words of a Person that Helen— and you—can grow to love.

Finally, *you*, the reader, weigh in with the voice. These words are meant to map onto *your* experience. Helen found that her experience could be expressed in ways she'd never think of herself. The Word of God comes to change us and our response to our own lives.

Psalm 10 contains two things: honest requests and thoughtful analysis. At the beginning and end, the injured person bluntly talks to God, saying in effect, "Why are you far away? Get up and do something. You see what's going on. Sufferers trust you because you've helped the helpless in the past. Strip the power away from the hurtful now. I know you hear what I want. I know you will listen and make things right." In the middle, the sufferer vividly describes people who harm others—how they think and act and affect innocent victims. People who harm *people* are also rebelling against *God*. They will be destroyed.

Psalm 10 unfolds in four movements: a cry of desolation, a blunt assessment of predatory people, a cry of reliance on God, and a confident affirmation. Here are the details.[1]

I. Opening Cry: Where Are You? (v. 1)

Why do You stand afar off, O LORD? *Why do you hide in times of trouble?*

Where *are* you? Where *were* you? Often this is the heart's first cry: "You have said that you love me, so why do you seem absent just when I am violated? Why don't I know your protection?"

This is a cry of faith. Jesus said almost identical words as his faith expressed its anguish: "My God, my God, why have You forsaken me?" (Ps. 22:1; Matt. 27:46). You are in the company of one who knows God yet has felt abandoned.

People can ask questions like these from two fundamentally different stances. For those who walk in the footsteps of this psalm, the questions express a cry of faith that looks to God. In trouble, they *want* God but feel overwhelmed and isolated. Other people express a cry of unbelief, hatred, and accusation. In trouble, they *blame* God. At first, it may not be clear which stance predominates. There may be mixed motives. Helen groped in God's direction, wondering at times if God wasn't a figment of her imagination. "I believe, help my unbelief." But over time it always becomes clear whether we are processing our anguish through faith or through pride and unbelief. Psalm 10:1 speaks intimately and directly with trust in the Lord who is great, not with contempt for a god who seems impotent and uncaring.

II. Analyze Harmful People: They Are Proud, Willful, Godless, and Predatory (vv. 2–11)

In pride the wicked burn, pursuing the afflicted.

No psalm gives a fuller description of the inner workings of those who hurt others. The afflicted man spells out why he is distressed.

Why? It helps to describe what you are up against. Hurtful people are self-ruled and self-exalting: "proud." They are consumed with and by the things they do to others: they "burn."[2] This burning describes the arousal of any evil desire. Even at the mildest level a dark passion operates: "You stupid !@#$% jerk! You are useless! I wish you'd never been born." (Sanitized quotation of a father's response to a son's mistake while working in the family store.) More extreme violence rages with the same fire. The burning can be sexual or financial: the lust of the powerful or the single-minded pursuit of a scam. Evildoers exalt themselves and their own agenda. In each case, someone with power picks on the helpless to further his own self-interest.

They [the afflicted] are caught in the plots which they [the wicked] have devised.[3]

The word "plots" vividly describes the fact that people *think about* using and abusing others. Violence and betrayal are not accidental. Helen's husband set out to destroy her marital and financial well-being.

For the wicked boasts of his heart's desire. The greedy man curses and spurns the LORD.

Simply put, evildoers do what they want. They are not "sick," except in a metaphorical sense. They are *wicked* and live for their cravings.

Notice that to serve self-centered desire excludes serving the Lord. Abusers of others are rebels against God. They turn *from* the Lord *to* their greed. The sufferer's plight reveals that those who caused the suffering have a problem with God. Something bigger is going on behind someone's particular miseries.

The wicked, in the haughtiness of his countenance, does not seek Him. All his thoughts are, "There is no God."

Imagine living inside a mind in which there are no thoughts about God—except for the thought that "God doesn't matter"! The plans, memories, assessments, hopes, attitudes, and reactions are devoid of God's will, God's judgment, his mercy and lordship. A person who seeks only what he instinctively craves is by definition "wicked."

Helen's husband pursued his own agenda, indifferent to what it looked like to God. The psalmist reminds himself and God what such people are really like. It helps to know that those who oppress *me* have really got a problem with *God*. It helps in bringing the problem to God as a matter of his concern.

His ways prosper at all times. Your judgments are on high, out of his sight. As for all his adversaries, he snorts at them. He says to himself, "I will not be moved; throughout all generations I will not be in adversity."

Users seem to "get away with it"—in the short run. Their ways apparently "prosper." While Helen picks up the pieces, her husband runs off with a job, money, girlfriend, freedom, and self-righteous superiority to small-minded, church busybodies: "I will not be moved." Violators think, "My life works, and nobody can stop me." Helen's husband can skip town and never look back—he thinks.

This presumption is wired into the wicked act itself. Neither fear nor love hinders the wicked's self-centeredness. It can help Helen to understand these thought processes. It can keep her relying on God rather than blaming him. It keeps her moral compass rightly aligned. Notice that even in analyzing evil, the sufferer talks *to* God: *Your judgments are remote to those who think they can get away with it.*

This evil logic will be turned on its head when the sufferer asks God for help in the third section of the psalm. Evil ways will not prosper, despite what evildoers may think. God's judgments will come down to where we live.

His mouth is full of curses and deceit and oppression; under his tongue is trouble and wickedness.

This sentence catalogues the ways people intimidate, mislead, and overwhelm others. The wicked are "full" of what then overflows. Something "under the tongue" is ready to use at a moment's notice. The psalm gives categories, not specifics, inviting you to fill in the details.

Psalm 10 speaks from the standpoint of the innocent victim who relies on God. But sufferers must honestly ask themselves, "Am I more like my oppressor than I want to admit? Does God find bitterness and falsehood in me? Are there ways I act as if there is no God? Does my reaction to evil reveal my own evil, or a living faith?"[4] The apostle Paul cites this verse in Romans 3:10 to raise this humbling question. In a lengthy, direct challenge to every human being, Paul convicts every one of us of sin, and convinces us that our standing with God depends on what Jesus did. "Are we better than they? . . . There is none righteous, not even one. . . . For all have sinned and fall short of the glory of God, being justified as a gift by His grace through the redemption which is in Christ Jesus." The fair punishment for sin is capital punishment. Jesus, the only true innocent, took what I deserve (Rom. 3:25).[5]

Here is how Helen reflected on her experience. "I did not do the hateful things my husband did, but I spent years in bitterness and played the injured victim-doormat, with all the self-righteousness and self-pity of that role. I fantasized vengeance at times—even murder. Part of my silence came from living for my social reputation. I gave romantic fantasies air time in my mind. I often took refuge in junk food rather than in God. My husband intimidated and manipulated me; in those ways I was a victim. But at other times the easy way out shaped my choices. Yes, my husband sinned in dreadful ways, but Jesus' mercy has enabled me to face it with a growing measure of mercy. I have come to know God's love as refuge from my sufferings *and* my sins."

He sits in the lurking places of the villages. In the hiding places he kills the innocent. His eyes stealthily watch for the unfortunate. He lurks in a hiding place as a lion in his lair. He lurks to catch the afflicted. He catches the afflicted when he draws him into his net. He crouches, he bows down, and the unfortunate fall by his mighty ones.[6]

Evildoers "lurk." They conceal what they do, seeking to trap the innocent. Of course, with respect to God, none of us are innocents. But on the human-to-human level, there *are* innocents. Helen was an innocent. A husband whose wife is abusive and irresponsible is an innocent. Children who are molested, beaten, or abandoned are innocents. Aging parents whose children neglect them are innocents. Victims of racism or auto theft or religious persecution are innocents. Jesus was an innocent. None of these deserves what he gets from the "man who is of the earth." You are meant to cry out, "Unfair! Outrageous!" and to feel the hair stand up on the back of your neck. Evil terrifies and intimidates the innocent and weak.[7]

He says to himself, "God has forgotten. He has hidden His face. He will never see it."

Evil people really think they'll never be called to account. Helen's husband was sure his mistresses and larceny could be kept out of sight. He believed a lie.

III. Cry to God: Act to Aid the Hurting (vv. 12–15)

Arise, O LORD. *O God, lift up your hand. Do not forget the afflicted.*

The voice that said, "God, you seem distant," now cries, "God, be near." The voice that rehearsed trouble now begs that the trouble be dealt with. This God can "rise" and "lift His hand": he can remember—and do something. The wicked may think that God will never act. Believing sufferers may wonder (v. 1), but they call on him to do something. The previous ten verses communicated a dark world where the violator produces bleak fear in the victim. But now that world begins to crack open. Terrifying light begins to dawn on the self-absorbed mind of the wicked. Delightful light begins to dawn into the frightening world of the afflicted. The Lord misses nothing. He does not forget.

Why has the wicked spurned God? He has said to himself, "You will not require it." You have seen it, for You have beheld trouble and vexation to take it into Your hand.

God *has seen* the hurt and turmoil the wicked inflict. The dark threat thrives on concealment and the powerlessness of its victims, but it is completely visible to God. The thought processes and actions of evildoers are presented to God in urgent need and trust: you see; you judge good and evil; you act. As Helen interprets her husband, she intercedes with God intelligently and forcefully.

The unfortunate commits himself to You. You have been the helper of the orphan.

God has been the helper of the helpless. He must become such again. This is no theoretical God. Human need seeks real divine help.

These sentences put the plight of the sufferer in very strong words. The "unfortunate" and "orphan" is the "hurting person," the helpless, needy, and forlorn. What do the needy need? Many forms of help may be timely. The church of Christ can help Helen in many practical ways. And because American society fosters a degree of social conscience, the legal system can help her find a measure of justice, protection, and recompense from her husband. Mercy ministries, social work, and advocacy for the powerless, poor, and disenfranchised are good things. But Psalm 10 drives home a bigger issue. First and finally, the needy need God. God runs his universe to ensure that in an evil world, no mere human advocacy can redress the full need.[8] Consider Jesus, the pioneer and perfecter of the life of faith: "into Your hands I commit My spirit" (Luke 23:46) and "for the joy set before Him [He] endured the cross, despising [thinking little of] the shame" (Heb. 12:2). Profound suffering needs one who will "wipe away every tear from their eyes; and there will no longer be any death; there will no longer be any mourning, or crying, or pain" (Rev. 21:4).

Break the arm of the wicked and the evildoer. Seek out his wickedness until You find none.

The helper of the weak is the destroyer of the abusive. The arm that once "caught" the afflicted will be snapped in two. The mind, tongue, and actions of "wickedness" will be annihilated. Here is a profound irony. The wrongdoer thinks that the Lord will not seek out his sins ("require" 10:13). But the sufferer calls on God to seek out sins until they can't be found because they have been obliterated.

Abusers think, "God won't require it," but when God acts, evildoers reap what they sow. The sufferer asks God to bring on the logical consequences: the arm that broke another will be broken. Throughout the Bible, the consequences of an evil act have a certain appropriateness. The punishment fits the crime. For example, when Israel turned to the idol gods of the surrounding nations, she came under the political power of those nations (Judg. 2–16).

But remember, this is a cry of faith, not pride. If I become the vindictive one, I assume that evils against me must be remedied by God right now. Faith trusts God's wrath in a different way. This is the cry of the weak one who trusts the Strong One, the hurting person who trusts the one who will make it all better. Helen can let go of her bitterness. She can refuse to play tit-for-tat with her husband in court. She can let go of the years of darkness, secrets, fear, and shame. She can trust someone else to make all wrongs right and get on with her life. The wrath of God is a central piece of the hope of God's people.[9]

IV. Confident Affirmation: The Lord Will Right Wrongs (vv. 16–18)

The LORD is King forever and ever. Nations have perished from His land.

This psalm ends with quiet confidence. God is a person with a name—Yahweh, I AM THAT I AM—who rules forever. He has proved it in history. Sufferers call on a God who has annihilated evildoers and idolaters. This King is now known as Jesus. He has redeemed the nations—Helen included—by perishing in the place of his elect. But those who reject him will cry, "Mountains, fall on us!" at their impending destruction.

Where do sufferers place their hopes? The first half of this statement is quoted in the New Testament: "[The Lord] will reign forever and ever" (Rev. 11:15). Christ wins; evil loses. This is the indestructible foundation for human hopes, even when our schemes for earthly joy are shattered by sufferings.

> These inward trials I design,
> From sin and self to set thee free,
> To break thy schemes for earthly joy,
> That thou may'st find thy all in Me.
> John Newton

Here, too, the great divide among sufferers becomes obvious. The psalm writer, all God's people, Jesus, and Helen put their hopes in the right place, and come out in the right place. Other sufferers break when their schemes for earthly joy are broken. They come out vindictive, addicted, embittered, immoral, unbelieving, and greedy. The Lord will reign with his people; idolaters will perish.

O LORD, You have heard the desire of the afflicted.

Victims want many things: protection, relief, vindication, justice, and hope. The Lord hears such desires, for they reflect God's own intention. God is the righteous Judge who hears the cry of his chosen ones (Luke 18:1–8). But will the Lord find faith on the earth when he comes? Will afflicted ones rest their hopes on him? Are you in fact the "poor in spirit," one who knows your need and brings it to the Lord? Psalms never vindicate victims who act like the wicked themselves, plotting vengeance, thinking that "there is no God." The afflicted are believers who cry to the personal God on whom they rely.

We saw earlier that the wicked "boasts of his heart's desire." He is arrogant, autonomous, demanding. But "the desire of the afflicted" is heard because it is aligned with the purposes of the loving God. "This is the confidence which we have before Him, that, if we ask anything according to His will, He hears us. And if we know that He hears us in whatever we ask, we know that we have the requests which we have asked from Him" (1 John 5:14–15). Thomas Watson commented that "desires are the soul and life of prayer."[10] Equally, desires are the soul and life of wickedness. Understanding the difference is life for the soul!

You will strengthen their heart.

God acts first to strengthen sufferers internally. If you "suffer in a Godward direction," he gives you hope. It is in the context of suffering that God strengthens hearts in many ways. The love of God pours out directly into the hearts of afflicted persons who rely on him in hope (Rom. 5:3–5). God becomes directly *known*—"seen"—in ways previously unimaginable (Job 42:5). Our foolishness is revealed, so that we might receive growing wisdom directly from God (James 1:2–5). We are remade into the image of Jesus, and established in the love of God (Rom. 8:29, in the context of 8:18–39). We learn to trust and obey Jesus, who walked the path of unjust suffering *ahead* of us and now walks it *with* us (Heb. 4:14–5:9; 12:1–11). Our self-centered cravings are revealed and our faith is purified and simplified (1 Peter 1:3–15). Helen trembles in the face of betrayal, but God can bring substantial joys out of her nightmare.

Here again, Jesus is the pioneer. His passion began with sorrow, betrayal, and abandonment:

- "Father, let this cup pass from me."
- The silence of a lamb before its shearers.
- "My God, my God, why have you forsaken me?"
- "I am thirsty."

This sufferer loved his enemies, as we are called to do.
- "Today you will be with Me in paradise."
- "Father, forgive them, for they do not know what they are doing."
- "Woman, behold your son. . . . Behold your mother."

It wrapped up in commitment and hope:

- "It is finished."
- "Into your hands I commit my spirit."

Faith finds God in suffering, producing endurance, love, and hope. Psalm 10 is one part in the larger gospel whole, one piece of the experience of each God-centered sufferer.

> *You will incline Your ear to vindicate the orphan and the oppressed, so that man who is of the earth will no longer cause terror.*

God not only strengthens hearts in suffering, he destroys the powers of evil. The weak will be vindicated. Yes, some people intimidate, but they will be destroyed, some sooner, some later, all sooner or later.

A marvelous promise closes this psalm: "That man who is of the earth may cause terror no more." People are fundamentally weak— mere clay, morning mist. An evildoer has a moment of power to hurt, but the God who is fundamentally strong will have the final say. That

hope animates "groan[s] within ourselves" that everything will someday be renewed (Rom. 8:23). Alongside, the Holy Spirit "intercedes
for us with groanings too deep for words" (Rom. 8:26). We will be delivered from all sin and misery. Every tear will be wiped away when
evil is no more (Rev. 20–21).

APPLICATION: MAKE THIS YOUR OWN

Read the psalm as a whole, turning it into your own words and
thoughts.

I. Opening Cry: Where Are You? (v. 1)

1. Talk *to* God. Talk out loud. Many sufferers stay submerged in
their thoughts and feelings, and stifle spoken prayer. Prayer means
asking someone for help. Too often "prayer" is indistinguishable from
thought life. "God" becomes blended with chaotic mental processes,
rather than existing as a distinct person. But God is a person. Talk to
him. Jesus prayed out loud with feeling: "He offered up both prayers
and supplications with loud crying and tears to the One able to save
Him from death, and He was heard because of His piety" (Heb. 5:7).
Cry out.

2. Psalm 22 captures in even greater detail the relationship between a sufferer and his God, who seems far away. It is even more explicitly Jesus' experience. After making Psalm 10 your own, do the
same with Psalm 22. God will meet you in the integrity of your real
life experience.

3. The psalms are intended for use by groups of people, as well
as by individuals. Who can pray with you? God does not intend you
to fully resolve your struggles even in private with him. Join the people of God in a setting where your needs can be presented to God by
others.

4. Matthew 26–27, Mark 14–15, Luke 22–23, and John 18–19
make it plain that Jesus not only experienced sufferings *like* yours, he
experienced evil in *greater concentration*. In fact, he did it *for* you, and
on purpose. And his *cry was answered*, as God delivered him in power:
Matthew 28, Mark 16, Luke 24, John 20–21. Read a different version
of the story each day. Think about these things.

II. Analyze Harmful People: They are Proud, Willful, Godless, and Predatory (vv. 2–11)

1. Are you suffering? Have you been "burned" because someone else "burned" to do you wrong?

- Have you been verbally attacked, humiliated, treated with contempt, slandered?
- Have you been sexually manipulated, molested, seduced, raped?
- Have you been financially victimized?
- Have you been physically threatened, stalked, attacked, beaten, or tortured?
- Have you been a victim of prejudice regarding race, age, gender, ethnicity, economic status, disability, or religious faith?
- Have you faced a multitude of evils? Helen's circumstances fit the category "all of the above."

Describe what has happened to you: who, what, when, where, how, why. Talk it out with God in detail, according to the pattern of Psalm 10.

2. We are usually aware of what wrongdoers *do*, because that directly affects us. What does Psalm 10 say about how they *think*, what they *want*, what they *worship*, what they do *with God*? How does recognizing this Godward dimension help you when you face the sting of their actions? How does it make you less alone?

3. How have you sinned? Have you criticized, lusted, stolen, threatened, or been prejudiced? Do you lose sight of God and sink into unbelief? How do your sins come out in reaction to being sinned against? Remember, God has transformative purposes in the sufferings of those who love him.

4. What has Jesus Christ done to save sinners? Study 2 Corinthians 5:14–21 for the condensed version: Jesus has dealt both with sin's penalty and perverse mastery. Study Romans 3:9–6:23 for the detailed version. You have been given an inexpressibly wonderful gift, and nothing can take it away. No suffering can separate you from God's love: Romans 8:18–39.

III. Cry to God: Act to Aid the Hurting (vv. 12–15)

1. What will Jesus Christ do to unrepentant sinners who harm God's children? Study 2 Thessalonians 1:6–10 for the condensed version. Study Revelation for the uncut version.

2. Talk *to* God. But don't babble. Talk intelligently, based on an understanding of God's reign of power and grace that deals with evil and suffering. Many sufferers simply writhe in pain and confusion. Jesus prayed knowing exactly what he was saying, focused on obeying the will of the Father: "My Father, if it is possible, let this cup pass from Me; yet not as I will but as You will" (Matt. 26:39). He modeled the things he had taught his disciples to pray (Matt. 6:9–13). Don't grumble. Don't fall into the superstition of using fine-sounding religious phrases. Don't name and claim, thinking that your words pry goodies out of heaven. Don't think that piety can't ask for anything specific. Pray direct prayers pursuing God's will and glory.

3. Ask God to act: "Destroy evil and promote good." Prayer is not about working up some state of mind, though prayer does affect our state of mind, as Psalm 10 illustrates. Prayer goes to Someone you love and trust, asking for action and confessing faith.

IV. Confident Affirmation: The Lord Will Right Wrongs (vv. 16–18)

1. What truths do you need to affirm? Where can you find calm, strength, hope, and comfort? Begin where Psalm 10 begins. What else can you put in your confession of faith in the midst of trouble?

2. Ponder this (slightly modified) statement of faith from the sixteenth century Heidelberg Catechism:

> *What is your only comfort in life and in death?*
> That I am not my own, but belong—
> > body and soul,
> > in life and in death—
> to my faithful Savior, Jesus Christ.
> > He has fully paid for all my sins with his precious blood,
> > and has set me free from the tyranny of the devil.
> > He also watches over me in such a way
> > that not a hair can fall from my head
> > without the will of my Father in heaven;
> > in fact, all things must work together for my salvation.
> Because I belong to him,
> > Christ, by his Holy Spirit,

assures me of eternal life
and makes me wholeheartedly willing and ready
from now on to live for him.

If you grasped these things with your whole heart, how would it affect the way you handle suffering?

3. David turned his suffering into words that have brought hope and guidance to countless people for three thousand years. Can you turn your experience into a ministry to others who suffer? God "comforts us in all our affliction so that we will be able to comfort those who are in any affliction" (2 Cor. 1:4).

Psalm 10 teaches us to think clearly and seek help from where help really comes. You need to *think* about what has happened. Who has mistreated you? What have they done? How do they think? What are they doing with God (not just with you)? Since evildoers are often deceitful (vv. 5 and 7), they can be hard to identify. Often the first people they deceive are their victims. See your danger for what it is.

You need to *seek* help. This help comes first and finally from the living God. He hears, helps, strengthens, and vindicates those who rely on him. If you look anywhere else first, you will set yourself up for a fall. You will get snared in bitterness and revenge (spurning God for *your* pride). You will flee in avoidance and addiction (spurning God for *your* false refuges and comforts). You will develop a perverted dependency on others (spurning God for *your* trust in man). Sadly, our culture has awakened countless people to think about what evildoers ("abusers") have done to them, but it has cast them upon their own resources as "abuse victims." Yet victims can properly understand their own sins and sufferings, and God's grace. They can learn the faith of Psalm 10 and find hope, mercy, and courage in dealing with evildoers.

As you seek the Lord, you will find that many secondary helps contribute to the healing process. There is a place to call the police, press criminal charges, pursue church discipline, seek counseling, weep with a friend, get financial advice, and so forth. The Lord is a refuge who leads us to rightly appropriate the many other helpers who can play a part in our lives—and to play a part for good in others' lives, as well. As Helen learns to think about evil and beseech God, she will also learn to participate in the community of God's people in a rich, immediate way. She'll have things to offer other sufferers down the road—a heart that has learned to think and pray Psalm 10, for example (a 2 Cor. 1:4 "comfort in any affliction"). What her husband meant for evil, God meant and works for good.

6 DON'T WORRY:
LUKE 12:22–34

Jesus is talking to a huge crowd out in the open air, on a hillside overlooking the Sea of Galilee. The crowd is mostly simple people: dirt farmers, fishermen, and peasant women. Jesus has been talking to them about two things: who they're most afraid of—God or other people—and their attitude toward him.

Somebody had just interrupted him: "Jesus, Master, tell my brother to give me half of the inheritance! I want my share. I want what's fair" (see Luke 12:13). Jesus cuts the man off and essentially says, "I'm not going to divide inheritances for you. I've got a different plan." But since the man's interruption has turned the conversation to money and possessions, Jesus turns to the crowd and says, "Look out for every form of greed. What you are is not what you own." Money is an issue that reveals a lot about what people most fear, and about how they view Jesus.[1]

Jesus then tells a story about a man who had lots of money (12:16–21). He lived a comfortable life and thought he had no worries. But God said to that man, "You fool! You're going to die tonight. Who's going to have what you worked for your whole life? You have nothing. Your life is an utter waste."

Jesus weaves a warning through the whole story: "Keep your life from every form of greed" (see v. 15). That theme runs through the earlier section (vv. 13–21) right to verse 22: "Keep your life free from *every* form of greed, from the selfish 'I want mine' form of greed, and even from the complacent 'Because I *have* mine, I can sit back and coast' form."

Jesus pursues this topic as he talks straight to the disciples—his friends, the people who love and know him.

And [Jesus] said to His disciples,

"For this reason I say to you, do not worry about your life, as to what you will eat; nor for your body, as to what you will put on.

For life is more than food, and the body more than clothing.

"Consider the ravens, for they neither sow nor reap; they have no storeroom nor barn, and yet God feeds them; how much more valuable you are than the birds!

"And which of you by worrying can add a single hour to his life's span?

If then you cannot do even a very little thing, why do you worry about other matters?

"Consider the lilies, how they grow: they neither toil nor spin; but I tell you, not even Solomon in all his glory clothed himself like one of these.

But if God so clothes the grass in the field, which is alive today and

"For this reason I say to you, don't worry about your life, as to what you will eat." He's saying that even if you *don't have* a lot of money, or as much as you think you need, money is still not your life. So don't get anxious. Money can't make or break you. Remember that Jesus is talking in a subsistence culture: scratch-plow farmers, poor fishermen, people selling a few items in the marketplace—like a third-world village. Many of us in the United States take food and clothing for granted, but we worry about money too. Although our situations are different, the same issues, attitudes, and temptations play out. "Your life is more than food. Your life is more than money."

Jesus lists reason after reason why you should not be in the grip of fear and worry. First, he says, "Consider the ravens." As Jesus is talking out in the open in Palestine, crows are flying overhead or hopping on the ground squabbling. "Take a look at those crows! They neither sow nor reap. They make no preparations and have no barns. Yet God feeds them. How much more valuable are you than birds?"

He adds a second reason: "Which of you by worrying can add a single hour to his lifespan? If you can't do the littlest thing like this, why do you worry about the rest?"

Jesus keeps piling on the reasons: "Consider the lilies." He's talk-

tomorrow is thrown into the furnace, how much more will He clothe you? You men of little faith!

"And do not seek what you will eat and what you will drink, and do not keep worrying.

For all these things the nations of the world eagerly seek; but your Father knows that you need these things.

But seek His kingdom, and these things will be added to you.

"Do not be afraid, little flock, for your Father has chosen gladly to give you the kingdom.

"Sell your possessions and give to charity; make yourselves money belts which do not wear out, an unfailing treasure in heaven, where no thief comes near nor moth destroys.

For where your treasure is, there your heart will be also."

—Luke 12:22–34

ing about the kind of tough wildflower that grows in a vacant lot or on the roadside among the weeds. "Look at those flowers over there, how they're growing. They neither toil nor spin"—they make no effort to look pretty. "But I tell you even Solomon in all his glory was not clothed like one of these. If God so clothes the grass of the field, which is alive today and tomorrow is thrown into the furnace, how much more will he clothe you, you of little faith?"

Then Jesus gives a fourth reason. It deals not so much with *feelings* of anxiety as with what you are *living for*. Jesus describes that driven, obsessed preoccupation with money and possessions. "Don't seek what you are going to eat and drink, and don't keep worrying." Of course we should have jobs and make money. But he warns against making it your life objective. "All these things the nations of the world eagerly seek." In other words, that's what everyone in the world is into. But that's their business. "Your Father knows that you need these things. But seek his kingdom. These things will be added to you." God says, Don't live for the one thing everybody else lives for. I'm going to give you something better—and along the way I will take care of you financially.

Lest we should doubt ("Is he *really* going to give something better?"), Jesus gives his next reason. He says, "Don't be afraid, little flock." It's the only place in the Bible where that phrase, "little flock," is used. It's a vivid picture of a flock of sheep small enough that the shepherd knows all their names, their personalities, and what each one faces. Jesus makes sure we know that God is not reluctant to love us. Do not worry, because "Your Father has gladly chosen to give you the kingdom."

Jesus has piled up reasons not to get hung up on money, even when survival is at stake. This leads to radical implications for your lifestyle. "Sell your possessions, give to charity." Instead of being characterized by every form of greed, where we say, "What's in it for me? I want my share! I've got a lot, so I can sit comfortably! What if I don't have enough? Maybe I won't get something I need!"—instead of all that, *you can give because you have been given to*. Why? Because your Father who loves you gives you a life that you can give away and not lose. "Make yourselves money belts that don't wear out—store up that unfailing treasure in heaven where no thief comes and no moth destroys. Where your treasure is your heart will be also."

YOU'VE GOT PLENTY OF GOOD REASONS TO WORRY!

We need these strong and comforting words, because we do have good reasons to worry. Take the people Jesus is talking to. They are *poor* people with primitive sanitation and no health care. When drought comes, they die.

This passage shows us that we all worry about many things. We all get obsessed about the wrong things. If you are six years old, perhaps it comes in at this level: "My older brother gets three dollars more for his allowance. If only I had that extra three dollars." If you're the ten-year-old brother, you think, "My sister is so lucky, because she has a job. If only I had a job!" Then you get a job—which you think will solve all your worries. But now you've got bills, and everything you want costs more.

Let's say you have that after-school job and can put some money in your pocket. You still worry. "How will I pay for college? What kind of a part-time job or student loan will I need?" If you're in college or just graduating, you worry, "Will I get a decent job? What if there's no work?" When you get that real job, "Will I ever have enough money for a house? How are we going to afford kids?" There are always more reasons to worry. Does all this sound familiar? Even when I have enough money to pay all the bills, I leave my bill-paying sessions with a vague anxiety. After I've paid everything, there's not much money left. Low-grade worry sneaks in. In my budget it's always the dentist or the auto mechanic. It was never in my budget, but it easily gets onto my worry list.

Then you get older and start doing financial planning for retirement—which you should have been thinking about twenty years before (another worry). The planners show you diagrams of your projected assets. The amount goes up for a little while, and then takes a nosedive at age seventy-five. You're better off dying before you're eighty-two—or you'll be in the poorhouse or dependent on your kids. Then there's your 401K: the stock market crashes. . . .

There's *always* something to worry about.

One of the things that makes money such a powerful source of worry is its obsessive component. It's always there. It says "Goodnight" and wakes you up in the middle of the night. It greets you in the morning with, "Hi, here I am. Think about me." Financial worries play with your mind, and all the other worries operate in exactly the same way. What you see in common with all of them is that they are *uncertain.* We ask, "Am I going to get that? Maybe, maybe not. If I have it, could I lose it? Maybe, maybe not." We worry about things that are inherently uncertain. You can never be sure. Money is a great example, but what other things plague you? What are the one, two, six, dozen things that you tend to worry about? Do you find yourself dwelling on any of the following?

- "Do I have any real friends?"
- "What if I don't make the team? What if I forget my lines in the play? What if someone else gets picked for that committee?
- "Will I ever find a spouse?"
- "If I do find one, will he or she be faithful?"
- "Am I worth marrying?"
- "Will I be able to have kids?"
- "If I have kids, how will they turn out?"

- "What about my health? Some of my friends are dying of cancer. Is that going to be me? What if I get Alzheimer's and die unable even to recognize the people I love?"

Worry rages about your health, your money, your relationships, and your achievements. Any of those things can hijack the controls of your mind. The fact is, you can't control any of them. There is every reason in the world to worry about them. So ask yourself: What do *you* worry about?

But there's a second question to ask yourself: When all is said and done, *why* do you worry? Why do you fret about these things in the first place? Why do you get preoccupied, or driven, or have panic attacks, or brood, or whatever form your anxiety takes?

The easy answer is to point your finger at *what* you are worrying about, as if that explains it. "I'm worried because I don't know if I'm going to get a job. I'm worried because I don't have enough saved for retirement. I'm worried because I have a family history of cancer." But Jesus doesn't allow that. He explains our worries not by pointing to how uncertain life is, but by pointing to something *in us*. Throughout this passage he says, "You worry because of *you*, not because of *things*." That's why he said, "Guard *yourself* from every form of greed."

"I want my share of what's fair" was one form of greed. *Covetous* greed will make you angry and manipulative. You'll even break in to interrupt Jesus when he's talking!

"I am set. I can kick back. I've got plenty!" That was a different form of greed. *Complacent, satisfied* greed makes you care less about what really matters, because it lulls you to sleep.

In this passage, where Jesus is talking to his disciples about not being anxious, he goes after a third form of greed. "What if I don't have enough? What if what I need isn't there?" That's *anxious* greed. I want something I might not get, so I worry.

Later in the passage Jesus captures the same thing from a different angle: "O you of little faith!" Little faith does not mean *no* faith. Rather, it's like a flashlight with drained batteries. It still makes light, but the light is flickering and uncertain. The faith is dying out. We lose sight of God because what we want (and worry about) is the only thing we see. Jesus helps us to spot things: "Where do I go off? What makes me forget? Why do I fret? Why do I lose it?" When faith is dying out, greed and worry come to life.

The middle of the passage offers another reason why you worry. "Which of you by worrying can add a single cubit to his lifespan, a single hour? If you can't even do a small thing, why are you worrying about the rest?" Worriers act as if they might be able to control the uncontrollable. Central to worry is the illusion that we can *control* things. "If only I could get my retirement right, I could control the future." "If I could get my diet and medicine right, I wouldn't get cancer." "If I could figure out the right childrearing technique, I could guarantee how my kids turn out." Worry assumes the possibility of control over the uncontrollable. The illusion of control lurks inside your anxiety. Anxiety and control are two sides of one coin. When we can't control something, we worry about it.

Jesus' final comment offers one more reason *why* you worry. A worrier is storing "treasure" in the wrong place. If what you *most value* can be taken away or destroyed, then you set yourself up for anxiety. Whether it be money, health, a particular friendship, the dream of marriage, success in sports or business, or how your children turn out, you're building your house on sand. Even if you feel good or everything's going your way, you're building your house on sand. Your treasure is vulnerable. And whenever what is "precious" to you is threatened, you'll be gripped with fear. Where do you store your treasure? In iffy things or certainties?

So why do *you* worry? What life objectives snuff out your awareness of God? What makes you want to control your world? Understand those things, and Jesus' alternative will become very, very precious to you.

You've Got Better Reasons *Not* to Worry!

Jesus has no interest in simply talking about what's wrong with us. He's always going somewhere good. He does make reference to our temptations and failures, but he's more concerned with giving you solid reasons not to worry. Yes, you have reason to worry because things are uncertain. But you have many, much better reasons *not* to worry!

Some things are *certain!*

Jesus lays them out for his disciples, wooing, informing, and encouraging them. Be persuaded and heartened as you read. "Don't worry" doesn't hang in space as a moral platitude! Jesus gives you solid reasons to live without fretting—even when you're facing the very things that are inherently uncertain and uncontrollable.

Below are seven promises Jesus makes, seven reasons for you not to worry. Which one do *you* find most inviting? Which one is most necessary and helpful, where you can say, "If I remember _____, I'll be a different person this week. I would not worry about money, health, friends, whatever"? Which of these *better* reasons do you most need?

1. Your life is so much more than food or clothing. There's so much more to who you are than what you have or don't have. Jesus refers back to the story of the rich fool whose money couldn't give him identity or meaning or security or life. Therefore, Jesus adds, "If your life isn't made by having money, then your life can't be unmade by the lack of it!" What matters a lot more is "Whom do you fear?" and "What do you do with Jesus?" Those are matters of life and death.

Everyone knows people who are living for empty, foolish things. The twenty-three-year-old woman who is living to be beautiful will only find that she will grow old and wrinkly. It's a losing bet from the start.

Those who live for health or athleticism or adventures inevitably start to get knee injuries after age thirty-five. Reflexes slow down. Systems start to break down. Sooner or later, death surely comes. It's foolish! There is more to life than health and sports and vacations!

It's like that with everything we live for—and worry about. If you live for money, you are banking on a clunker. The "car" is a lemon; it will *always* break down and give you reason to worry. There are better things to give your energies to. There is something much more important going on in your life than the stuff you worry about. Go through your worry list one by one. Jesus promises, "Your life is more than _____." That's promise Number 1.

2. Jesus tells people to look around at the world. In this case, look at crows. Jesus says, "Consider the ravens. God feeds them even though they don't put a single seed in the ground. They don't ever water their crops. They don't store a thing for next year—not even for tomorrow. They live in the moment, but God provides for them."

How does God feed them? It's not romantic in the least. A crow is a scavenger. They are dirty, tough, aggressive, and smart. They are noisy, obnoxious pests. How does God feed crows? Road kill. Trash picking. Raiding your crops. That's why you have scarecrows. God feeds the crows as they steal your food and pick over your garbage!

God's provision for the crows came home vividly to me one summer. A treasured plum tree grows in our yard. That year it was the only one of our five fruit trees to bear fruit. As summer unfolded, no less than forty, beautiful, sweet plums (I counted them!) were coming to ripeness. I couldn't wait!

One day when I came home, there were only twenty plums left on the tree. A gang of crows was having a feast on *my* precious plums! Earlier in the year this gang of six crows had moved into our neighborhood. I called them The Crow Boys. They made all kinds of racket early in the morning and they were always scavenging. And the Crow Boys had found *my* plum tree. I was not happy. We had planted this tree as a family. I prune it regularly and spray it faithfully. I had been eagerly looking forward to those forty juicy plums. And now there were only twenty left.

I mobilized our defenses. I threw ice cubes at the crows, banged trash cans, and ran to buy netting to put over the tree. By the time I got back, there were only twelve plums left on the tree. I draped the netting. When any crow tried to land, he would get a big, unpleasant surprise. Sure enough, a few minutes later, the first crow swooped in. He hit the netting, got tangled and flustered, and flapped off irritably, "Caw! Caw! Caw! Caw!" So I thought, *Maybe I've won!*

But by the end of that day, there were *zero* plums left on my tree! Those crows were too smart. They had figured out how to come up from the bottom of the tree. They would land on the ground, and hop up through the branches close to the trunk where the netting didn't reach. They cleaned me out!

God's sense of timing and sense of humor are very interesting: quite a "coincidence" that I had to preach on this passage a month later. Jesus says to me, "Oh, David, by the way, look how God provides for the crows." Yes, he provides by using *my* fruit trees! But here's the promise: *You are much more important than crows.* Yes, the scavengers get fed. But how much more does God care about you? Do you see what Jesus is saying here? God feeds a bird, even one of the

Old Testament's unclean animals, a bird that lives on road kill and theft. People matter a *lot* more to God. That's a promise you can take home.

3. Which of you by worrying can add a single hour to his life? Literally, Jesus says, "Which of you by worrying can add a cubit to his span?" A cubit is a distance measure: eighteen inches, your elbow to your fingers. The Bible envisions life as a "walk." You walk through your life, step by step. Jesus is saying, "You won't get even eighteen inches further by worrying. You can't even get half a step further by worrying." Worrying does . . . nothing. It accomplishes . . . zero. It won't get you eighteen inches further down the path of your life.

4. "Consider the lilies of the field, how they grow. They neither toil nor spin, yet I say unto you that even Solomon in all his glory is not clothed like one of these." Again, Jesus is pointing to weed flowers growing in vacant lots. The flowers that grow on their own are beautiful, without any tending or care except God's. Jesus starts with the same logic as with the crows: Look at something familiar—but he ups the ante this time. If God makes mere wildflowers so glorious that their beauty outdazzles Solomon, how much more will you outdazzle the lilies, O you of little faith! This promise is far more than "God will take care of you." This is "God will clothe you in nothing less than his radiant glory!" "So why do you worry about the clothes you wear? I'll dress you in my own glory! Why do you worry about your health? I'll raise you from the dead to eternal life. Why do you worry about a few dollars? I'll give you the whole earth as your inheritance. Why do you worry when someone doesn't like you? I'll make you live in the kingdom of my love!"

This fourth promise, rightly understood, is a spectacular reason not to worry. God is giving you a life that is radiant, indestructible, and full of glory. You will *dazzle*. If God so adorns mere wildflowers with glory, how much more will he make you as radiant as himself!

5. "Don't seek what you are going to eat and drink. Don't keep worrying about these things"—the word for worry here means more than feeling anxious; it means to be obsessed, driven, preoccupied— "All these things the nations of the world eagerly seek." We could put it this way: Look at what everybody everywhere is after. Are you going to march in step with the crowd just because everybody else does it?

Take, for example, the Sunday newspaper. What percentage of it is about money? Ninety percent? It's not just the business and financial sections. Look at the automobile section, the housing section, the want ads, the jobs, the coupons, and all the other advertising. Most of the news articles—covering wars, crime, budgets, taxes—are also about money. Even the sports section dwells on possible strikes and salaries. The newspaper covers what everyone is into—and it's ninety percent money.

So life is about money, according to the Sunday paper. That's what counts as news. That's what people are interested in. But what about the Bible? It talks a lot about money—maybe five percent is directly about money and property. But the Bible is one hundred percent about what *really* matters. It asks, "What is your attitude toward money? People live for *either* God *or* money—what will it be for you?" The Bible is about what really lasts, what's certain. It's about the living God, the One who made us in his image, who made us to live our lives for something bigger and better than the things we tend to worry about and define our lives by.

Yes, we do have economic needs. Jesus says, "I promise you, your Father knows you need these things." You do need a job. It's not wrong to provide for retirement, to pay your mortgage and bills, to own a car. Your Father knows you need these. But what are you going to be *about?* Is your life *about* money? Everyone else's life is: "The nations of the world *eagerly seek* these things." Jesus says, "Your Father will give what you need." If you just get the *big* things straightened out, you will have what you need in the little things. What everyone in the world is obsessed with, God makes a distant second. He'll give you what you need to live on if you *need* him in order to live.

6. God promises you . . . himself. Jesus keeps giving better reason after better reason. His sixth promise is the most significant of all. Some of what Jesus has been saying might sink in by reading the paper, looking at crows, looking at flowers, or thinking a minute about how useless it is to worry. It is God's world, so life works the way he says it does. But you'd never see how God connects to the crows or the flowers unless he tells you. This sixth reason is the capstone, the climax of Jesus' argument. In effect what Jesus says is, your Father knows you need these things. If you are preoccupied with his kingdom, then the other things you need will be added on. Get your life to be about what your Father is about.

This promise directly meets our tendency toward anxiety. We know what happens if we live for money, health, being pretty, having a boyfriend or girlfriend, or job success. But what guarantee do you have that Jesus' kingdom won't turn out to be one more iffy bet, one more disappointment? Jesus firmly and tenderly emphasizes this promise: "*Your Father knows what you need.* . . . Don't be afraid, *little flock,* because *your Father has chosen gladly to give.* . . ." You can rest on this. Jesus makes it as personal, intimate, and generous as possible. He wants you to really understand this, to stake your life on this and never be disappointed. As we said earlier, the shepherd of a "little flock" knows every single sheep by name. He knows everything about you, and it is his *pleasure* to give you the kingdom. He invites you, "Leave your anxious fretting, and seek my kingdom." We could say a hundred things about what that kingdom means.

I once talked with a close friend who described a series of painful experiences. She had become very discouraged, doing a lot of worrying, brooding, and floundering. She couldn't get traction in her life. She felt swept away by tension and confusion. She was seeking God, but couldn't seem to find him. Then, like a bolt of lightning, the thought came into her mind, "Your father . . . is God. Your father is God." She described how her worries changed. The circumstances didn't go away: the child's disability, the husband's financial problems, uncertainties about her health, conflicts in her extended family, and miserable things from her past still lingered. But the promise weighed more: "Your father . . . is God." That supreme and simple promise came in and rearranged how she saw life and what she lived for. It drained the life from her worrying. You can say, "My father is God. He is more than willing to give me his kingdom. It is his pleasure. He chooses gladly to love me." One of the things the kingdom means to you is, "My father is God."

I once watched a toddler wade into the shallow end of the baby pool. She headed boldly toward the deep end, without fear. She started out—ankle deep, up to her knees, then to her waist. Pretty soon the water was up to shoulder level. She kept heading into the deep end. What if she stumbled? She wasn't all that stable on her feet yet. But right behind her walked her mom, with arms outstretched, two alert hands poised inches from the little girl's shoulders. At one point the girl slipped slightly. I don't think she even realized it, but her mother reached out and steadied her. "Your father is God." Someone is right there, like that mom with her toddler.

What else does it look like to be given the kingdom? It's being able to say Psalm 121: "My helper is the LORD who made heaven and earth." Or meditate on this: "My rescuer is the Messiah of the world, Jesus." Or, "My Savior, who bears the substitutionary sacrifice, is the Lamb of God, the one good man, the only Savior of the world."

Or say, "My shepherd is the LORD. I shall not want. Why would I be afraid? What am I so uptight about?" If life is like the entire electromagnetic spectrum, from infrared to ultraviolet with every wavelength in between, why do we obsess and fret, as if all of life were found in the green band, the money band? Money is part of life, but wake up! Your Father is concerned with the entire spectrum. It is his pleasure to give you the kingdom, little flock, beloved children.

7. Having given you so much, your Father calls you to the radical freedom of giving your life away. It's both a reason and an alternative. Everything before was get. We become anxious because we want to get. We don't want to lose what we've got. We become presumptuous, and kick back into a life of leisure, because we have gotten. Everything is get, got, gotten. But the end of Jesus' message is all give. Because you have been given a sure thing, because there's nothing to really worry about, then give. It's his pleasure to give to you, so you can give, too. When that sinks in, a marvelous transformation takes place. You have good reasons to let your worries go. We—who tend to be obsessed and anxious about money—become able to open our hands.

Jesus says, "Sell your possessions, give alms." That doesn't mean you have to live exactly like Francis of Assisi—but to have Francis of Assisi's attitude. In that is the only true freedom and the only real happiness. It's an attitude of trusting your Father and living a life that's worth something. You can give yourself away. You can use your gifts. Your life can be about *give*. There's a world to reach out to, and people to love, and jobs to be done, and we can give ourselves to that purpose. Your Father knows what you need. He promises to provide for you, as needed. But get first things first. Live for the kingdom. When you do, it works directly against the uncertainty of the things we worry about.

Jesus describes this kingdom investment as "money belts that do not wear out." You can own something that will never get old. It will never wear out or run out. An unfailing treasure. You can live for and give away something that is inexhaustible. Yes, that crash in the retirement income means your assets might get exhausted. But here's a treasure that's inexhaustible. The spring is always flowing. Nothing and no one can ever take it away from you. This "purse" can never get stolen or moth-eaten or useless or lost.

Jesus says, "I promise you, the best thing you could ever want you will never lose." This is an amazing truth! All the things we worry about are what we want but could lose. That's why we worry. The best thing you could ever want you will never lose, and you can always give it away. "If you die for me, you will live"—that's a promise. It's the fundamental way redemption works. If you die for Christ, you will live. Your Father will provide, so you can give generously.

FENDING OFF THE BARBARIANS IN YOUR MIND

Proverbs 25:28 offers a good description of what happens with anxiety. "Like a city that is broken into and without walls is a man who has no control over his spirit." How do you get a grip when barbarians are rioting in the streets of your mind? Fear and anxiety have taken over. Nothing is safe or certain.

Anxiety is a universal human experience, and you need to approach it with a plan. A plan is not a formula. A football coach doesn't know a single thing that's going to happen after the opening whistle. He doesn't even know who's going to kick off until they flip a coin. But he's not unprepared. He goes in with a *game plan*, a basic orientation to the game ahead. Here are six things to use as a game plan when you start to worry and obsess.

1. *Name the pressures.* You always worry about *something*. What things tend to hook you? What "good reasons" do you have for

anxiety? The very act of naming it is often helpful. In the midst of the experience of anxiety, it seems as if a million things are overwhelming you. You're juggling plates, round and round and round. But really, you're juggling only six plates—or maybe obsessing on just one. It helps to name the one thing or the six that keep recycling. Anxieties feel endless and infinite—but they're finite and specific.

2. *Identify how you express anxiety.* How does anxiety show up in your life? For some people it's the feeling of panic clutching their throat, or just a vague uneasiness. For others it's repetitive, obsessive thoughts: "Oh, now that's the fourth time I've repeated that scenario in my mind." For some people the sign is anger. They get irritated, but when they work back, they realize, "I was fearful and worried about something." For other people, worry shows up in their bodies (e.g., a tension headache) or in the cheap remedies that sin manufactures to make us feel better (e.g., gobbling ice cream, or an overpowering desire for a stiff drink). Identify the signs. How can they become cues to you? "I'm losing it, I'm forgetting God, my flashlight is going dim."

3. *Ask yourself,* Why am I anxious? Worry always has its inner logic. Anxious people are "you of little faith." If I've forgotten God, who or what has started to rule in his place? Identify the hijacker. Anxious people have fallen into one of the subsets of "every form of greed." What do I want, need, crave, expect, demand, and lust after? Or what do I fear either losing or never getting? Identify the specific lust of the flesh. Anxious people "eagerly seek" the gifts more than the Giver. They bank treasure in the wrong place. What is preoccupying me, so that I pursue it with all my heart? Identify the object of your affections.

4. *Which promise of Jesus speaks to you most?* Take to heart those seven promises. They are all good reasons. But it's tough to remember seven things at once, so pick one. For some time, the most helpful to me was, "If God feeds the crows, won't he provide for you?" It made me laugh even to think about it. Those Crow Boys intercepted a lot of temptations to anxiety. They did me good. Grab one promise and work with it.

5. *Go to your Father.* Talk to him. Your Father cares about the things you worry about. *Your Father* knows what you need. Cast your cares on him, because he cares for you. You'll have to leave your worries with him—they are *always* outside of your control! How will your kids turn out? Will you get Alzheimer's? What will happen with the economy? Will your dad come to know the Lord? You have good reasons to be concerned about such things, but you have better reasons to take them to Someone who loves you. Like that toddler whose mom trailed her, even the deep end of life is safe.

6. *Give.* Do and say something constructive. Care for someone else. Give to meet human need. In the darkest hole, when life is toughest, there's always some way to give yourself away. The problem might seem overwhelming. You could worry, worry, worry. But what you're called to do is just a small thing. There's always something to give yourself to, and some way to give. Jesus said more about this in Matthew 6, a parallel passage: "Let the day's own trouble be sufficient for the day thereof." Give yourself to today's trouble. Leave tomorrow's uncertainties to your Father.

It is *your Father's pleasure* to give you the kingdom. Your father is God. Don't worry.

Part 2 Reinterpreting Life

I suppose all of us who counsel find ourselves particularly gripped by certain issues. I am particularly fascinated by the question *Why?* Why do we do what we do, think what we think, feel what we feel, say what we say? Why do we treat God the way we do? Why do we treat each other the way we do? What is the reason, the cause, the motivation, the dynamic?

In addition, I've been repeatedly struck by the host of different reasons proposed to explain motivation. "He did that *because* _____. She gets angry *because* _____." All the different psychological theories are essentially different theories of motivation. In fact, every individual is a "psychologist," in the general sense. People *always* assert or assume "reasons" whenever they talk about themselves or others. What is the *real* explanation for what makes a person tick? Is it sexual and aggressive instincts? need for self-esteem? role models? longing for love and acceptance? chemical imbalance? early childhood experiences? choices? drive for superiority? search for meaning and significance? spiritual hunger? genetic proclivity? survival? socialization and enculturation? karma? pursuit of affiliation and achievement? temperament type? money, status, and power? birth order? social injustice? patriotism? astrological sign? ethnic background or race? thrill-seeking and fun-loving? patterns of reinforcement? being a jerk? pursuit of pleasure and avoidance of pain? DSM-IV diagnosis? craving to be God? "People do that *because* _____." Take your pick— and you reveal your operative motivation theory.

God has a motivation theory. Or, more accurately, the Searcher of hearts sees what makes us tick, and he accurately evaluates what he sees. His opinion is the final word. He gives the real reason *Why?* As he opens our eyes to see more and more clearly, orienting us to his gaze, it changes the way we think about *"because _____."* We question the kinds of reasons other people give. New eyes bring a new way of interpreting. A new way of seeing makes us reinterpret all the old ways of seeing. That's what this section is about.

The next nine chapters look at common, real life problems. In every case, they circle back to the *Why?* question in some essential way. They always reinterpret the other explanations commonly offered. This strategy of argument (in the good sense of the word) has a long lineage. The Bible itself often tells the Truth by contrasting it with what other voices were saying at the time. Jesus often teaches by contrast: "You have heard that it was said . . . but I say. . . ." Similarly, many other parts of the New Testament teach truth about God, ourselves, and circumstances by debating other views that were then current: Acts 17:16–32, 2 Corinthians, Galatians, Philippians, Colossians, 2 Thessalonians, 2 Peter, and 1 John. In the Old Testament, Jeremiah and Proverbs teach positive truth vividly by a continual reference to what other voices were saying. The specific points of debate may have changed, but the need for reasoned argument remains in tackling issues current today.[1] Motivation theory is one of those red hot issues, given the numerous forms of nature and/or nurture determinism that have arisen from the social, behavioral, and medical sciences.

Chapter 7 goes for the big picture on motivation theory. "X-ray Questions" explores what God says he sees when *he* looks at why we do what we do.

Chapter 8 further develops one of the X-ray questions, picking up on a comment by Abraham Maslow, "I Am Motivated When I Feel Desire." How should we interpret the essential human phenomenon that we want, wish, long for, yearn, crave, lust after, need, expect, seek, and pursue?

Chapter 9, "God's Love: Better Than Unconditional" examines one of the catch phrases of the psychotherapeutic revolution (Carl Rogers's "unconditional positive regard," an attitude of all-accepting tolerance and affirmation), a phrase that also has a noble Christian lineage.

Chaper 10 considers the implications of "What If Your Father

Didn't Love You?" Is a positive parenting experience essential for a person to have a good experience of God as "Father"?

Chapter 11 looks at the ways we put on false fronts and deceive both ourselves and others. "Human Defensiveness: The Third Way" reinterprets one of the cornerstones of a psychoanalytic interpretation of the human condition.

Chapter 12 is a case study. A woman tells her story of coming out of lesbianism, crediting the causal power of childhood experience for her former struggle. "The Ambiguously Cured Soul" rethinks the causal interpretation that a counselor inserted into her story.

"What Do You Feel?" is one of the banner questions in psychotherapeutic philosophy and practice. It is a good question to ask. Chapter 13 thinks through both the reasons we ask the question and the ways we interpret the answers we give or hear.

Chapter 14 looks at the pop psychology of "love languages." In "Love Speaks Many Languages Fluently," we seek to deconstruct and reconstruct the term, in order to think more consistently about how God's creatures (we!) work.

Finally, Chapter 15 looks at "Biological Psychiatry." "Nature" determinism misreads the fact that we are physiological organisms (just as "nurture" determinism misreads the fact that we are social creatures). The combination of two misreadings ("nature and/or nurture" determinism) does not add up to a true reading of how people work.

7 X-RAY QUESTIONS

"Why did I do that?" Why *do* you react that way? Why use those words and that tone of voice? Or think those things? Or feel this way? Or remember that particular facet of what happened? Or make that choice in this situation?

The question *Why?* launches a thousand theories of human nature. Why do people do what they do? An "answer" to this question anchors every theory of human personality, and every attempt to fix what ails the human race. One's view of motivation will align and color every detail of theory and practice: Did you become fixated somewhere on the hierarchy of need? Are you genetically hardwired toward aggression? Are raging hormones the culprit? Do your instinctual psychic impulses conflict with the dictates of society? Have your drives been reinforced by rewarding stimuli? Are you an Aries with Jupiter rising? Are you an Adult Child of unhappy and determinative traumatic experience? Are you compensating for perceived inferiorities, seeking to acquire better self-esteem? Did a demon named Addiction infiltrate a crevice in your personality? Did you have a failure of willpower? Are you ignorant of good doctrine? Are you temperamentally melancholy or sanguine, a pessimist or optimist, an introvert or extrovert? Are you immersed in the ideological false consciousness that characterizes your social class? Does your self-talk misrepresent the bases for identity and self-worth? "I did that, thought that, felt that *because. . . .*" People relentlessly try to determine the underlying reasons for what appears on the surface.

Theories of what makes people tick inevitably become counseling models. Explanations are signposts to solutions: take medication, experience reparenting, cast out a demon, get your needs met, don't make big decisions on bad star days, reprogram your inner mono-logue, explore your pain. Presumed reasons and appropriate re-sponses are fiercely debated. In any university library, thousands of shelves collect and collate the debates.

But the Lord God also has a great deal to say on the issue. He vig-orously rebuts the counterfeits by demonstrating that human motiva-tion has to do with *him*. Counseling that is faithful to Scripture must do justice to what God says about the whys and wherefores of the hu-man heart. Scripture claims to search out the "thoughts and inten-tions of the heart" according to the specific criteria by which the Searcher of hearts evaluates what he sees in us (Heb. 4:12–13).

DISCERNING OUR FUNCTIONAL GODS

The list of "X-ray questions" in this chapter provides aid in dis-cerning the patterns of a person's motivation. The questions aim to help people identify the ungodly masters that occupy positions of au-thority in their hearts. These questions reveal "functional gods," what or who actually controls their particular actions, thoughts, emotions, attitudes, memories, and anticipations. Note that "functional gods" in a particular situation often stand diametrically opposed to the "pro-fessed God."

Consider when you become anxious, preoccupied, and filled with fretful concern. Something happened, and you can't get it off your mind. Now something else is happening—you're consumed with it. Your mind turns over and over what will happen tomorrow, chewing on every possible contingency. As the sin of worry tightens its unpleasant hold on your soul, perhaps you jump for some es-capist quick fix: raid the icebox, watch TV, masturbate, read a novel, go shopping, drink a beer, play a game. Or perhaps you mobilize to seize control: make a string of phone calls, work all night, build a faction of supporters, clean your house, get mad. Why is all this go-ing on?

As a Christian you *profess* that God controls all things, and works everything to his glory and your ultimate well being. You profess that God is your rock and refuge, a very present help in whatever troubles you face. You profess to worship him, trust him, love him, obey him.

But in that moment—or hour, day, season—of anxiety, you live as if *you* needed to control all things. You live as if something—money, someone's approval, a "successful" sermon, your grade on an exam, good health, avoiding conflict, getting your way—matters more than trusting and loving God. You live as if some temporary good feeling could provide you refuge, as if your actions could make the world right. Your functional god competes with your professed God. Unbelievers are wholly owned by ungodly motives—their functional gods. Yet true believers are often severely compromised, distracted, and divided by our functional gods as well. Thankfully, grace reorients us, purifies us, and turns us back to our Lord. Grace makes our professed God and functional God one and the same.

Christ's transformational work in our lives simultaneously operates in two dimensions, the "vertical" and "horizontal," the Why and the How. God is always reorienting our worship *and* our walk, our motives and our lifestyle. Paul summarizes the purpose of his ministry this way: "The goal of our instruction is love from a pure heart and a good conscience and a sincere faith" (1 Tim. 1:5). Love summarizes here the renovation of horizontal relationships. Pure heart, good conscience, and sincere faith capture the reconfiguration of vertical relationship. An impure, double-minded heart serves multiple masters. A bad, distorted conscience misinterprets and misguides, failing to process life God's way. A hypocritical faith professes, sings, and prays one way, but trusts something else when push comes to shove. Defections of heart, conscience, and faith produce particular sins. Restoration of heart, conscience, and faith produces particular obediences. This chapter probes the vertical dimension that guides and animates—*causes*—the horizontal dimension.

Notice that each X-ray question circles around the same basic issue: Who or what is your functional God/god? Many of the questions simply derive from the *verbs* that relate you to God: love, trust, fear, hope, seek, obey, take refuge, and the like. Each verb holds out a lamp to guide us to him who is the way, truth, and life. But each verb also may be turned into a question, holding up a mirror to show us where we stray. Each question comes at the same general question, but one may be more appropriate and helpful than another in a given situation. These questions are best used when the different times, places, and people that make up individual situations are taken into

account. Different ways of formulating the motivation question will
ring the bells of different people.

The questions that follow are "Why?" questions, framed con-
cretely as "What?" questions. These questions can help you draw
out what gives specific direction to a person's life. You do not see
into anyone's heart, but you can make intelligent inquiry into
"Why are you angry? Why do you manipulate him? Why are you
anxious in that situation? Why do you have a problem of lust at that
particular time? Why do you drink to excess?" The Bible—the penetrating and light-giving word of the Searcher of hearts—goes below behaviors and emotions in order to expose our motives before
God. A reorientation of motives through the grace of the Gospel
can follow only when there is conviction of particular forms of disorientation.

These questions can be used in several different ways. Each can
be focused "microscopically," to dissect the details of one particular
incident in a person's life. Or each can be focused to give a "wide-
angle" panoramic view, to illuminate recurrent patterns that characterize a person's entire life. You will find in the course of counseling—and your own growth in grace—that the details and the
panorama complement each other. The panorama alone is too general; change happens in specifics. The details alone seem trivial; the
panorama gives large meaning to such tiny details.

The Bible references barely scratch the surface of Scripture's
treatment of what motivates people. They are meant to prime the
pump for your own study and reflection. Be sure to ask the questions
first "existentially." What is motivating you or another? Do not run to
the "Christian right answer" without first working hard and honestly
to analyze deviant functional gods. Intelligent repentance will make
the right answers really right and will make the love of Jesus your joy
and hope.

1. *What do you love? Hate?* This "first great commandment"
   question searches you out, heart, soul, mind, and strength.
   There is no deeper question to ask of any person at any time.
   There is no deeper explanation for why you do what you do.
   Disordered loves hijack our hearts from our rightful Lord and
   Father. (See Matt. 22:37–39; 2 Tim. 3:2–4; Luke 16:13–14.)

2. *What do you want, desire, crave, lust, and wish for? What de-sires do you serve and obey?* This summarizes the internal op-erations of the desire-driven flesh in the New Testament epistles. "My will be done" and "I want _____" are often quite accessible. Various desires rule people, so go for details of *this* person, *now*, in *this* situation. Sometimes another per-son's will has control over you (in peer pressure, people-pleasing, slave-like, or chameleon behavior). In such cases, your heart's craving is to get whatever good they promise and avoid whatever bad they threaten: "I crave to be included, ap-preciated, accepted, and admired by you." (See Pss. 17:14–15; 73:23–28; Prov. 10:3; 10:28; 11:6–7; Gal. 5:16–25; Eph. 2:3; 4:22; 2 Tim. 2:22; Titus 3:3; 1 Peter 1:14; 2:11; 4:2; 2 Peter 1:4; 2:10; James 1:14–15; 4:1–3.)

3. *What do you seek, aim for, and pursue? What are your goals and expectations?* This particularly captures that your life is active and moves in a direction. We are purpose-full. Human motivation is not passive, as if hardwired needs, instincts, or drives were controlled from outside us by being "unmet," "frustrated," or "conditioned." People are active verbs. (See Matt. 6:32–33; 2 Tim. 2:22.)

4. *Where do you bank your hopes?* The future dimension is prominent in God's interpretation of human motives. People energetically sacrifice to attain what they hope for. What is it? People in despair have had hopes dashed. What were those shattered hopes? (See 1 Peter 1:13; 1 Tim. 6:17.)

5. *What do you fear? What do you not want? What do you tend to worry about?* Sinful fears are inverted cravings. If I want to avoid something at all costs—loss of reputation, loss of con-trol, poverty, ill health, rejection, etc.—I am ruled by a lustful fear. (See Matt. 6:25–32; 13:22.)

6. *What do you feel like doing?* This is slang for question 2, what do you desire? To be "feeling-oriented" means to make your wants your guide: "I feel like cursing you. I don't feel like do-ing my chores." (See Pss. 17:14–15; 73:23–28; Prov. 10:3; 10:28; 11:6–7; Gal. 5:16–25; Eph. 2:3; 4:22; 2 Tim. 2:22; Ti-

tus 3:3; 1 Peter 1:14; 2:11; 4:2; 2 Peter 1:4; 2:10; James
1:14–15; 4:1–3.)

7. *What do you think you need? What are your "felt needs"?*
Questions 2 and 3 exposed your aims in terms of activity and
pursuit. This question exposes your aims in terms of what you
hope to receive, get, and keep. Felt needs are frequently taken
as self-evident necessities to be acquired, not as deceptive
slave-masters. Our culture of need reinforces the flesh's instincts and habits. In most cases, a person's felt needs are slang
for idolatrous demands for love, understanding, a sense of being in control, affirmation, and achievement. (See Matt.
6:8–15; 6:25–32; 1 Kings 3:5–14; all the prayers in the Bible
express reoriented felt needs.)

8. *What are your plans, agendas, strategies, and intentions designed to accomplish?* This is another way to size up what you
are after. The egocentricity lurking within even the most no-
ble-sounding plans can be appalling. No one ever asserts,
"The expansion of our church into a mega-church will get me
fame, wealth, and power," but such motives are garden-variety
human nature. Their presence, even covertly, will pervert and
stain one's actions. (See Matt. 6:32–33; 2 Tim. 2:22.)

9. *What makes you tick? What sun does your planet revolve
around? Where do you find your garden of delight? What lights
up your world? What fountain of life, hope, and delight do you
drink from? What food sustains your life? What really matters
to you? What castle do you build in the clouds? What pipe
dreams tantalize or terrify you? What do you organize your life
around?* Many gripping metaphors can express the question,
"What are you really living for?" To be ruled, say, by deep
thirsts for intimacy, achievement, respect, health, or wealth
does not define these as legitimate, unproblematic desires.
They function perversely, placing ourselves at the center of
the universe. We are meant to long supremely for the Lord
himself, for the Giver, not his gifts. The absence of blessings—rejection, vanity, reviling, illness, poverty—often is the
crucible in which we learn to love God for who he is. In our

idolatry we make gifts out to be supreme goods, and make the Giver into the errand boy of our desires. (See Isa. 1:29–30; 50:10–11; Jer. 2:13; 17:13; Matt. 4:4; 5:6; John 4:32–34; 6:25–69.)

10. *Where do you find refuge, safety, comfort, escape, pleasure, security?* This is the question that Psalms invites. It digs out your false trusts, your escapisms that substitute for the Lord. Many "addictive behaviors" are helpfully addressed by this question. They often arise in the context of life's troubles and pressures, and function as false refuges. (See Pss. 23, 27, 31, 46, and about two-thirds of the rest of the Psalms.)

11. *What or whom do you trust?* Trust is one of the major verbs relating you to God—or to false gods and lies. Crucial psalms breathe trust in our Father and Shepherd. Where instead do you place life-directing, life-anchoring trust? In other people? In your abilities or achievements? In your church or theological tradition? In possessions? In diet, exercise, and medical care? (See Prov. 3:5; 11:28; 12:15; Pss. 23; 103; 131.)

12. *Whose performance matters? On whose shoulders does the well-being of your world rest? Who can make it better, make it work, make it safe, make it successful?* This digs out self-righteousness, or living through your children, or pinning hopes on getting the right kind of husband or wife, and so forth. (See Phil. 1:6; 2:13; 3:3–11; 4:13; Ps. 49:13; Jer. 17:1–14.)

13. *Whom must you please? Whose opinion of you counts? From whom do you desire approval and fear rejection? Whose value system do you measure yourself against? In whose eyes are you living? Whose love and approval do you need?* When you lose God, you enter a jungle of distortion. You tend to live before your own eyes or before the eyes of others—or both. The "social idols" which encompass approval and fear can take numerous forms: acceptance or rejection, being included or excluded, praise or criticism, affection or hostility, adoration or belittlement, intimacy or alienation, being understood or caricatured. (See Prov. 1:7; 9:10; 29:25; John 12:43; 1 Cor. 4:3–5; 2 Cor. 10:18.)

14. *Who are your role models? What kind of person do you think you ought to be or want to be?* Your "idol" or "hero" reveals you. Such persons embody the "image" toward which you aspire. (See Rom. 8:29; Eph. 4:24; Col. 3:10.)

15. *On your deathbed, what would sum up your life as worthwhile? What gives your life meaning?* This is Ecclesiastes's question. That book examines scores of options—and finds all but one option ultimately futile. At some point, translate Ecclesiastes 2 into its modern equivalents. (See all of Ecclesiastes.)

16. *How do you define and weigh success or failure, right or wrong, desirable or undesirable, in any particular situation?* The standards that you serve and employ may be wildly distorted. God intends to renew your "conscience," that by which you evaluate yourself and others. If you approach life "in your own understanding" or "in your own eyes," you will live as a fool. (See 1 Cor. 10:24–27; Prov. 3:5; Judg. 21:25.)

17. *What would make you feel rich, secure, prosperous? What must you get to make life sing?* The Bible often uses the metaphor of treasure or inheritance to speak of motivation. (See Prov. 3:13–18; 8:10f; 8:17–21; Matt. 6:19–21; 13:45–46; Luke 16:10–15; 1 Peter 1:2–7.)

18. *What would bring you the greatest pleasure, happiness, and delight? The greatest pain and misery?* Blessedness and accursedness are the Bible's way of discussing happiness and woe. What calculation do you make about where and how to find blessing? Your calculation reveals what you live for. (See Matt. 5:3–11; Pss. 1; 35; Jer. 17:7–8; Luke 6:27–42.)

19. *Whose coming into political power would make everything better?* This used to be less true of Americans than of many other nations, where politics is a major locus of idolatrous hopes. But as cultural consensus breaks down, many people increasingly invest hopes in political power. (See Matt. 6:10.)

20. *Whose victory or success would make your life happy? How do you define victory and success?* How does inertial self-interest reveal itself? Some people "live and die" based on the perfor-

mance of a local sports team, the financial bottom line of their company, their grade point average, or their physical appearance. (See Rom. 8:37–39; Rev. 2:7; Pss. 96–99.)

21. *What do you see as your rights? What do you feel entitled to?* This question often nicely illuminates the motivational pattern of angry, aggrieved, self-righteous, self-pitying people. Our culture of entitlement reinforces the flesh's instincts and habits. "I deserve _____"? (See 1 Cor. 9; Rom. 5:6–10; Ps. 103:10.)

22. *In what situations do you feel pressured or tense? Confident and relaxed? When you are pressured, where do you turn? What do you think about? What are your escapes? What do you escape from?* This question comes at matters from a slightly different direction. Many times certain patterns of sin are situation-dependent. Teasing out the significant aspects of the situation can hold up a mirror to the heart's motives. When public speaking "makes you" tense, perhaps your heart is ruled by your own performance in the eyes of others (fear of man and pride). When paying bills generates anxiety, perhaps a strand of mammon-worship operates within you. (See the dozens of psalms of refuge.)

23. *What do you want to get out of life? What payoff do you seek out of the things you do? "What do you get out of doing that?"* This is a concrete way to restate questions 3 and 8, digging out your operative goals. Idols, lies, and cravings *promise* goodies. Serve Baal, and he'll give you fertility. Get that cute guy to like you, and you'll feel good about yourself. Make $100,000, and you'll show up those people who thought you'd never make it in life. (See Prov. 3:13–18; Matt. 6:1–5, 16–18.)

24. *What do you pray for?* Your prayers often reveal the pattern of your imbalance and self-centeredness. Of the many possible things to ask for, what do you concentrate on? Prayer is about desire; we ask for what we want. Do your prayers—or lack of—reflect the desires of God or of the flesh? (See James 4:3; Matt. 6:5–15; Luke 18:9–14.)

25. *What do you think about most often? What preoccupies or ob-*
    sesses you? In the morning, to what does your mind drift in-
    stinctively? What is your "mindset"? Hold up a mirror to your
    drift, that you might reset your course! (See Col. 3:1–5; Phil.
    3:19; Rom. 8:5–16.)

26. *What do you talk about? What is important to you? What atti-*
    tudes do you communicate? This question and the next pre-
    sume the closest possible connection between motives and
    behavior. Notice both what people choose to talk about and
    how they say it. Our words proclaim what our hearts worship.
    (See Luke 6:45; Prov. 10:19; Eph. 4:29.)

27. *How do you spend your time? What are your priorities?* Notice
    what you and others choose to do. It is a signpost to the heart's
    operative loyalties. (See Prov. 1:16; 10:4; 23:19–21; 24:33.)

28. *What are your characteristic fantasies, either pleasurable or*
    fearful? Daydreams? What do your night dreams revolve
    around? We are still responsible human beings even when
    more or less detached from consciousness. Your patterns of
    concern and desire are revealed in reverie. (See Eccl. 5:3–7;
    Gal. 5:16–25; Eph. 2:3; 4:22; 2 Tim. 2:22; Titus 3:3; 1 Peter
    1:14; 2:11; 4:2; 2 Peter 1:4; 2:10; James 1:14–15; 4:1–3; Prov.
    10:3; 10:28; 11:6–7; Pss. 17:14–15; 73:23–28. Matt. 6:25-32;
    13:22.)

29. *What are the functional beliefs that control how you interpret*
    your life and determine how you act? Hebrews 4:12 speaks of
    the "thoughts and intentions" of the heart. Perhaps we could
    translate this "beliefs and desires." Both the lies you believe
    and the lusts you pursue undergird visible sins. A person's
    functional, operative beliefs control responses. The ways you
    understand God, yourself, others, the devil, right and wrong,
    true and false, past, present, future . . . have pervasive effects.
    (See the entire Bible, as God seeks to renew darkened minds
    from falsehood.)

30. *What are your idols or false gods? In what do you place your*
    trust, or set your hopes? What do you turn to or seek? Where do

you take refuge? Who is the savior, judge, controller, provider, protector in your world? Whom do you serve? What "voice" controls you? This entire list of thirty-five questions pursues things that usurp God. Each of these can metaphorically be termed an "idol" to which you give loyalty. The voices you listen to mimic specific characteristics of God. Start to trace that out into the details of everyday life, and your ability to address the vertical dimension relevantly and specifically will mature. (See the entire Bible, as God seeks to deliver people from idols, to serve the living and true God; Ezek. 14:1–8; Acts 26:18; Col. 3:5; Eph. 5:5; 1 Thess. 1:9–10; 1 John 5:21; Jer. 17:5; James 4:11–12.)

31. *How do you live for yourself?* This is a general way of asking any of these questions. "Self" takes a thousand shapes and wears a thousand disguises. (See Luke 9:23–25; 2 Cor. 5:14–15.)

32. *How do you live as a slave of the devil?* Human motivation is not purely "psychological," "psychosocial," or "psychosocial-somatic." When you serve lusts and lies, you serve a personal enemy who wishes to deceive, enslave, and murder you. Human motivation is thoroughly "covenantal." You may serve the devil, or you may serve the Lord, but you're going to have to serve somebody, as Bob Dylan put it. (See John 8:44; Acts 26:18; Eph. 2:2–3; 2 Tim. 2:26; James 3:14–16.)

33. *How do you implicitly say, "If only. . . ." (to get what you want, avoid what you don't want, keep what you have)?* The "if onlys" are slang that can uncover many motivational themes in the interest of creating biblical self-understanding and repentance. (See 1 Kings 21:1–7; Heb. 11:25; Phil. 3:4–11.)

34. *What instinctively seems and feels right to you? What are your opinions, the things you feel are true?* You not only "feel like" doing some things (question 6 above), you also "feel that" certain things are true. In God's view, foolishness is opinionated, but wisdom is correctable as it listens and learns. (See Judg. 21:25; Prov. 3:5; 3:7; 12:15; 14:12; 18:2; Isa. 53:6; Phil. 3:19; Rom. 16:18.)

35. *Where do you find your identity? How do you define who you are?* The Bible says radical things about self-knowledge, identity, and the categories of self-evaluation ("conscience"). The places people typically look for identity are dry wells. (For example, take the book of Ephesians and notice every word or phrase that describes "identity," either about Paul himself, or about who we used to be, or about who we now are. You will find more than thirty different statements in this short letter.)

ESTABLISHING A PLAN FOR CHANGE

This set of questions will get you thinking fruitfully about how human life is exhaustively God-relational. Let me reinforce three points that I have found particularly helpful in keeping my compass bearings, both in counseling and in seeking to repent of my own sins.

First, my rule of thumb is a twofold question: *What lies, and what lusts, are being expressed through this sinful pattern of life?* Dig under irritability, selfishness, hopelessness, escapism, self-righteousness, self-pity, crippling fears, complaining—whatever—and you will find a mosaic of specific lies believed and cravings pursued. Scripture equips you to get at them, to draw them into the light.

Second, *the verbs that relate people to God must become an active part of your thinking.* People are *always* doing something with God. Human beings either love God—or despise him and love something else. We take refuge in God—or flee from him and find refuge in something else. We set our hopes in God—or we turn from him and hope in something else. We fear God—or we ignore him and fear something else. Scripture will come to life in new ways as you develop an alertness to how the man-before-God verbs play out in real life. Such perspective grants powerful insights both for evangelistic counseling and for helping the saints grow.

Third, *by seeing the God-relatedness of all motivation, you see that what is wrong with us calls for a God-related solution: the grace, peace, power, and presence of Jesus Christ.* Human motivation is about the vertical dimension. The good news of Christ is no add-on, no religiously-toned way to meet pre-existent desires and needs. Living faith in Jesus Christ is the only real solution, the only sane motivation, the radical alternative to a thousand forms of deviance.

Sanctification aims to purify both heart and members, to change both motives and behavior. Both matter. Imagine sitting on a hill overlooking a lake. You watch a powerboat speed across the water. You see and hear its "behavior": it accelerates from the dock, makes a wide turn, bounces over another wake at high speed, suddenly cuts its motor, drifts into the shallows by an islet, and splashes an anchor overboard. Why did it behave in that way? If you were able to zoom in, you would find out about its "motives." You would find what powered and directed the boat: a 200 horsepower inboard V–8 motor, a rudder and steering wheel, the thoughts and intentions of the pilot. Why did the boat go to the island? To find buried treasure? Escape from the police? Take the family for a picnic? Test drive the boat for possible purchase? Flag down a passerby because it ran out of gas? To fully understand and "help" the powerboat, you must converse about both the visible and the invisible, both behavior and motive. The Bible gets at both results and reasons. To evaluate and "counsel" the powerboat, you need to pursue all that can be known.

The Knower of *hearts* will repay each person according to his *deeds* (see Jer. 17:10). Scripture never separates motive and behavior. The mirror of Scripture exposes both. The lamp of Scripture guides both. The grace and power of Jesus Christ change both root and fruit. The "first great commandment" addresses motivational roots: Do you love God with all your heart, soul, mind, and strength? Or does something else divide and steal your affections? The "second great commandment" addresses behavioral fruits: Do you love your neighbor as yourself? Or do you misuse, bully, fear, avoid, hate, or ignore your neighbor? The gospel of Jesus Christ bridges from darkness to light. Grace takes out of us the heart of stone, teaching us to know God; grace replaces the hands and tongue that do evil, teaching us to live more beautiful lives.

Two Examples

Any of these thirty-five questions can be asked directly of a person in this or an appropriately altered form. But they are not always questions to ask directly. Sometimes it is better simply to listen and observe, sorting through the fruit in a person's life for the patterns that might indicate the heart's functional commitments. I remember noticing how a man I counseled would apologize profusely, with evident agitation and distress, each time he arrived a few minutes late. These little bits "fit" with other pieces of the puzzle that hadn't quite taken shape yet in our counseling conversation. As it turned out, he was late because he couldn't break off from phone calls or visits with other people, for fear they would not like him. He apologized profusely to me because he was afraid that I would not like him. He had very few true peers, but either idealized superior beings or condemned inferior creatures.

Those small bits of fruit—the reasons for lateness, momentary agitation, inordinate apology, a polarized view of others—led us into the pattern that mastered his life: people too big and God too small (see Prov. 29:25). That interweaving of pride and fear of man is a primary disorder in our disordered hearts. And that directed us straight to the trustworthy Jesus Christ. Remember what we said earlier: explanations are signposts to solutions. As this man found forgiveness and the power to trust a new Master, he learned to walk out practical changes. Rather than cowering or towering, he began to love people with increasing realism and tenderness as he grew to see others as essentially no different from himself.

Let me close with a final case study. I once counseled a man who habitually escaped life's pressures with TV, food, video games, alcohol, pornography, antique collecting, sci-fi novels, working out at the gym. He neglected loving his wife and children; he was slack about his job; he was evasive and deceitful in his communication to others; he went through the motions in church. Where to begin? There were so many problems, so many sins of both commission and omission. I wasn't sure what to pick up on.

Then it struck me: Try the Psalms—as a whole! Almost every single psalm, in some way or other, portrays the Lord as our refuge in trouble, as the center of our hopes. The Psalms implicitly and explicitly rebuke taking refuge in anything less; the Psalms offer steadfast love and mercy; the Psalms spur us to know and obey God in the trenches of life. This man felt vaguely guilty for some of his bad behavior. But he didn't see the pattern or the seriousness of what he lived for. He craved ease, control, comfort—and expressed his craving in dozens of ways. His efforts at change were half-baked and unsuccessful. Conviction of the specific sin of his heart—turning from the living God in order to seek idolatrous refuge—woke him up, and made him see his behavioral sins in a fresh way. His need for what God offered—grace upon grace, for a life of faith working through love—began to burn inside him. As the lights came on about his patterns, he even began to identify little escapist tricks he had never realized he did and had never connected to the more Technicolor sins: e.g., ways he (mis)used humor, or made subtle excuses for himself, or felt sorry for himself.

God seemed far away at the beginning of the process, when he was fog-bound; God seemed very, very close, relevant, and desirable as the process unfolded. Christ's grace became very real and necessary. He became motivated to practical change—to face pressures and responsibilities, to learn to love others, to God's glory. God had graciously laid the motives of his heart bare, and that insight led to a glorious transformation.

8 I Am Motivated When I Feel Desire

The simplest way to discover why a person does, says, thinks, or feels certain things is to ask, "What do you *want*? What desires made him do that? What yearning led her to say that? What longings animate me when I follow that train of thoughts and fantasy? What did they fear when they felt so anxious?"[1] Such questions are plain common sense. Abraham Maslow sensibly described matters this way:

> The original criterion of motivation and the one that is still used by all human beings . . . is the subjective one. I am motivated when I feel desire or want or yearning or wish or lack.[2]

So, pose the question, "What do you want?" to yourself and others. Then pay attention to the answers. If you listen to people, they'll often tell you exactly what they want. "I got angry because she dissed me, and I want respect." "She became tongue-tied because she yearns for acceptance." "He feels anxious because money's tight, and he fears that poverty will prove he's a failure." "Those fantasies of heroism and success play in my mind because I long to be important." Even when a person is inarticulate or unaware, you can often deduce the answer with a high degree of accuracy if you watch and listen closely, and if you know yourself well. Part of knowing any person well is learning what he or she typically lives for—the pattern of desires.

The Meaning of Our Desires

But naming what you want is the easy part. The harder part is this: how should you now *interpret* what you've identified? Naming is not the same as understanding what your wants mean and how you should evaluate them. The meaning of our desires is not common sense at all. Instead, it's a battleground for contending theories of human nature, competing interpretations of the underlying dynamics of human psychology. Abraham Maslow, for example, went on to explain our desires this way:

> It is these needs which are essentially deficits in the organism, empty holes, so to speak, which must be filled up for health's sake, and furthermore must be filled from without by human beings *other* than the subject, that I shall call deficits or deficiency needs.[3]

Is it true that we have these "needs" for respect, acceptance, money, or significance that must be met from outside? Many other great psychologists—B. F. Skinner, Alfred Adler, Sigmund Freud, Victor Frankl, Aaron Beck, Carl Jung, and Virginia Satir, to name a few—didn't think so at all. They disagreed fiercely with each other, too!

The God who reveals his way of thinking in the Bible doesn't agree either with Maslow or with any of the others. In fact, no one ever rightly understands and weighs desires without God's self-revelation in Scripture. Neither lowbrow common sense nor highbrow personality theory gets it straight. God must show us how to properly interpret our wants, because we are compulsive misinterpreters: we don't *want* the true interpretation. It's too threatening to the pursuit of God-less autonomy that is our deepest, darkest, most persistent, and most inadmissable passion.

GOD'S INTERPRETATION AND INTERVENTION

This chapter will zero in on desire.[4] What do you crave, want, pursue, wish, long for, hope to get, feel you need, or passionately desire? God has an interpretation of this that cuts to the marrow of who you are and what you live for. He sees our hearts as an embattled kingdom ruled either by one kind of desire or by another kind. On the one hand, what *lusts of the flesh* hijack your heart from God's rule? On the other hand, what *holy passions* express your love for God? Our desires are not a given, but a fundamental choice. Desires are most often unruly, disorderly, inordinate affections for XYZ, a good thing that I insanely *need*. Sometimes they are natural affections for xyz, made sane and orderly by subordination to passionate love for God that claims my heart, soul, mind, and might. Our desires are often idolatrous cravings to get good gifts (overthrowing or ignoring the Giver). Sometimes they are intense desires for the Giver himself as supremely more important than whatever good gifts we might gain or lose from his hand.

That's the first unique thing God shows us about human psychology. This cosmic battleground is something none of the secular psychologists have seen or can see, because they can't see that deeply into why we do what we do. Their own motives give them reasons not to want to see that deeply and honestly. It would mean admitting sin.

To examine desires is one of the most fruitful ways to come at the topic of motivation biblically. New Testament authors repeatedly allude to life-controlling cravings when they summarize the innermost dynamics of the human soul. Which will triumph, the natural deviancy of the lusts of the flesh or the restored sanity of the desires of the Spirit? Christ's apostles have the greatest confidence that only the resources of the Gospel of grace and truth possess sufficient depth and power to change us in the ways we most need changing. The mercies of God work to *forgive* and then to *change* what is deeply evil, but even more deeply curable by God's hand and voice. The in-working power of grace qualitatively transforms the very desires that psychologists assume are hardwired, unchangeable, morally neutral givens. Christ's grace slays and replaces (in a lifelong battle) the very lusts that the theories variously explain as "needs" or "drives" or "instincts" or "goals."

That's the second unique thing God shows us about human psychology. We can be fundamentally rewired by the merciful presence of the Messiah. None of the secular psychologists say this or can say this. They have no power to address us so deeply, and they don't want to address us at the level of what we (and they) live for. It would mean confessing Christ.

We will use a series of fifteen questions to probe the world of our desires.

1. How does the New Testament commonly talk about what's wrong with people?

Lusts of the flesh (cravings or pleasures) is a summary term for what is wrong with us in God's eyes. In sin, people turn *from* God to

serve what they want. By grace, people turn *to* God from their cravings. According to the Lord's assessment, we all formerly lived in the
lusts of our flesh, indulging the desires of the flesh and the mind
(Eph. 2:3). Those outside of Christ are thoroughly controlled by what
they want. ("Of course I live for money, reputation, success, looks,
and love. What else is there to live for?") And the most significant inner conflict in Christians is between what the Spirit wants and what
we want.

But the term "lust" has become almost useless to modern readers
of the Bible. It is reduced to sexual desire. Take a poll of the people
in your church, asking them the meaning of "lusts of the flesh." Sex
will appear on every list. Greed, pride, gluttonous craving, or mammon worship might be added in the answers of a few of the more
thoughtful believers. But the subtleties and details are washed out,
and a crucial biblical term for explaining human life languishes. In
contrast, the New Testament writers use this term as a comprehensive
category for the human dilemma! It will pay us to think carefully
about its manifold meanings. We need to expand the meaning of a
term that has been truncated and drained of significance. We need to
learn to understand life through these lenses, and to use these categories skillfully.

The New Testament repeatedly focuses on the "lusts of the flesh"
as a summary of what is wrong with the human heart that underlies
bad behavior. For example, 1 John 2:16 contrasts the love of the Father with "all that is in the world, the lust of the flesh and the lust of
the eyes and the boastful pride of life." (See also Rom. 13:14; Gal.
5:16–17; Eph. 2:2; 4:22; James 1:14–15; 4:1–3; 1 Peter 1:14; 2 Peter
1:4.)[5] This does not mean that the New Testament is internalistic.[6] In
each of these passages, behavior intimately connects to motive, and
motive to behavior. Wise counselors follow the model of Scripture
and move back and forth between lusts of the flesh and the tangible
works of the flesh, between faith and the tangible fruit of the Spirit.

2. Why do people do specific ungodly things?

Lusts of the flesh is meant to answer the Why question at the heart
of any system that explains human behavior. Specific ruling desires—
lusts, cravings or pleasures—create bad fruit. Inordinate desires explain and organize diverse bad fruit: words, deeds, emotions,

thoughts, plans, attitudes, brooding memories, fantasies. James 1:13–16 establishes this intimate and pervasive connection between motive and fruit this way: "Let no one say when he is tempted, 'I am being tempted by God'; for God cannot be tempted by evil, and He Himself does not tempt anyone. But each one is tempted when he is carried away and enticed by his own lust. Then when lust has conceived, it gives birth to sin; and when sin is accomplished, it brings forth death. Do not be deceived, my beloved brethren." (See also Galatians 5:16–6:10; James 1:13–16; 3:14–4:12.)

In modern language such sinful cravings often masquerade as expectations, goals, felt needs, wishes, demands, longings, drives, and so forth. People talk about their motives in ways that anesthetize themselves and others to the true significance of what they are describing.

3. But what's wrong with wanting things that seem good?

What makes our desires wrong? This question becomes particularly perplexing to people when the object of their desires is a good thing. Notice some of the adjectives that get appended to our cravings: *evil, polluted* lusts.[7] Sometimes the object of desire itself is evil: to kill someone, to steal, to control the cocaine trade on the Eastern seaboard. But often the object of desire is good, and the evil lies in the lordship of the desire. Our will replaces God's as that which determines how we live.

John Calvin put it this way: "We teach that all human desires are evil, and charge them with sin—not in that they are natural, but because they are inordinate."[8] In other words, the evil in our desires often lies not in what we want but in the fact that we want it too much. Natural affections (for any good thing) become inordinate, ruling cravings. We are meant to be ruled by godly passions and desires (see Question 15). Natural desires for good things are meant to exist subordinate to our desire to please the Giver of gifts. Grasping that the evil lies in the ruling status of the desire, not the object, is frequently a turning point in self-understanding, in seeing the need for Christ's mercies, and in changing.

Consider this example. A woman commits adultery, and repents. She and her husband rebuild the marriage, painstakingly, patiently. Eight months later the man finds himself plagued with subtle suspiciousness and irritability. The wife senses it, and feels a bit like she lives under FBI surveillance. The husband is grieved by his suspiciousness because he has no objective reasons for it. "I've forgiven her; we've rebuilt our marriage; we've never communicated better; why do I hold on to this mistrust?" It emerges that he is willing to forgive the past, but he attempts to control the future. His craving could be stated this way: "I want to guarantee that betrayal never, ever happens again."

The object of desire is good; its ruling status poisons his ability to love. The lust to ensure her fidelity places him in the stance of continually evaluating and judging his wife, rather than loving her. What he wants cannot be guaranteed this side of heaven. He sees the point, sees his inordinate desire to ensure his marital future. But he bursts out, "What's wrong with wanting my wife to love me? What's wrong with wanting her to remain faithful to our marriage?" Here is where this truth is so sweet. There is nothing wrong with the object of desire; there is everything wrong when it rules his life. The process of restoring that marriage took a long step forward as he took this to heart.

Are preferences, wishes, desires, longings, hopes, and expectations always sinful then? Of course not. What theologians used to call "natural affections" are part of our humanity. They are part of what makes humans different from stones, able to tell the difference between blessing and curse, pleasure and pain. It is *right* that we don't want the pains of rejection, death, poverty, and illness, and we do want the joys of friendship, life, money, and health. Jesus was no masochist; of course he cried out, "Let this cup pass from me!"

The moral issue always turns on whether the desire takes on a ruling status. If it does, it will produce visible sins: anger, grumbling, immorality, despair, what James so vividly termed "disorder and every evil thing" (James 3:16).

Jesus was no idolater; he entrusted himself to his Father and obeyed. "Nevertheless, not my will but yours be done." If natural affections remain submitted to God, such faith will produce visible love. If you wish your son to grow up to be a Christian, and he strays, it may break your heart, but it will not make you sin against either God or your son.

4. Why don't people see this as the problem?

Consider a second adjective that Scripture attaches to the phrase "lusts of the flesh": *deceitful* lusts.[9] Our desires deceive us because they present themselves as so plausible. Natural affections become warped and monstrous, and so blind us. Who wouldn't want good health, financial comfort, a loving spouse, good kids, success on the job, kind parents, tasty food, a life without traffic jams, control over circumstances? Yet cravings for these things lead to every sort of evil. The things people desire are delightful as blessings received from God, but terrible as rulers. They make good goods but bad gods. They beguile, promising blessing, but delivering sin and death.

Some sins are high-handed, done with full awareness of choice (Ps.19:13). Other sins reflect the blind, dark, habitual, compulsive, hardened, ignorant, confused, instinctive insanity of sin.[10] One of the joys of biblical ministry comes when you are able to turn on the lights in another person's dark room. People usually don't see their desires as lusts. Souls are cured as the ignorant and self-deceived are disturbed by the light of God's analytic gaze and then comforted by the love that shed substitutionary blood to purchase the inexpressible gift.

I have yet to meet a couple locked in hostility (and the accompanying fear, self-pity, hurt, self-righteousness) who really understood and reckoned with their motives. James 4:1–3 teaches that cravings underlie conflicts. Why do you fight? It's not "because my wife/husband . . ."—it's because of something about *you*. Couples who see what rules them—cravings for affection, attention, power, vindication, control, comfort, a hassle-free life—can repent and find God's grace made real to them, and then learn how to make peace.

5. Is the phrase "lusts of the flesh" useful in practical life and counseling?

Apply the term to twenty-first-century experience, redeeming the evasive language people substitute. People frequently talk about what they want, expect, wish for, desire, demand, need, long for. Pop psychologies typically validate these needs and longings as neutral givens. Little do people realize that much of the time they are actually describing sinful usurpers of God's rule over their lives: inordinate desires, lusts of the flesh, cravings. They just aren't interpreting their experience rightly.

For example, listen to children talk when they are angry, disappointed, demanding, contrary: "But I want. . . . But I don't want to. . . ." In our family we began teaching our children about the "I-wantsies" before they were two years old. We wanted them to grasp that sin was more than behavior. For example, analyze any argument or outburst of anger and you will find ruling expectations and desires that are being frustrated (James 4:1–2).

The language people typically use day to day gets you into the details of a person's life, but it usually comes with a distorted interpretation attached. Wise counseling must reinterpret that experience into biblical categories, taking the more pointed reality of "lusts, cravings, pleasures" and mapping it onto the "felt needs" that underlie much sin and misery. The very unfamiliarity of the phrase is an advantage, if you explain it carefully and show its relevance and applicability. Behavioral sins demand a horizontal resolution—as well as vertical repentance. But motivational sins have first and foremost to do with God, and repentance quickens the awareness of relationship with the God of grace.

6. Does each person have one "root sin"?

With good reason, the Bible usually refers to the "lusts" (plural) of the flesh. The human heart can generate a lust tailored to any situation. Again John Calvin powerfully described how cravings "boil up" within us, how the mind of man is a "factory of idols."[11] We are infested with lusts. Listen closely to any person given to complaining, and you will observe the creativity of our cravings. Certainly one particular craving may so frequently appear that it seems to be a "root sin": love of mammon, fear of man and craving for approval, love of preeminence or control, desire for pleasure, and so forth, can dictate much of life. But all people have all the typical cravings.

Realizing the diversity in human lusts gives great flexibility and penetration to counseling. For example, one lust can generate very diverse sins, as 1 Timothy 6:10 states: "The love of money is a root of all sorts of evil." Every one of the Ten Commandments—and more— can be broken by someone who loves and serves money. The craving for money and material possessions is an organizing theme for symptomatic sins as diverse as anxiety, theft, compulsive shopping, murder, jealousy, marital discord, a sense of inferiority or of superiority compared to others, sexual immorality that trades sex for material advantage, and so forth.

On the flip side, a single behavioral sin can emerge from very different lusts. For example, sexual immorality might occur for many different reasons: erotic pleasure, financial advantage, revenge on a spouse or parent, fear of saying no to an authority, pursuit of approval, enjoyment of power over another's sexual response, the quest for social status or career advancement, pity for someone and playing the savior, fear of losing a potential marriage partner, escape from boredom, peer pressure, and so forth. Wise biblical counselors dig for specifics. They don't assume all people have the same characteristic flesh, or that a person always does a certain thing for the same reasons. The flesh is creative in iniquity.

7. How can you tell if a desire is inordinate rather than natural?

By their *fruits* you know them. Human motivation is not a theoretical mystery; there is no need to engage in introspective archeological digs. Evil desires produce bad fruits that can be seen, heard, and felt (James 1:15; 3:16). For example, a father who wants his child to grow up to become a Christian reveals the status of that desire by whether he is a good father or a manipulative, fearful, angry, suspicious father. In a good father, the desire is subordinate to God's will that he love his child. In a sinful father, the desire rules and produces moral and emotional chaos. Similarly, a wife who wants to be loved reveals the status of that desire by whether or not she loves and respects her husband. Visible fruit reveals whether God rules or a lust rules.

It is a serious mistake to engage in introspective "idol hunts," attempting to dig out and weigh every kink in the human soul. The Bible calls for a more straightforward form of self-examination: an outburst of anger invites reflection on what craving ruled the heart that our repentance might be intelligent. The Bible's purposes are "extrospective," not introspective: to move toward God in repentant faith (James 4:6–10) and then to move toward the one wronged by anger, making peace in repentance, humility, and love.

8. Is it even right to talk about the heart, since the Bible teaches that the heart is unknowable to anyone but God?
(1 Sam. 16:7; Jer. 17:9)

No one but God can *see, explain, control,* or *change* another person's heart and its choices. There is no underlying reason why a person serves a particular lust rather than God; sin is irrational and insane. And there is no therapeutic technique that can change hearts. But the Bible teaches us that we can *describe* what rules the heart and speak the truth that convicts and liberates. Effective biblical ministry probes and addresses why people do things, as well as what they do. Jesus' ministry continually exposed and challenged what people lived for, offering himself as the only worthy ruler of the heart.

For example, 1 Samuel 16:7 says that man judges by externals while God judges the heart. Yet a few verses earlier, we are told that Saul visibly disobeyed God for a reason: he feared the people and listened to their voice, instead of fearing God and listening to him (see 1 Sam. 15:24). His motives are describable, even if inexplicable. There is no deeper cause for sin than sin. Jeremiah 17:9 says that the human heart is deceitful and incomprehensible to any but God, but the same passage describes how behavior reveals that people trust in idols, themselves, and others, instead of trusting in God (see Jer. 17:1–8). Scripture is frank to tell us the causes of behavior: interpersonal conflicts, for example, arise because of lusts (see James 4:1–2). If anger and conflict come from a lust, the next and obvious question is, "*What* do you want that now rules you?"

To search out motives demands no subtle psychotherapeutic technique. People can tell us what they want. The Israelites grumbled—a capital crime—when they had to subsist on boring food. Why? They craved flavor: fish, cucumbers, melons, leeks, onions, and garlic (see Num. 11:5). Later they grumbled when they got thirsty and no oasis appeared. Why? They craved juicy foods, or foods that demanded irrigation: grain, figs, vines, pomegranates, and water (see Num. 20:5). In each case the craving reflected their apostasy from God and expressed itself in visible, audible sins. When we see the God-substitutes that claim our affections, then we see how good and necessary the grace of Jesus is in subduing hijackers and retaking the controls.

9. Doesn't the word lusts properly apply only to bodily appetites: the pleasures and comforts of sex, food, drink, rest, exercise, health?

People follow the *desires of body and mind* (see Eph 2:3). Bodily appetites—the organism's hedonistic instinct to feel good—are certainly powerful masters unto sin. But desires of the mind—for power, human approval, success, preeminence, wealth, self-righteousness, and so forth—are also potent masters. The desires of the mind often present the most subtle and deceitful lusts because their outworkings are not always obvious. They don't reside in the body, but the Bible still views them as "lusts."

10. Can desires be habitual?

Paul describes a *former manner of life* characterized by deceitful lusts. Peter tells his readers not to be conformed to their *former desires*.[12] Like all other aspects of sin—beliefs, attitudes, words, deeds, emotions, thoughts, fantasies—desires can be habitual. You will counsel people who typically and repeatedly seek to control others, or to indulge in the pleasures of sloth, or to be seen as superior, or to be liked. Jesus' call to die daily to self recognizes the inertia of sin. God is in the business of creating new habitual desires, for example, an active concern for the well being of others before God.

Many counseling systems are obsessed with locating the reasons for current problems in the distant past. The Bible's worldview is much more straightforward. Sin emerges from within the person. The fact that a pattern of craving became established many years before— even that it was forged in a particular context, perhaps influenced by bad models or by experiences of being sinned against—only describes what happened. For example, past rejections do not cause a craving to be accepted by others any more than current rejections cause that craving. The occasions of a lust are never its cause. Temptations and sufferings do push our buttons, but they don't create those buttons. That brings huge hope for change in the present by the grace of God.

11. What about fears? They seem as important in human motivation as cravings.

Fear and desire are two sides of a single coin. A sinful fear is a craving for something *not* to happen. If I want money, I fear poverty. If I long to be accepted, I'm terrified of rejection. If I fear pain or hardship, I crave comfort or pleasure. If I crave preeminence, I fear being inferior to others. With some people the fear may be more pronounced than the corresponding desire, and wise counseling will work with what is pronounced.

For example, a person who grew up during the Great Depression might manifest mammon worship through a fear of poverty that shows up in anxiety, hoarding, repeated calculations of financial worth, and so forth. A wealthy entrepreneur might manifest mammon worship through unchecked consumer spending. With the former, address fear; with the latter, address greed. They are complementary expressions of craving treasure on earth.

12. Do people ever have conflicting motives?

Certainly. The conflict between sinful lusts and the Holy Spirit's desires is a given of the Christian life (Gal. 5:16–17). People often have mixed motives, some good, and some bad. Most preachers and counselors will acknowledge that loving Christ and people battles against love for success and human approval.

In other instances, two sinful cravings may conflict. For example, a businessman might want to steal something from a convenience store, but holds back in fear of what people would think if they found out. In this example, mammon worship and social approval present themselves as options for the flesh; the heart inclines to the latter.

People often prioritize their cravings, and arrange the priorities differently in different situations. For example, the man who would never shoplift because of the social consequences might cheat on his taxes because he's not likely to get caught, and no one who "matters" would know if he did. In this case self-will and mammon worship seize the steering wheel, and social approval moves to the back seat. The "broad way" has a thousand creative variants!

13. How does thinking about lusts relate to other ways of talking about sin, such as "sin nature," "self," "pride," "autonomy," "unbelief," and "self-centeredness"?

These words are general terms that summarize the problem of sin. One of the beauties of identifying ruling desires is that they are specific and can therefore enable more specific repentance and specific change. For example, a person who becomes angry in a traffic jam may later say, "I know the anger is sin, and it comes from self." That is true as far as it goes. But it helps to take self-knowledge a step further: "I cursed in anger because I craved to get to my appointment on time, I feared criticism from the person waiting for me, and I feared losing the profits from that sale." Repentance and change can become more specific when the person

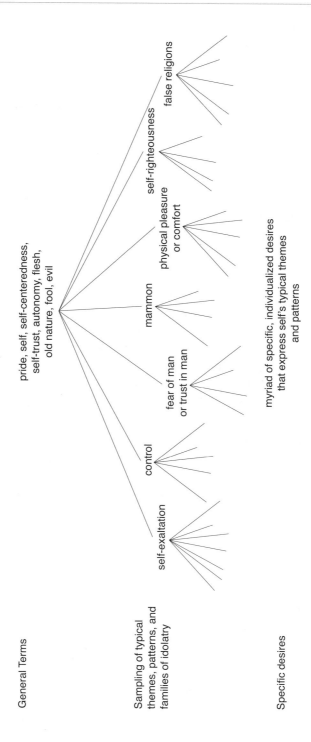

General Terms

pride, self, self-centeredness,
self-trust, autonomy, flesh,
old nature, fool, evil

Sampling of typical
themes, patterns, and
families of idolatry

self-exaltation

control

fear of man
or trust in man

mammon

physical pleasure
or comfort

self-righteousness

false religions

Specific desires

myriad of specific, individualized desires
that express self's typical themes
and patterns

Fig. 1. Desires of the Flesh

identifies these three lusts that expressed the lordship of self in this particular incident.

The Bible discusses sin in an astonishing variety of ways. Sometimes Scripture addresses sin at the general level: e.g., Luke 9:23–26 on self or Proverbs on the fool. At other times Scripture increases the microscope's power and treats a particular theme of sin: e.g., Philippians 3 on the pursuit of self-righteousness or 1 Timothy 6 on love of money. In still other places, the Bible speaks of sinful desires that lead to sin and invites us to make the specific application: e.g., James 1:14–15; 4:1–2; Galatians 5:16–21; Romans 13:12–14. We could diagram this roughly as follows: (1) general terms, (2) mid-level typical patterns, and (3) detail-level specifics (see Figure 1).

14. In counseling, do you just confront a person with his sinful cravings?

Wise counselors don't "just confront" anything. They do many different things to make confrontation timely and effective. Counselors never see the heart, only the evidences, so a certain tentativeness is often appropriate when discussing motives. Perhaps it would be more accurate to say that counseling aims to illuminate the heart, to help people see themselves as they are in God's eyes, and in that to make the love of God a sweet necessity. Since counselors have the same package of typical lusts, we meet on common ground in our need for grace because of pride, fear of man, unbelief, and love of comfort and control.

We can and must tackle such issues. Second Timothy 3:16 begins with teaching. Good teaching (for example, on how Galatians 5 and James 1 connect outward sins to inward cravings) helps people examine and see themselves. Good teaching invites self-knowledge and self-confrontation. Experience with people will make you "case wise" to typical connections (such as the varied motives for immorality mentioned in Question 6). Probing questions—What did you want or expect or fear when you blew up at your wife?—help a person reveal his ruling lusts to himself and to the counselor.

In the light of self-knowledge before God's face (Heb. 4:12–13), the Gospel offers many promises: mercy, help, the Shepherd's care in progressive sanctification (Heb. 4:14–16). "The unfolding of Your words brings light" (Ps. 119:130). Repentance, faith, and obedience become vigorous and intelligent when we see both our inner cravings and our outward sins in light of God's mercies.

The patterns, themes, or tendencies of the heart do not typically yield to a once-for-all repentance. Try dealing one mortal blow to your pride, fear of man, love of pleasure, or desire to control your world, and you will realize why Jesus spoke Luke 9:23! But genuine progress will occur where the Holy Spirit is at work. Understanding your motivational sins gives you a sense for the themes of your story, how your Father is at work in you over the long haul.

Work hard and carefully both on motivation issues (Rom. 13:14: the lusts of the flesh *versus* putting on Jesus Christ) and on behavioral issues (Rom. 13:12–13: the varied deeds of darkness *versus* proper "daylight" behavior).

15. *Can you change what you want?*

Yes and Amen! This is central to the work of the Holy Spirit. You will always desire, love, trust, believe, fear, obey, long for, value, pursue, hope, and serve *something*. You are motivated when you feel desire. God does not anesthetize us; he redirects our desires. The Holy Spirit works to change the something, as he leads us with an intimate hand.[13] The desires of the heart are not unchangeable. God never promises to give you what you want, to meet your felt needs and longings. He tells you to be ruled by other, different desires. This is radical. God promises to change what you really want! God insists that he be first, and all lesser loves be radically subordinate.

The best way to understand this is to think about prayer. Prayer means asking, and you ask because you *want* something. You ask God because you believe he has power to accomplish some desired good. When Solomon prayed for a wise and discerning heart, God freely gave Solomon what he wanted (1 Kings 3). God was delighted that Solomon did not ask for a long life, riches, and success, the felt needs of most people in power. Solomon had not treated God as a genie in a lamp who exists to grant him three wishes. What we want by nature—the cravings of the flesh—expresses our sin nature. But Solomon had learned to know what he really needed. He had learned to pray according to the will of God, and it pleased God to answer him. The Lord changes what we want, and we learn to pray for what delights God, to want what he wants.

God challenges the things that everybody everywhere eagerly pursues (Matt. 6:32). What desires of body and mind (Eph. 2:3) *do* people naturally follow? Consider our characteristic passions: desires of the body include life itself, air, health, water, food, clothing, shelter, sexual pleasure, rest, and exercise. Desires of the mind include happiness, being loved, meaning, money and possessions, respect, status, accomplishment, self-esteem, success, control, power, self-righteousness, aesthetic pleasure, knowledge, marriage, and family. Must these rule our lives? They did not rule Jesus' life. Can these cravings really be changed? The Bible says Yes, and points us to the promises of God: to indwell us with power, to write truth on our hearts, to pour out his love in our hearts, to enable us to say "Abba, Father."

As we have seen, many of these things are not bad in themselves. The evil in our desires does not lie in what we want, but in the fact that we want it too much. Our desires for good things seize the throne, becoming idols that replace the King. God refuses to serve our instinctive longings, but commands us to be ruled by other longings. What God commands, he provides the power to accomplish: he works in us both the willing and the doing of his good pleasure (Phil. 2:12–13).

Can you change what you want? Yes. Does the answer to this question surprise you? It counters influential contemporary views of human motivation. Most Christian counseling books follow on the heels of secular psychologists and take your desires, your "felt needs," as givens. Many leading Christian psychologists make the unchangeability of what we long for the foundation of their systems. For example, many teach that we have an "empty love tank" inside, and our craving for love must be met, or we are doomed to a life of sin and misery. Desires to feel good about ourselves ("self-esteem") or to accomplish something meaningful are similarly baptized. This creates the psychological equivalent of the "Health and Wealth" theology, which similarly selects certain common desires and accepts them as givens that God is obligated to fulfill. The psychological versions of health and wealth miss that God is about the business of changing what people really long for. If felt needs are unchangeable, then it is impossible for us to learn to pray the way Solomon did. This reinforces our tendency to pray for our cravings. It reinforces a sense of victimization in those who were mistreated. It reinforces the tendency to press God into the service of our lusts.

The deepest longings of the human heart can and must be changed if mankind is to become all that God designed us to be. Our deviant longings are illegitimate masters; even where the object of desire is a good thing, the status of the desire usurps God. Our cravings should be recognized in order that we may more richly know God as the Savior, Lover, and Converter of the human soul. God would have us long for him more than we long for his gifts. To make us truly human, God must change what we want; we must learn to want the things Jesus wanted. It is no surprise that the psychologists can't find any biblical proof texts for their view of human motivation. The Bible teaches a different view.

The Christian life is a great paradox. Those who die to self, find self. Those who die to their cravings will receive many times as much in this age, and, in the age to come, eternal life (Luke 18:29). They will find new passions worth living for and dying for. If I crave happiness, I will receive misery. If I crave to be loved, I will receive rejection. If I crave significance, I will receive futility. If I crave control, I will receive chaos. If I crave reputation, I will receive humiliation. But if I long for God and his wisdom and mercy, I will receive God and wisdom and mercy. Along the way, sooner or later, I will also receive happiness, love, meaning, order, and glory.

Every vital Christian testifies that the instinctive passions and desires of the flesh can be replaced with the new priorities of the Spirit. This reorientation is not instant and complete, but it is genuine and progressive. Two of the greatest books of practical Christian theology—Augustine's *Confessions* and Jonathan Edwards's *Treatise Concerning Religious Affections*—meditate on this transformation. And one assumes that Francis of Assisi meant his prayer: "O Divine Master, grant that I may not so much seek to be consoled, as to console; to be understood, as to understand; to be loved, as to love." The craving to learn *how* to love and understand replaces the craving *for* love and understanding.

Those who hunger and thirst for such righteousness will be satisfied. We have Jesus' word. We have no promise, however, that God will satisfy the instinctive cravings of the soul. The Bible teaches us to pray, to learn to ask for what we really need. Can we pray the petitions of the Lord's Prayer and really mean it? Yes. Can we long for God's glory, for his will to be obeyed, for daily material provision for all God's people, for sins to be forgiven, for aid in warfare with evil? Yes.

A wise Puritan pastor, Thomas Chalmers, once wrote of "the expulsive power of a new affection." New ruling desires expel lesser masters from the throne. What are the new and different motives that rule in renewed hearts? What changed objects of desire characterize the master motives of the new, listening heart? How does God change what people want? The Bible treats these matters everywhere.[14]

Idolatrous cravings hijack the human heart. Both the Christian life and Christian ministry are by definition about the business of accomplishing a transformation in what people want. Such transformations lie at the center of the Holy Spirit's purposes in working his Word into our lives. The lusts of the flesh lead somewhere bad: dead works. The lusts of the flesh have a specific solution: the Gospel of Jesus Christ, which replaces them. "He died for all, so that they who live might no longer live for themselves, but for Him who died and rose again on their behalf" (2 Cor. 5:15). The desires of the Lord lead to somewhere good: good works. One key ingredient in reclaiming the cure of souls is to make this transformation central.

We have probed only one of the many terms by which the Bible explains the workings of the human heart in specific detail. This is a theme whose riches are inexhaustible. The human heart is an active verb. We do not "have needs"; we "do desires," just as we do love, fear, hope, trust, and all the rest. Here we have examined the verbs of desire. We could have examined any of scores of complementary verbs that capture the fundamental activism of the heart of man. But we would do so confident of this: The gospel of Jesus Christ is as wide as human diversity and as deep as human complexity. The Scriptures that bear witness to this Christ in the power of his Spirit are sufficient to cure souls.

9 God's Love: Better Than Unconditional

Your lovingkindness, O LORD, extends to the heavens,
Your faithfulness reaches to the skies.
Your righteousness is like the mountains of God;
Your judgments are like a great deep.
O LORD, You preserve man and beast.
How precious is Your lovingkindness, O God!
And the children of men take refuge in the shadow of Your wings.
They drink their fill of the abundance of Your house;
And You give them to drink of the river of Your delights.
For with You is the fountain of life;
In Your light we see light.
O continue Your lovingkindness to those who know You,
And Your righteousness to the upright in heart.

Psalm 36:5–10

With these words, the psalmist David attempts to talk about the wonder and power of God's love. It is something he tried to do frequently throughout his life, yet we never get the sense that David felt he had succeeded. He piles superlative upon superlative. He pushes the limits of language. But David seems to know that the love he has experienced from God can never be fully communicated in words. All he can do is invite others to come and taste for themselves.

Is it any different for us today? Is it any easier for us to talk about love—any kind of love—let alone the all-encompassing love of God? Certainly, God's love is something people are hungry to hear about. Yet in some ways, it's even harder for us to talk about it, since most people now try to describe the most intimate, spiritual aspects of their lives in secular language. These words seem thin and pale and weak when they try to convey the richness and weight of a biblical truth. And nowhere is that more obvious than when it comes to God's love.

For example, have you ever had people tell you that God deals with his children with "unconditional love"? Most of the time, they are looking for a way to express how generous and complete his love is. But before we adopt this description we should remember David and ask, Is this explanation of divine love the best we can do?

I'd like to propose that God's love is much different and better than unconditional. Unconditional love, as most of us understand it, begins and ends with sympathy and empathy, with blanket acceptance. It accepts you as you are with no expectations. You in turn can take it or leave it.

But think about what God's love for you is like. God does not calmly gaze on you in benign affirmation. God cares too much to be unconditional in his love.

WATCHFUL, CARING LOVE

Imagine yourself as a parent, watching your child playing in a group with other children. Perhaps you are observing your child in a nursery or a classroom, or on the playground, or in a soccer game. You might accurately say that you have unconditional love for all the children in the group. That is to say, you have no ill will toward any of them; you generally wish them well.

But when it comes to your own child, something more goes on. You take much more notice of your own child. Injury, danger, bullying, or injustice arouses strong feelings of protection—because you love your child. If your child throws a tantrum or mistreats another child, you are again aroused to intervene—because you love. If your child thrives, you are filled with joy—again, because you love.

Of course, any of these reactions may be tainted by a parent's sin. Pride, fear of other's opinions, lust for success, superiority, ambition, or calloused self-absorption can warp parental love.

But imagine such reactions untainted by sin. Read Psalm 121, Hosea 11 and 14, Isaiah 49, the life of Jesus. The Lord *watches* you.

The Lord *cares*. What his children do and what happens to them *matter* to him. His watching, caring, and concern are intense. Complex. Specific. Personal. Unconditional love isn't nearly so good or compelling. In comparison it is detached, general, impersonal. God's love is much better than unconditional.

Active, Intrusive Love

God's love is active. He decided to love you when he could have justly condemned you. He's involved. He's merciful, not simply tolerant. He hates sin, yet pursues sinners by name. God is so committed to forgiving and changing you that he sent Jesus to die for you. He welcomes the poor in spirit with a shout and a feast. God is vastly patient and relentlessly persevering as he intrudes into your life.

God's love actively does you good. His love is full of blood, sweat, tears, and cries. He suffered for you. He fights for you, defending the afflicted. He fights *with* you, pursuing you in powerful tenderness so that he can change you. He's jealous, not detached. His sort of empathy and sympathy speaks out, with words of truth to set you free from sin and misery. He will discipline you as proof that he loves you. God himself comes to live in you, pouring out his Holy Spirit in your heart, so that you will know him. He puts out power and energy.

God's love has hate in it too: hatred for evil, whether done to you or by you. God's love demands that you respond to it: by believing, trusting, obeying, giving thanks with a joyful heart, working out your salvation with fear, delighting in the Lord.

In C. S. Lewis's *The Chronicles of Narnia*, Lucy and her siblings were frightened at first to learn that Aslan, the Christ figure, was not a tame lion. But though he was not tame, they were reassured that he *was* good. In the same way, the Lord's love for his children is no tame love, no relational strategy. It's not characterized by calm detachment or a determination not to impose his values on you. His love is good in a way that's vigorous and complex.

That's the love that is poured out on you as his child, and you are meant—in some fashion—to have this same kind of love for one another: "Walk in love just as Christ also loved you" (Eph. 4:32–5:2).

Such real love is hard to do. It is so different from "You're okay in my eyes. I accept you just because you're you, just as I accept everybody. I won't judge you or impose my values on you." Unconditional love feels safe, but the problem is that there is no power to it. When we ascribe unconditional love to God, we substitute a teddy bear for the king of the universe.

LOVE HAS A GOAL

What words will do to describe the love of God that is spectacularly accepting, yet opinionated, choosy, and intrusive?

> For the love of Christ controls us, having concluded this, that one died for all, therefore all have died; and He died for all, so that they who live might no longer live for themselves, but for Him who died and rose again on their behalf. (2 Cor. 5:14–15)

What words will do to describe the love of God that takes me just as I am but makes me over? That accepts people, yet has a lifelong agenda for change? Does it work to apply the label "unconditional love" to what God does—and to what godly parents and leaders are supposed to do, speak, and model?

The term seems flabby and weak in the face of God's powerful, purposeful love. However, many people do use the phrase "unconditional love" with good intentions, attempting to capture four significant and interrelated truths.

FOUR UNCONDITIONAL TRUTHS

It's true that conditional love is a bad thing. It is not love at all, but an expression of the routine hatred and self-centeredness of the human heart. It's better to call it "conditional and manipulative approval." It plays capricious Lawgiver and Judge: "If you please me and jump through my hoops, I will smile favorably on you. If you displease me, I will either attack you or avoid you." People use the term "unconditional" as shorthand to contrast with manipulation, demand, or judgmentalism. They use it to shine the light on a sinful form of human relationship and to say, "Real love isn't like this."

It's true that God's love is patient. He, and those who imitate him, forbear and endure with others in hope. God does not give up. Because God perseveres, his saints will persevere to the end and come through into glory. People use "unconditional" as shorthand for hanging in there through the process of change, rather than bailing out when the going gets rough. They use it to build hope over the long haul.

It's true that true love is God's gift. It is at God's initiative and choice; it isn't given out on the basis of my performance. God's gospel love is not wages that I earn with a model life; it is a gift. It is a gift that I cannot earn; more than that, it is a gift that I do not even deserve. God loves weak, ungodly, sinful enemies. The gift is the opposite of what I deserve. God ought to kill me on the spot. Instead, he sent his Son to die in my place. People use "unconditional" as shorthand for such unearned blessing. They use it to overcome legalism.

It's true that God receives you just as you are: sinful, suffering, confused. In street talk, he meets you where you are. You don't clean up your act and then come to God. You just come. People use "unconditional" as shorthand for God's invitation to dirty, broken people. They use it to overcome despair and fear that would shrink back from asking help from God and his people.

These are precious truths. They show that the adjective "unconditional" actually has a noble theological lineage in describing the grace of God. Unfortunately, the way people commonly use the term muddies the waters for four reasons.

Four Biblical Improvements

There are more biblical, vivid ways to capture these truths.
- The opposite of manipulation is not dispassionate complacency. Real love's kindness has zeal, self-sacrifice, and a call to change woven in (Isa. 49:15; 1 Thess. 2:7–12).

- The call for you to hang in there through the thick and thin of a person's struggles can be frankly stated: "Love is patient," "Be patient with them all" (1 Cor. 13:4; 1 Thess. 5:14).
- "Grace" and "gift" capture the free, unearned quality of God's love less ambiguously than "unconditional" (2 Cor. 9:15; Rom. 6:23; Eph. 2:4–10).
- God's welcome to the godless comes with a story attached: "Christ Jesus came into the world to save sinners" (1 Tim. 1:15). "Christ loved us and gave himself up for us" (Eph. 5:2). The gospel is an action story, not simply an attitude of acceptance.

We do not need to use a vague, abstract word like unconditional when the Bible gives us more vivid and specific words, metaphors, and stories to communicate what God's love is like.

Unmerited grace is not strictly unconditional. While it's true that God's love does not depend upon what you do, it very much depends on what Jesus Christ did for you. In that sense, it is highly conditional. It cost Jesus his life.

In fact, the love of God described in the Bible requires the fulfillment of two conditions: perfect obedience and a sin-bearing substitute. Jesus, by his active obedience to the will of God, demonstrated and earned the verdict "righteous." His fulfillment of God's conditions is passed on to you when God justifies you.

And Jesus, in his passive obedience, suffered the penalty of death. The substitutionary Lamb took our death penalty to bring you freedom and life. So the love of God contains two "conditions fulfilled" as it is handed freely to you and to me. God's love contains both the life and death work of the One who was both God's servant and God's lamb. Unconditional love? No, something much better, something costly and hard and generous.

God's grace is intended to change people. There *is* something wrong with you! From God's point of view, you not only need someone else to be killed in your place in order to be forgiven, you need to be transformed to be fit to live with. The word "unconditional" may be an acceptable way to express God's welcome, but it fails to communicate its purpose: a comprehensive and lifelong rehabilitation, learning "the holiness without which no one will see the Lord."

People often use the word "unconditional" to communicate an affirmation that "you're okay," robbing God's love (and a pastor's or parent's love) of its very purpose. You "turn" to receive God's love. You do nothing to receive blanket acceptance—and it doesn't take you anywhere.

Unconditional love carries cultural baggage. As you've read the previous paragraphs, you've noticed how unconditional is wedded to words such as "tolerance, acceptance, affirmation, okay." It is wedded to a philosophy that says love should impose no values, expectations, or beliefs on another.

I could have used the technical phrase that arose within humanistic psychology: "unconditional positive regard." Most people think of this concept when they think of unconditional love: "Deep down you're okay; God accepts you just as you are. God smiles on you even if you don't jump through any hoops. You have intrinsic worth. God accepts you, warts and all. You can relax, bask in his smile, and let the basically good, real you emerge." This is a philosophy of life utterly at odds with God's real love.

Contraconditional Love

The opposite of conditional and judgmental might seem to be unconditional and affirming. The opposite of unreasonable expectations might seem to be no expectations at all. The opposite of being bossy might seem to be non-directive. Or so people wish.

Yes, conditional love is obviously hate, not love. But unconditional love—used with the meaning the term now carries—is a more subtle deceit. It keeps company with teachings that say to people, "Peace, peace," when, from God's holy point of view, there is no peace (see Jer. 23:14, 16).

If you receive blanket acceptance, you need no repentance. You just accept it. It fills you without humbling you. It relaxes you without upsetting you about yourself—or thrilling you about Christ. It lets you relax without reckoning with the anguish of Jesus on the cross. It is easy and undemanding. It does not insist on, or work at, changing you. It deceives you about both God and yourself.

We can do better. God does not accept me just as I am; he loves me *despite* how I am. He loves me just as *Jesus* is; he loves me enough to devote my life to renewing me in the image of Jesus.

This love is much, much, much better than unconditional! Perhaps we could call it "*contra*conditional" love. God has blessed me because his Son fulfilled the conditions I could never achieve. *Contrary* to what I deserve, he loves me. And now I can begin to change, not to earn love, but because I've already received it.

People who speak of unconditional love often mean well. A few use the words with the old theological meanings intact. Many just want people to care for each other. Many want to help those who view God as the Great Critic, whom they either serve grudgingly or flee because they can never please him. I have no doubt that the phrase has served some strugglers usefully, despite the riches it leaves out and the baggage it usually contains.

THE BETTER LOVE OF JESUS

But there is a good reason why the Bible tells us stories of amazing events, speaks in gripping metaphors, and unfolds detailed theology to inform us of God's love. It's because you need something better than unconditional love. You need the crown of thorns. You need the touch of life bestowed on the dead son of the widow of Nain. You need the promise to the repentant thief. You need to know, "I will never leave you or forsake you." You need forgiveness. You need a Shepherd, a Father, a Savior. You need to become like the One who loves you. You need the better love of Jesus. And by God's grace, that is what he offers you.

10 WHAT IF YOUR FATHER DIDN'T LOVE YOU?

This is love, not that we loved God, but that He loved us and sent
His Son to be the propitiation for our sins. 1 John 4:10

If God is for us, who is against us? He who did not spare
His own Son but gave Him up for us all, will He not also
give us all things with Him? Romans 8:31–32

The love of God has been poured into our hearts through the
Holy Spirit who has been given to us. Romans 5:5

You have received a spirit of adoptions as sons by which we cry out,
"Abba! Father!" The Spirit Himself testifies with our spirit that
we are children of God. Romans 8:15b–16

How do you come to know the love of God the Father? The passages of Scripture just cited speak of two aspects. First, there is an inescapable, historical fact: Jesus Christ went to an agonizing death out of love for sinners. Second, there is a powerful internal dynamic: the Holy Spirit pours out God's love in us to create the child's trusting response. *Did* God act in love? *Does* God act now in love? Yes and amen. The love of Christ—that converts enemies into thankful children—contains both anguish and glory. He who wore the brutal crown of thorns now wears the radiant crown of glory. God's love is effective, both then and now.

But what about people who seem to know neither the fact nor the dynamic? The crown of thorns leaves them cold. The Holy Spirit is a theory. There is little or no "Abba, Father" in their hearts. How do you reach them? Listen to two statements I've heard repeatedly, both from Christian counselors and from struggling Christians. The first says, "You can't really appreciate God as Father if you had a poor relationship with your human father." This statement logically correlates to a second statement about counseling methods and Christian growth: "If you have had parent problems in your personal history, you need some sort of re-parenting or corrective emotional experience. You need the love of some father substitute, therapist, mentor, or support group before you can experience God as a loving Father."

Are these statements true? If your father was abusive, critical, neglectful, or selfish, are you prevented from knowing God as a loving Father? Must you first experience a corrective human relationship in order to make "God is my Father" a nourishing reality?

These two statements prove false under examination. They distort the nature of the human heart and why it is that people believe lies about God. They flatly deny the power and truth of God's Word and the Holy Spirit. They replace the Almighty God with an almighty psychotherapist, whose tolerance and affirmations retool the heart for a god who will merely tolerate and affirm.

This is not to say that people with poor human parents don't often project those images onto the true God. Naturally, they go on to state that such a god is untrustworthy and unloving. The first statement appeals plausibly to a common phenomenon: "I had a rotten parent. I think God is rotten." But is the plausible connection between these facts the real connection? You must dig below the surface of the pat answer. Do people twist their view of God *because* they have had sinful parents, or for some other reason? Are there any people with bad parents who have a great relationship with God? Are there any people with good parents who have a rotten view of God?

The second statement also appeals plausibly to a common phenomenon: "It really made a difference to meet a person I could trust, and my relationship with God grew." Of course, good, caring, and wise friends are a tremendous help in the change process. A godly counselor is like a godly parent in many ways. But is the plausible explanation of change the right one? Again, you must dig. Do affirming human relationships correct the problem of mis-seeing God, or is there a different primary solution? Are there any people who know a person they trust, yet still think God is untrustworthy? Can a relationship with a person you trust mislead you further about God?

My King, Shepherd, Master, Savior, and God

Our response to these two statements should first note that *none* of the words God uses to describe himself have wonderful experiential correlates. Sinful human fathers are not unique in misrepresenting God. Consider, for example, *God is King*. Human rulers are frequently impotent, remote, tyrannical, or corrupt. To whom do you look for examples of what God the King is like: Queen Elizabeth? Bill Clinton? Saddam Hussein? The judges in traffic court? God-imaging rulers have always been rare. Yet your experience—however bad—needn't cripple you from knowing God as King and Judge. God himself informs you about good, bad, and mediocre kings, so you can learn to tell the difference. The Bible also shows and tells what sort of king God is. Do you allow the Word or experience to dictate your perception of God? You project human experience onto God at your peril. But to those who have ears, the Holy Spirit speaks through the Word to reinterpret life experience. Truth increasingly informs subsequent experience.

Consider another example: *The LORD is my shepherd*. Human shepherds generally provide us dubious exemplars. Few are like Philip Keller, who portrayed so winsomely the care and wisdom of the shepherd's craft (A *Shepherd Looks at Psalm 23*). What if the real-life shepherds you knew were ignorant menials or drunken drifters? Or what if all you've known are picture book scenes of lambs and fair youths gamboling in green meadows? Is either picture descriptive of God? Is Psalm 23 then powerless to strengthen you until you know a Philip Keller-type shepherd? Of course not.

Consider also the shepherds of God's flock whom you've known. Some people can point with joy to a "godly pastor who made such an impact on my life." But other people grew up under false teachers, greedy, willful, and arrogant men, as described in Ezekiel 34. Does this mean that you can gain no comfort from the fact that the Lord is a shepherd until you have the corrective experience of knowing a godly pastor? Ezekiel 34 (and then John 10) argues the opposite. God assumes we can hear comfort straight from him even if people have betrayed our trust: "I am against these evil shepherds, and I, the good shepherd, will myself come and take care of you, my flock" (author's paraphrase). The existence of perversity does not make us blind to purity. Get first things first. The Holy Spirit often *uses* godly shepherds but does not *require* them; he is powerful enough to reveal the Chief Shepherd even without noble human models.

Or consider that *the Lord is my master, and I am his bond slave.* How do people typically experience authority figures—bosses, commanding officers, CEOs, management? Often there is estrangement, rivalry, manipulation, and suspicion between masters and underlings. Literal slavery has always been full of degradation and resentment. Yet God chose a word that is loaded with such negative experience and expects us to experience it as a delight. He portrays himself as a kind master and us as willing slaves! What a shock Paul's slavery language must have been to any resentful or despairing slaves. But how liberating, once he or she grasped the point. Again, frequently one-sided experience must yield to two-sided truth. There are both good and bad master-slave relationships. Will you believe God or the world you've known? The Holy Spirit is able to effectively renew minds.

Consider this biblical image: *God is my Savior, Rescuer, and Helper.* We often have good reason to flee from human beings who like to play the savior by rescuing or fixing others. They have a "messiah-complex." They are proud. Meddlesome. Self-righteous. Controlling. It's no fun being helped by such a would-be helper! Such saviors often become depressed or embittered. If you have only known pseudo-saviors, are you prevented from richly knowing Jesus Christ as your Savior? Amazingly, somehow God seems to be able to reveal himself as utterly Godly without utterly godly people showing the way.

Consider one last example, the ultimate example: *The LORD is God."* What is the typical human experience of "God"? Depending on whom you listen to, God is a philosophical abstraction, your higher power, an idol, an experiential high during meditation, a remote tyrant, a good buddy, creative energy, a benign grandfather, or even yourself. All these images grossly misshape God. Is it impossible for me to know the living and true God if I have spent my life hearing and worshiping such false images? The Bible everywhere repudiates such an idea and offers to "open their eyes so that they may turn from darkness to light" (Acts 26:18). God is in the business of changing people's minds; he is not hindered by distortions. He can reveal himself, shining into our hearts to give the light of the knowledge of the glory of God in the face of Christ (see 2 Cor. 4:6). Life experience is not supreme. Lies that people believe are not supreme. God is, and he alone trumps what we bring to the table.

In each of the above examples, to say that life experience dictates a person's reality is absurd. In fact, the very experience of disappointing and distorted images can make you long to know the *real* King, Shepherd, Master, Savior, and God. You might say, "My pastor growing up never taught me about God. How I rejoice that Hebrews 13:20–21 is true, that the great Shepherd of the sheep shed his blood for me and teaches me to do his will. My boss is manipulative and deceptive. How I rejoice that Ephesians 6:5–8 is becoming true in me and that I can serve Christ with integrity instead of brooding bitterly or fearfully! The God I grew up hearing about seemed like a remote killjoy. Praise the real God that Psalm 36 is true, and he is an immediate refuge and a fountain of love, light, and joy!"

Clearly, our fallen experience need not be determinative. Yet why should *God is Father* be the exception for so many people? Must your own father dictate the meaning of that phrase until a substitute human father puts a new spin on it?

But Is God My Father?

Concepts from our psychologized culture saturate the way people—even Christian people—think about themselves and others. The intellectual source for the notion that your experience of your father determines your view of the heavenly Father is psychodynamic psychology, not the Bible. The notion was developed by men such as Sigmund Freud and Erik Erikson. They rightly observed that people often fabricate their own gods. Psychodynamic theory made this "from the bottom up" pattern into a normative explanation for ideas of God. It denied that the real God revealed himself "from the top down." The psychodynamic god was a projection of the human psyche. Popular versions of this way of thinking now infuse our culture.

"If my father didn't love me, I can't know God as a loving Father." Of course, this idea rings a bell in the human heart. As sinners we tend to manufacture false images of God, and human fathers are prime candidates. As sinners we duck responsibility for our unbelief, blaming others and savoring the role of victim. When we project lies and faulty images onto God, we may prefer to point at human fathers as the cause rather than looking to the activities of our own hearts. The psychological "insight" panders to one variation on a sinful tendency: We like to find excuses for our unbelief.

In an earlier generation, one of the stock human excuses for unbelief was, "The church is full of hypocrites, so I don't want anything to do with God." That was more willful and bitter: "Get lost, God." The new variant is more self-pitying: "I just can't seem to trust God." But the net effect is the same. No cry of "Abba, Father" springs from the heart. "My father didn't love me, so my self-centeredness, self-pity, and unbelief have an underlying reason. Somebody else caused my problems; somebody else must fix them."

The therapeutic technique follows logically, given these assumptions. "Your Dad was distant and mean. You think of God as distant and mean. I, your therapist, will be interested in you and nice. Knowing my love will let you think of God as like me, interested in you and nice." Whoa! Stated baldly, that's a shocking statement. (That's why it's usually insinuated, not trumpeted, so it sneaks up on people.) Catch my point carefully. Such "re-parenting" not only despises the Word and the Spirit; it merely replaces one false image of God with a different one. The dissatisfying god manufactured by the human soul, supposedly because of bad parents, can now be remanufactured in the image of a satisfying therapist.

It's easy to see that the living and true God is not like an abusive, rejecting, capricious parent. The real God sent Jesus Christ on a mission of love to save unacceptable people. But neither is God like the benign, all-accepting therapist. The real God has just anger and an unchanging standard, and those he loves are "helpless, ungodly, sinners, enemies" (Rom. 5). The real God is not a devil. But neither is he Carl Rogers. The "re-parenting" methodology has a faulty view of who the Father is and what a parent ought to be. It knows tyranny and neglect are wrong. But it replaces such sins with supreme confidence in the therapist's powers and coddling affirmations of the self. There is no authoritative truth, no dying to self, and no crucified Savior in this version of love.

Am I saying that caring and concerned counselors and friends are irrelevant to change? Of course not. One needn't choose between truth and love: people grow in the way Ephesians 4:15–16 describes. My point is simply a matter of getting first things first so that our vision of human love connects with God's love, rather than competes with it.

People change when the Holy Spirit brings the love of God to their hearts through the Gospel. Whoever receives the Spirit of adoption as God's child learns to cry out, "Abba, Father." People change when they see that they are responsible for what they believe about God. Life experience is no excuse for believing lies; the world and devil don't excuse the flesh. People change when biblical truth becomes more loud and vivid than previous life experience. People change when they have ears to hear and eyes to see what God tells us about himself:

> The LORD has comforted His people,
> And will have compassion on His afflicted.
> But Zion said, "The LORD has forsaken me,
> And the Lord has forgotten me."
> Can a woman forget her nursing child,
> And have no compassion on the son of her womb?
> Even these may forget, but I will not forget you.
> Behold, I have inscribed you on the palms of My hands.
>   (Isa. 49:13–16)

> He has not dealt with us according to our sins,
> Nor rewarded us according to our iniquities.
> For as high as the heavens are above the earth,
> So great is His lovingkindness toward those who fear Him.
> As far as the east is from the west,
> So far has He removed our transgressions from us.
> Just as a father has compassion on his children,
> so the LORD has compassion on those who fear Him.
>   (Ps. 103:10–13)

These things are true, both the promises and the actions that fulfill them. God addresses the fears and anxieties of sufferers and sinners.

Do people come to know *this* God because human counselors skillfully re-parent them? No, and the very attempt to make that a counseling paradigm is idolatrous. But aren't good counselors like good fathers (and mothers)? Yes, of course. Consider,

> But we proved to be gentle among you, as a nursing mother tenderly cares for her own children. Having so fond an affection for you, we were well-pleased to impart to you not only the Gospel of God but also our own lives because you had become very dear to us. For you recall, brethren, our labor and hardship, how working night and day so as not to be a burden to any of you, we proclaimed to you the Gospel of God. You are witnesses, and so is God, how devoutly and uprightly and blamelessly we behaved toward you believers; just as you know how we were exhorting and encouraging and imploring each one of you as a father would his own children, so that you may walk in a manner worthy of the God who calls you into His own kingdom and glory. (1 Thess. 2:7–12)

Why should a counselor be like this? Because God is like this. The difference between Paul and re-parenting therapy lies on the surface. Did Paul "re-parent" the Thessalonians so that, now knowing and changed by Paul's love, they would be able to envision God as loving? No, that's exactly backwards and even blasphemous.

Paul was vigorous, caring, and authoritative as a parent-counselor who carried the Father's message. The love of the Father changes people; it changed Paul. Knowing divine love, he gave love, a love that was both the fruit and the vehicle of the message he pressed on his hearers. God is primary; the human agent is significant but secondary. The modern re-parent/therapist reverses this. The human counselor is primary; if God is significant at all, he is only secondary. The issue at stake is not whether counselors should be patient, kind, and so forth. First Corinthians 13 settles that. But in God's drama of redemption, who will be the lead, and who will be the supporting actor?

If your father didn't love you, you *can* know the love of the Father.

A godly counselor (or parent or friend) may be instrumental. But the key to change lies between you and God, not between you and that other person.

GETTING DOWN TO CASES

Let me briefly describe two cases. Sally is a twenty-eight-year-old woman who grew up in an abusive household. As an adolescent she was sexually molested by her father. This put the bitter icing on a miserable relationship. Sally became a Christian in high school. "But for years I felt that I could never know God as my Father because I had such a rotten relationship with my real father. I thought of God as untrustworthy, demanding, merciless, unpredictable. Then I realized that my biggest problem was *me*, not God or my father. My belief system was all messed up. I was projecting lies onto God and not believing what was true about him!"

Sally fed her faith with truth. God the Father *is* faithful, merciful, consistent. He patiently worked on her, disciplining her and teaching her to know the truth about him. Sally saw that her view of God was not caused by her life experience but by what her own heart had done with her experience of being wronged. As Sally repented and her mind was renewed, she was progressively freed to let go of old disappointments, bitterness, fears, and demands. She became able to say wholeheartedly, "Give thanks to the LORD, for he is good, for his steadfast love endures forever."

Bill is a thirty-six-year-old man whose father abandoned his family when he was three years old. He is a committed Christian, mature in many ways, and using his gifts. But he sought counseling, complaining of a longstanding sense that "God is remote, like my father was." In a nutshell, there were three significant components to change.

First, he grasped the fact that he, like all of us, tended to view his life experience as a Technicolor blockbuster, while the Bible seemed a dull, black-and-white silent movie in comparison. The flesh produces this state of affairs by interpreting life through the lens of its lies and desires. Bill began with two key truths about God as Father. First, God *is* abounding in mercy (Ps. 103; 2 Cor. 1:2–5). Second, God *is* committed to meet his children directly, to teach, to bless, and to transform (John 15:2; Heb. 12:1–14). Bill prayed and meditated these truths into his life. As he learned to repent of the lies he had believed, he found the Father becoming vivid.

Second, in the process, Bill faced sins he had been avoiding. The flesh is deceitful. He found that his sentence, "God is remote, like my father was," in part came from buying into pop psychology's convenient and self-excusing diagnosis. It's true, God did seem remote. And Bill's father had been absent. But on examination the two things proved to be minimally related, much like saying, "I'm angry because I'm an Aries." In fact, early in Bill's Christian life God had not seemed remote at all. But some very specific patterns of sin—sexual fantasy, manipulating and avoiding people, laziness, love of money—lay beneath Bill's recurrent sense of God's remoteness. Dynamic psychology had turned his relationship with parents into a magic wand to explain all of life. The Bible offered Bill a more concrete and life-transforming explanation.

Third, Bill found some good friends and models (Prov. 13:20; 1 Thess. 2:7–13). He had been quite isolated. He found people to know and be known by, to love and be loved by. These people did not substitute for God and re-parent Bill. They were fellow children of the Father, seeking to grow up into the Father's image. Through it all Bill began to read God into his experience—to trust and obey God—rather than continuing to read God out of his life experience. No surprise, his relationship with God was transformed both objectively and experientially.

Can you (and your counselees) know God as Father even if your human father was violent, deceptive, cold . . . or even just occasionally disappointing? The Bible says, YES! Listen and believe, and join in fellowship with other children of the Father!

HOW TO GET TO KNOW YOUR FATHER

Here is a simple summary of the way to grow in the knowledge of God your Father even if your father sinned against you.

1. Identify and take responsibility for the specific lies, false beliefs, desires, expectations, and fears that poison your relationship with God.

2. Find and apply specific truths in the Bible that contend with those lies and cravings. There ought to be a battle going on within you daily as God's light and love battle your darkness.

3. Turn to God for mercy and help, so that the Spirit of truth would renew you, pouring out his love freely.

4. Take responsibility for the particular sins that you express toward your father, and, as generalized patterns, toward other people: bitterness, willfulness, avoidance, blame-shifting, brooding, fears, people-pleasing, slander, lying, self-pity, etc.

5. Turn to God for mercy and help, that the Spirit of love would enable you to bear his fruit thankfully.

6. Identify the specific sins committed against you. Fathers who are selfish or hostile, who lie or betray trust, who duck responsibility, do evil. The love of God gives you courage to look evil in the eye. Identifying wrong helps you know what to forgive. It also makes clear what God calls you to tackle constructively. You need humility to recognize that some wrongs may be perceived wrongs—products of your own expectations—not real wrongs. Repenting of your own sins clears your mind to sort out evil done from evil merely perceived. You also need a renewed mind to understand that some things you were told or you assumed were right may actually be wrong.

7. Ponder the good things your father did for you. Often bitterness and disappointment cloud the love that *was* shown. There are some fathers who seem to incarnate evil. But most are a mix of love and selfishness.

8. The Father gives the power to return good for evil rather than evil for evil. He remakes his children like his Son, Jesus. Come up with a plan for specific changes in how you deal with your father and his wrongs: forgiving, giving love, seeking forgiveness, forbearing, confronting constructively, refocusing your attention, pouring your energies into God's calling, etc.

9. Find wise believers to pray for you, hold you accountable, encourage, and counsel you. Faith in God our Father is catching. Wisdom for living as a peacemaker and a son of God is also catching. "The companion of the wise becomes wise." The Father is seeking worshipers and creating children who know him.

11 | Human Defensiveness: The Third Way

> *Change is brought about, not by new observations or*
> *additional evidence in the first instance, but by transpositions*
> *that were taking place inside the minds of the scientists themselves.*
> *In this connection it is not irrelevant to note that of all forms of*
> *mental activity the most difficult to induce, even in the minds of*
> *the young who may be presumed not to have lost their flexibility,*
> *is the art of handling the same bundle of data as before,*
> *but placing them in a new system of relations with one*
> *another by giving them a different framework.*[1]

This chapter will introduce no new observations or evidence. Indeed, it will work with some of the oldest and most familiar pieces of both "psychological" and "theological" data. But what it offers is a transposition of that data, for it presents a new framework, a new system of relations. It asks for a flexible mind to connect what often functions as two discrete "departments" in the minds of Christians. It aims to portray such a tight relationship between biblical data and psychological data that neither one can ever remain the same.

In some ways we are simply reassessing the nomenclature with which familiar things are discussed. The French chemist Antoine Lavoisier revolutionized chemistry in the 1780s, and the core of his achievement was the introduction of a new set of terms to explain phenomena: the cosmos was now composed of oxygen, hydrogen, carbon, and other elements rather than earth, air, fire, and water. After Lavoisier, even those who wished to dispute him were forced to do so using his definitions and terms. Something very similar happened with the revolutionary psychological systems of the twentieth century:

they changed the terms in which we think about people and their problems. A reawakened biblical worldview will not only engage our culture in its terminology, but offer something more clear-headed, comprehensive, fruitful, and true.

Lavoisier's goal was to improve science by improving its nomenclature:

> However certain the facts of any science may be, and however just the ideas we may have formed of these facts, we can only communicate false impressions to others while we want words by which these may be properly expressed.[2]

My goal in this chapter is to improve both the "science" of understanding people and the "technology" of trying to help them by focusing on terminology and its impact on both. Christians often have been forced to discuss human problems in the distorted terminology of secularized psychology. For example, how common—and insidious—is the use of the nomenclature for "improved self-esteem." Yet this very terminology casts our insight in a constricted and warped framework. False impressions are inevitably communicated, and false counseling implications are drawn from the false impressions. Language about "more accurate self-knowledge, both causing and caused by a higher esteem for Christ" is a far more accurate and comprehensive way to describe people who experience a deep sense of failure. It also handles observations of people who are cocky and confident about their abilities and successes.

This chapter, however, is not about self-knowledge but its opposite: self-deception. We will examine nomenclature related to the ways people hide from themselves and from others. We will seek to redefine the turf of "defense mechanisms" in a way that will markedly "improve the science"—as well as improve the counseling that flows from one's framework of interpretation.

Our discussion will have two parts. First, we will generally discuss human "defensiveness" as it has been seen and analyzed by ego psychology and by behavioral psychology. The classic studies of "ego defense mechanisms" are rooted in the Freudian tradition; the more contemporary behaviorist discussion of "self-exonerating mechanisms" has been initiated by Albert Bandura. Second, we will comment and interact from the biblical worldview.

Much of the persuasive power of Freud's and Bandura's analyses of human motivation rests on their explorations of human hiding and self-justifying: they see many ways that we all put on a "good front" to ourselves and others. Ego psychologists interpret these things as arising from an inner dynamic process; they are intrapsychic mechanisms. Put in simplest terms, these psychological activities ("ego defense mechanisms") are designed to protect our selves ("ego") from invasive anxiety, which arises when our desires ("id") act contrary to the image we have of our selves ("ego ideal") and our internalized conscience ("superego") responds by accusing us.

Bandura interprets these same things as behavior that is both internally represented (i.e., cognitive behavior) and outwardly expressed. These psychological and verbal activities ("self-exonerating mechanisms") are designed to protect our selves from the unpleasant experience ("self-contempt") that arises when our behavior transgresses internalized standards of performance that we have learned from people we respect ("models").

The parallels between these two interpretations are obvious: both are psychic "mechanisms"; both deal with failure to attain standards we have for ourselves; both describe some process of internalizing standards from others; both describe aversion to unpleasant emotions that threaten to destroy our sense of integrity and "OK-ness." The differences in interpretive framework are also obvious: the one is a psychodynamic paradigm; the other is a behavioral paradigm. Different as they are, each is persuasive in its own way, for each "covers the facts."

But each is also a serious distortion of how people work. In response, I want to reinterpret the data. People do the things that are described, but the correctness of the terminology and the theoretical system in which those terms function are highly debatable matters. Freud and Bandura differ seriously with one another but they are united in this: they attempt to account for human defensiveness without seeing human life in its totality—behavior, psychological dynamics, interpersonal relations, physiology—as related to God. Accuracy about human defensiveness only comes from a proper understanding of the relationship between man and God. Defensiveness cannot be reduced to psychosocial mechanisms. Thus the biblical view drastically differs with both Freud and Bandura.

Mechanisms of Human Defensiveness

Before we get to the biblical view, we want to look briefly at the bundle of data. What follows is a representative sample of some "defense mechanisms" (1–10) and "self-exonerating mechanisms" (11–15), recast in more descriptive, less technical language that bears a resemblance to the original nomenclature but does not indicate their theoretical framework. Secular psychologists always bring their interpretation to the behaviors they observe. In seeking to distinguish among the many varieties of defensive behavior, they arrive at interpretive categories that are distortions—we might even say counterfeits—of the truth.

1. We fear that others harbor the same sinful motives we harbor (and have not dealt with) ourselves. We often *accuse* others of these things, such as lust, anger, greed, and competitive pride. For example, a man may have persistent fears that his wife is unfaithful to him. He grills her about the slightest apparent inconsistency in her behavior and conjures up his own wild interpretations of her actions. In reality, the man has an active sexual fantasy life, an ongoing problem with masturbation, and unacknowledged guilt over premarital sexual intercourse. This mechanism has been termed "projection"; extreme cases of such fear, accusation, hostility, and pride are termed "paranoia."

2. People *cover up* their failures, sin, and guilt by trying to be good or by making up for them without genuine repentance to God or others. They *deny* the truth about themselves to God, others, and themselves. They try to manipulate and control others with niceness and great shows of "love," at the same time they hide from themselves all awareness of what they are doing. Judgmentalism, anger, disappointment, sexual lust, and the desire to control others are frequently covered up. For example, a woman may exude a kind of sticky-sweet love and piety even while she is extremely frustrated and angry with her husband. This has been termed "reaction-formation" because the truth is concealed from consciousness by an "opposite reaction."

3. People *misdirect their attention* from important issues to secondary matters. Any area of failure or guilt can be avoided in this way. For example, a Christian may be preoccupied with minutiae of es-

chatology and the necessity of carrying tracts while he has poor relations with family and co-workers (because of his perceived judgmentalism and hypocrisy) and visits prostitutes once a month. This mechanism has been termed "substitution" because all sorts of secondary preoccupations are substituted for attention to personal and interpersonal problems (i.e., issues of sin).

4. People *fantasize* rather than face their problems biblically. Fantasy can cover failed hopes, laziness, unrealistic ideals of success, unforgiven hurts, and loneliness. It can also express sexual, financial, or status lusts, as well as a fundamental thanklessness. For example, a lonely single woman with a "boring" job may read romance novels, watch soap operas, and daydream about being glamorous, successful, and beloved. This has been termed "fantasy" for obvious reasons.

5. People *whitewash* or candy-coat reality rather than facing things honestly and responding constructively (i.e., biblically). For example, a widow may whitewash the memory of her husband in her own mind and in conversation with others. He may have been a drunk, an adulterer, and a deadbeat, but she insists that "he was really a good man." This has been termed "inversions" because the truth is turned inside out.

6. People *generate physical symptoms* rather than face problems. Pride, unrealistic self-image, anxiety, anger, and a host of other things can be expressed in "psychosomatic" ways. For example, a man who views crying as a sign of feminine weakness may get intense headaches whenever he thinks of his wife's death. A pastor who will not face his fear of others' opinions tends to get sick on Saturdays and is developing an ulcer. This response has been termed "conversion" because a genuine problem is converted into physical symptoms.

7. People *scapegoat*, blame, and attack innocent, helpless, or even guilty parties (or inanimate objects) rather than face and solve problems biblically. For example, a man yells at his wife, kids, and dog after a tough day at work. He throws an ashtray through the television screen when his football team loses; he perpetually grumbles and rages at minor injustices—drivers who tailgate him, a mechanic who ripped him off—and never deals with the fundamental pride that rules his life. This has been termed "displacement" because the emo-

tion is directed away from its genuine object. The problem that needs to be solved is avoided.

8. People *deny or avoid reality* to save face or hide from consciousness of guilt. For example, a mother excuses her son's drunkenness and troubles with the law by saying, "He's really a good boy; he just got in with a bad crowd." This has been termed "denial" and can serve as a catch-all for the whole gamut of defensive behavior.

9. People *cover failures* with other successes instead of facing problems and limitations constructively and realistically. For example, a woman with a bad marriage may pour herself into her children and volunteer work. This has been termed "compensation" for obvious reasons.

10. People *rationalize*, make excuses, and shift blame to put themselves in the best light. For example, a couple may rationalize their fornication by saying, "We really love each other. Society's standards are wrong, and people need to be free." A woman may say she is justified in her bitterness at her husband because he is an alcoholic. A homosexual says God made him that way, and Romans 1 only applies to natural heterosexuals who engage in homosexuality. This has been termed "rationalization" and, like denial, can serve as a catch-all for many of the masks people put on.

11. People *use euphemisms* about themselves and others to avoid guilt or any attribution of responsibility. For example, "I'm just irritated, not angry." "I just had a few drinks." "He acts that way because he has a low self-esteem." This has been termed "euphemistic labeling."

12. People *compare themselves to others* to try to look good and justify themselves. For example, "I know I have my faults, but I'm not as bad as a lot of other people." "I might have slacked off some on my job, but at least I didn't smoke dope in the bathroom like most of the employees." This has been termed "advantageous comparisons."

13. People *shift blame* from themselves to others, God, circumstances, sickness, etc. For example, "It's only human to get angry. It's just the way God made me. If my wife would only treat me with respect, I wouldn't get angry." "My life is messed up because my parents got a divorce." This has been termed "attribution of blame."

14. People *spread around responsibility* to avoid culpability. If everybody does it, the law allows it, or society accepts it, then it is OK. For example, "Everybody cheats on his income taxes." "The Supreme Court decision makes abortion all right, and 68 percent of the American people agree we ought to be free to choose." This has been termed "diffusion of responsibility."

15. People *ignore and minimize the consequences of their actions.* For example, "I suppose my wife is hurt when I curse her out and threaten to leave, but she should know I don't mean it." This has been termed "disregard of consequences."

These are but a sampling of the "ego defense mechanisms" and "self-exonerating mechanisms" that various psychologists have detailed. There are examples of similar behavior evident in all sectors of daily life. The theoretical freight these fifteen samples carry in psychology (the technical labels embody Freudian or Banduran theory) can mask the fact that these supposed mechanisms can be described in very untechnical terms: we "wear masks"; we duck, weave, and dodge the light of self-knowledge and honesty before God and man; we wear fig leaves.

Fig Leaves
The following are a smattering of further examples of the fig leaves we wear.
- We change the subject or crack jokes if an awkward or threatening subject arises.
- We monopolize conversation, filling silences to keep others at bay and to keep from feeling like failures.
- We live or die vicariously with a sports team.
- We run from problems by watching TV, drinking, smoking, promiscuity, workaholism, compulsive eating.
- We mock or "put in a box" those whose opinions or problems threaten our own commitments and behavior.
- We get defensive, accusatory, testy, or talk loudly, or try to bully others to defend ourselves and make a show of competency.
- We overdo penance by saying, "Poor me; I'm so horrible and such a failure," by expressing maudlin repentance and wallowing in failures.

- We minimize the seriousness of problems—"It's nothing"—or the difficulty of change—"I promise I'll never do it again."
- We lie outright, to look good or to avoid looking bad.
- We lie subtly, putting ourselves in the best light by innuendo, embellishment, or careful selection of data. This often accompanies subtle expressions of contempt or criticism for other people.
- We think highly of our own opinions on every issue.
- We tie up our identity in certain grandiose roles, like "counselor" or "parent" or "pastor." Any of our functions and successes, real or imagined, can become fodder for self-deception.
- We pray for help before performing a certain responsibility, and then rehearse our own success afterwards without thought of God.

My purpose in listing the above behaviors is to demonstrate that it does not take a psychologized theory of ego defense mechanisms or self-exonerating devices to track down countless instances of self-deception, self-aggrandizement, manipulation, and deception. In fact, the powerhouses of modern thought are those who dissect false consciousness, who pierce the illusions of individual and collective life and expose the shame and the game, such as Marx, Kierkegaard, and Nietzsche. Nietzsche once observed, "'I did that,' says my memory. 'I could not have done that,' says my pride, and remains inexorable. Eventually—the memory yields."[3] Or as T. S. Eliot put it, "Human kind cannot bear very much reality."[4]

THE BIBLE'S CRITIQUE

The greatest critic of human hypocrisy and dissembling, however, is the Bible, in which the Searcher of hearts exposes illusions and false consciousness using an entirely different grid from those of Marxists, existentialists, or psychoanalysts. There is much that can be said biblically on the subject of human defensiveness, but in this context we will make seven general points.

The Warmaking of Sin

First, the Bible ascribes the data of human defensiveness to the workings of sin. "Defensiveness" incarnates all the blindness to the truth about oneself that might be denominated "pride." It has that combination of self-deception and deception of others that fits under the heading "the deceitfulness of sin." It embodies a primal resistance to honesty about oneself, an evasiveness, excuse-making, and blameshifting, all of which are captured in a host of colorful metaphors: stiff-necked, hardened or darkened in heart, foolish, and so forth.

Also, the bundle of data describing defensiveness is not well explained by merely calling it a set of intrapsychic mechanisms. It has an evident interpersonal component. Defensive people are almost invariably offensive as well. Self-deception and defensiveness are only one side of the story. There is a curious blindness to the trouble such behavior causes for others: spouse, children, parents, boss, co-workers, and counselors, who all suffer hardship and frustration in attempting to build meaningful, honest, and constructive relationships with "defensive" people. The latter are variously aggressive, evasive, deceptive, manipulative, and yet somehow blind and driven, unable to help themselves. Of course, none of us is immune to this! We all recognize ourselves in these descriptions of defensive behavior. It is no accident that others suffer hardship and frustration in cultivating good relationships with us.

We also intuitively recognize that the psychological diagnosis does not adequately capture the whole picture of what a human being is. It fails to capture that perverse combination of desire for good relationships, yet suspicion and fear of others; of tolerance for others' failings, yet self-aggrandizement and despising of others; of moments of brilliant self-awareness, yet habitual blindness to what about us is obvious to others; of patience with counselees, yet petty anger with family members. In picking a good metaphor to capture the vast data of defensiveness, the metaphor "mechanisms" would never do. The metaphor "warmaking" is far more cogent. It captures the interpersonal component, including both the defensive and offensive behaviors; it includes the self-justifying rationalizations for what we do; it implies we are both victims and victimizers; it implies the peacemaking that the Gospel accomplishes in order to transform habitual warmakers into peacemakers. The idea of defense mechanisms represents a severe constriction of the data; it only has appeal because of a presuppositional tunnel vision that looks at people as psychological entities rather than as covenantal beings existing in relationship to God and neighbor.

It should not surprise us that "warmaking activities" explains the data far more lucidly and comprehensively than does "defense mechanisms." Secular psychology is always hamstrung by its pre-commitment to view human problems as "ontological" problems—as things that are not working right. Hence something as basic as self-deception is inevitably analyzed as a psychological mechanism. But the Bible never views human problems as ontological but as relational or ethical at their cores. Problems exist *between* man and God and *between* man and man. That our psyches are unhinged—or futile, darkened, alienated, ignorant, hardened, deceived, and desire-ridden, as Ephesians 4 puts it—does not mean our problems are at their core psychological. The disorientation that manifests itself in our psychic life is only symptomatic of an interpersonal disorientation: our alienation from God. The very efforts of Freud, Bandura, and others to describe these problems as essentially ontological mechanisms are a manifestation of that same disorientation.

Conscious vs. Unconscious

Second, if we are going to understand so-called defense mechanisms as part and parcel of human sin, how do we make sense of the conscious character of so many of the "psychological" problems that defensive people manifest? In the discussion above, I have indiscriminately mingled relatively conscious acts, like lying, with relatively unconscious acts, like projection by an angry paranoid. Psychodynamic psychology has stressed that defense mechanisms in neurosis and psychosis are relatively unconscious. It has no way to adequately account for both conscious and unconscious acts.

For example, compare the concealed anger of a "reaction formation" with the concealed intentions of a Casanova on the make. The former genuinely does not seem to know or to be able to admit the truth; the latter could admit in a moment the sexual motives under the debonair and caring exterior. The whitewashing and image manipulation of a political ad campaign is a calculated affair, while the "inversion" of a widow whitewashing her husband's memory is automatic and unconscious. Conscious concealment is not "ego-defense mechanisms" according to the theory. But the failure to connect these two things derives from the constriction of vision in psychological theory.

In practice, conscious and unconscious are not that easy to distinguish. They are on a continuum. It is remarkable how the most "unconscious" person knows he is responsible for his sinful reaction as soon as it is brought out into the light. And the most "conscious" person is deeply deceived. However much the guilt has been denied and twisted, the "defensive" person is guilty. The well-psychoanalyzed person may be able to identify each of his defensive machinations as it happens, but in a sense he remains wholly deceived as to what those mechanisms really are.

The fear of the LORD is always the beginning of true wisdom, no matter what another interpretive framework may say. The phenomenological status of a particular problem is no safe guide to what that problem is. However unconscious or conscious a particular pattern of warmaking activity seems, it is still fundamentally warmaking. The biblical doctrine of sin easily accommodates the reality of unconscious actions: sin is a darkening of the mind, a blind compulsion, a slavery, an automatic and indelible proclivity. When sin is understood in terms of its inner hold on human life—variously analyzed as pride, unbelief, idolatrous desires, self, or a drive for autonomy from God— then the automatic character of so-called defense mechanisms is poignant testimony to the deceitfulness of sin and to human culpability, not to the excuse of psychological problems.

Sin's Complex Inner Workings

Third, people (psychiatrists, people on the street, many Christians) have trouble seeing "unconscious emotional and psychological problems" as intimately related to sin. People may say Casanova had a sin problem. But a troubled person has "emotional problems." And a paranoid schizophrenic or a case of reaction formation is a matter of psychosis or neurosis. It is common to put such defensive behavior in a category other than sin.

There are two simple reasons for this. First, the typical view of sin is that it consists solely in outward, consciously chosen acts, where one could have chosen the righteous alternative. Second, the typical attitude or stance taken toward sin is a moralistic one, condemning the person and/or telling him to shape up by an exercise of will power.

The paranoid person—to pick the extreme case—seems clearly not to have chosen to become that way. And telling such a person to shape up has never worked in the history of mankind!

The view of sin that focuses on willed actions is a denial of the biblical view of sin. It is the heresy known as Pelagianism in the history of theology. That it is the natural theology of the person on the street, psychiatrists, and even most Christians does not make it even an approximation of biblical truth. Where sin is viewed primarily as willed outward acts, people's complex inner troubles tend to be absorbed under other categories. This typical view of sin—it creeps almost spontaneously into all of our thinking—misses the deep inner hold of sin. It misses the dislocation and confusion of our hearts that is the core of the biblical view of sin. Both the high-handed sins and the subtle sins, like anxiety, are embraced within the biblical view. Other categories communicate false impressions.

The attitude toward sin naturally follows from the view of sin. An external view of sin implies a moralistic stance toward it. But the resulting attitude of criticism or exhortation to will power is a frank denial of the Gospel. For most people the term "sin" connotes criticism or moralistic exhortation. But for the Bible—and for a counselor or counselee who desires true self-knowledge rather than some species of rationalization—it connotes the saving grace of Jesus Christ. It implies compassion and love offered to those who would know themselves and God. Christ did not come to judge or to say, "Shape up!" He came to save, to invite people to an inner transformation of mind, heart, motives, will, identity, and emotions. He came to draw to himself people who, standing on their own, are already judged and powerless to change themselves. "Christianity transformed the lives of men not by appealing to the human will, but by telling a story. The lives of men are transformed by a piece of news."[5]

Historically, attitudes toward troubled people have often been moralistic in Western society and in the church. Secular psychology might even be viewed as a tolerant reaction against moralism, for it sought to accept people rather than judge them, to show acceptance rather than to promote guilt, to make problems be psychological or behavioral maladjustment rather than sin. Such themes are prominent in the life histories of men like Carl Rogers, B. F. Skinner, Ernest Jones, and many of the other founders of psychiatry.

It is no accident that the history of secular psychology and psychiatry is intertwined with theological liberalism and has continued to appeal where there is a liberalizing trend going on in the church. The pendulum swings from error to error, from moralism that condemns men before God to liberalism that sets men free of God. The paradox is that, in the name of tolerance, i.e., non-judgmentalism and supposedly objective psychological science, the truth that troubled people have a deep sin problem is withdrawn. And the Gospel that deals with that sin problem is also withdrawn. People whose hearts are "more deceitful than all else . . . ; who can understand it?" as Jeremiah 17:9 so eloquently puts it, are taught psychological euphemisms to diagnose their problems. They are then given the unconditional regard and acceptance of the therapist as a substitute for the self-giving love of the Lamb of God. "They heal the brokenness of the daughter of my people superficially, saying, 'Peace, peace' but there is no peace" (Jer. 8:11). Both legalism—"this is willful"—and psychologism—"this is a defense mechanism"—are profound distortions. Jesus Christ is a distinct third way.

The Gospel's Third Way

Fourth, both Bandura and the ego psychologists assume that there are only two alternatives: stifling moralism ("character flaws," lack of will power, judgmentalism, the way most religionists and the person on the street interpret behavior) or liberating psychological science (deeply penetrating into unconscious and dissociated behavior; non-judgmental; the way most psychologists interpret behavior). The Gospel, however, is a third way. It is exactly the truth—of the radical and denominating nature of sin and of the radical and reorienting power of the forgiving love of Christ—that defensive people need and respect.

In counseling it is striking how schizophrenics, the paradigm case for powerful unconscious defensiveness, track to the themes of pride and hiding. They are large children, full of folly in the Proverbial sense, and they know it. It is also striking how "madmen" become sane as they begin to grasp the implications of justification by faith, the substitutionary atonement, the alien righteousness of Christ, adoption as children of the Father, and the Lordship of the crucified Savior (of course, not in such polysyllabic language at first!). Biblical

Christianity is a third way. It is hard truth that heals deeply. It is not a set of euphemisms, like "ego defense mechanisms." It is not a set of criticisms like, "If he wanted to, he could shape up."

A Deadly Irony

Fifth, when we look closely at the thought structure in which ideas like "ego defense mechanisms" or "self-exonerating mechanisms" are generated, we realize that they involve a deadly irony. These very categories are examples of the very things they describe. Their own categories condemn them. The nature of rationalization is to hide oneself from hard facts, from blows to one's pride. Human responsibility is muted; there are "other reasons" for our problems.

The psychodynamic explanation of human hiding and self-deception is itself a systematized and well institutionalized defense mechanism. Similarly, Bandura's theory of self-exonerating mechanisms is itself an example of euphemistic labeling taking place. He takes the data of human sin and euphemizes it. He writes, for example, "It is self-exonerative processes rather than character flaws that account for most inhumanities."[6] It would be much more accurate to write that sin—in all its self-deceptive power—evidences itself in inhumanities, character flaws, and self-excusing. Euphemism makes deep (serious) things shallow, and Bandura is shallow in his analysis of human knots.

Sinner and Sinned Against

Sixth, one of the most persuasive arguments in favor of a view of problems as emotional and psychological has always been that people with such problems almost invariably have had real scars from their upbringing. When one has a moralistic view of sin, it seems especially cruel to say, for example, that a woman with multiple personalities (an extreme form of the defense mechanism "fantasy") has a basic sin problem. Such a person typically underwent constant criticism, was sexually abused, had horrendous role models, and lived a life of constant failure and danger.

But a biblical view of sin and counseling is tailor-made to help people with such deep problems. She was sinned against grievously and repeatedly—both in being given negative models of how to live, and in the direct attacks against her. Jesus Christ has great compassion on the sinned-against: He can give this woman courage, a reason to face what happened to her, and the power to forgive.

She is also enslaved in sin—she lives multiple lies, is ruled by fear and bitterness, gives nothing to others, manipulates, has blasphemous ideas about God, and does not trust in Jesus. That she was both provoked and taught to sin does not lessen the fact that her life is controlled by sin. In fact, her sin against God is the "10,000 talents," for her life is owed to him and is completely alienated from him; the sin against her is the "100 denarii," a huge amount (a denarius is a day's pay). Such large pain of being wronged will be converted into forgiveness when she sees her bigger wrong against God. Jesus Christ has great compassion on sinners: as she faces him and finds forgiveness, she will gain reason and courage to live and to forgive.

Theological at the Core

Seventh, all this is to say that the "ego ideal," which "ego defense mechanisms" are defending, and the violations of one's internalized moral code which "self-exonerating mechanisms" are busy justifying, are both far from being mere psychological categories. These are theological issues to the core: the pervasive outworkings of human pride in consciously or unconsciously seeking to live autonomously from the Creator and Redeemer.

Let us carefully use the descriptions and observations of secular psychologists. They have often been more careful to observe what people do and say than Christians have. But an interpretive framework is incarnated in their reports. Their technical terminology is the bearer of unbiblical, speculative theory. Let us be wary of the terminology, for it sets the terms of the discussion of human problems in a worldview that is false. "Projection," for example, is a mechanical term for a decidedly human, interpersonal, and covenantal activity! It is a term freighted with distorted theory. Machines project; people act. Human beings do not have mechanisms, however automatically they react.

Seeming automatisms in human behavior are better seen as illustrations of slave-like behavior, not machine-like activity. Just as the notion of warfare activities thrusts us into a personalistic world, so the notion that behavior is ruled, not mechanical, forces us to see people more accurately and personally. The Bible portrays sin, the desires of the flesh, the world around us, and the devil as rulers that enslave and command behavior.[7] They are personalized powers that deceive people and induce them to warfare activities, whether people know that they are ruled or not. To show a slave how he is a machine may give him a sense of control and a way to interpret his experience. But though his anxiety level is reduced and he functions more self-confidently, he has been deceived more profoundly.

If they could be isolated from their system, none of the terms we have considered would be bad. Euphemistic labeling, fantasy, rationalization, and others are reasonably concrete words with which to describe behavior. But functioning as technical terms, they are theory-laden. The triumph of Lavoisier's nomenclature was the triumph of Lavoisier's system! Simple descriptive language that incarnates a personalist worldview may be more useful than technical terminology, as long as the secular theoretical framework continues to be implicit in the vocabulary.

Freudians and Bandurans have some notion of truth that serves as a framework in which to determine what is euphemistic, fantastical, or rationalistic. But their notion of truth is a shallow and distorting gloss when seen next to Scripture. They observe the evidences of human sin in massive detail, but they do not see sin or hear Jesus. There is a vast difference between saying, "That is a case of euphemistic labeling," and saying, "You are using euphemisms." The former places us in a world of secular mechanisms needing repair; the latter locates us in the world of human sin needing redemption.

Let us be ruthless to root out theoretical structures that view people as psychological or socio-psychological abstractions: the phenomena observed are not "ego defense mechanisms" but are pride's offensive, defensive, and deceptive strategies. And let us also reject the therapeutic assumptions that are consequent to the theory: they are poor and deceptive substitutes for the Gospel of Jesus Christ.

If—and it is a large IF—biblical categories control, we can revel in the descriptive acuity and case study riches of psychologists. With biblical categories, we ourselves will mature as psychologists in the best sense of the word: acute observers of human life, experienced in cases and case studies, consistently wise in our counseling methods. We will know people deeply enough to know exactly how they need Jesus Christ. We will remember that Christianity is a third way.

The alternative to moralism is not psychologism; the alternative is Christianity. "Warmaking activities" are omnipresent. Jesus Christ came and made true peace. Blessed are the peacemakers who help others into the peace of God that is in Jesus Christ. With biblical categories we will become men and women who know people—including ourselves first of all—and who know how to truly help others, with the *paraklēsis* with which we ourselves have been comforted by God.

12 THE AMBIGUOUSLY CURED SOUL

When truth lines up next to error, the Bible next to philosophies of life, Christ next to figments of the imagination, you can learn to spot the difference in a flash. Good is good, evil is evil, and never the twain shall meet. But discerning the difference in the midst of everyday life is often not so simple.

Corporately, church history simultaneously plays out both the divine comedy and an all-too-human tragedy. Things turn out wonderfully well, because Jesus Christ is on the move. Yet conflicts, confusions, and deviancies always arise. There are always things we need to repent of, reform, and renew.

In each saint, the cravings and works of indwelling sin grapple against the Holy Spirit's desires and fruit (Gal. 5). It is no surprise, then, that in life stories you often notice competing voices jostling for the final say. A transcription of what takes place in a person's soul reads like a courtroom drama where different witnesses tell contradictory stories about what happened.

These are the givens of our struggle on the long walk from regeneration to glorification. I want to consider an aspect of the problem that seldom gets much attention: not remnant sin grappling with the Spirit for control, but remnant falsity calling out from the same mouths that also utter the Spirit's truth. "Lady Wisdom" and "Dame Folly" both say, "Listen to me" (Prov. 8–9), and in principle they are utterly different voices. But sometimes the same person speaks a bit with *both* voices. The same person who is a means of grace may be at other times a means of confusion. We consciously aim to disciple others in the truth, but they can easily catch our errors in the bargain!

For example, a man may repent of a criminal lifestyle and find genuine new life in Christ. But, at the same time, in the name of Christ he embraces a bizarre eschatological scheme and a political conspiracy theory. He may genuinely turn from violence and drug addiction—high hosannas! At the same time he may become newly self-righteous toward former partners-in-crime and adopt the abrasive manner of the person who led him to Christ—a Bronx cheer for such results. Souls are cured, but they also sicken in new ways. Souls always need more curing.

In the counseling context, you often witness such ambiguities. The positive effects of good, true, and beautiful counsel coexist— uneasily, you hope—with the negative effects of counsel that is bad, untrue, and deformed. This contributes to the problem of the am- biguously cured soul.

AMELIA'S TESTIMONY

The following testimony came from a woman, Amelia, who strug- gled with lesbian desires. Her story appeared in the newsletter of a counseling center that aims to counsel Christianly. Some of the out- come is good: in Christ she openly battles her sins, rather than se- cretly indulging and regretting the flesh's inclinations. But some of the ideas her story communicates are troubling. They express stan- dard psychotherapeutic fare, not something identifiably Christian. They deviate from Scripture— and thus from the truth about human psychological functioning, which God always gets straight and which rebellious psychological theories twist. The result is an ambiguous fix for a real problem. Hear her story.[1]

¶1 My name is Amelia, and for many years I struggled with a se- cret inner life that contradicted my relationship with the Lord. Fi- nally, in my early thirties, I faced up to the fact that I needed help, and I sought Christian counseling. I'd been married for eight years, had two kids, and had been actively involved in several of our church's ministries. But I'd carried on a secret lesbian fantasy life that first sprouted in elementary school and had become a well es- tablished "secret garden."

¶2 I hated myself for it; and I knew God hated what I did in the theater of my mind. But I also loved my fantasy release. When I felt lonely and rejected, or when my husband or friends disappointed me, I'd turn to the "precious friends" I made up. I professed to believe—and taught others!—that Jesus forgave sins and changed sinners. But I lived as if the opposite were true. I couldn't give up my secret comfort; but I couldn't live with myself, either. Either I had to change or I had to "come out" as a lesbian and forget God.

¶3 The idea of counseling scared the wits out of me. I'd never told anyone my struggle. I was popular and vivacious, but I never let anyone in. I always thought, "If they knew the real me, they'd think I was some weird and dangerous pervert," though I'd never acted out my fantasies. I never consciously chose to have lesbian desires. It seemed like something that just happened *to* me as a child, something I "discovered" inside me, not something I "decided."

¶4 So what happened? My therapist accepted me. That eased my anxieties. In counseling over the next year and a half, he helped me to understand the reasons for my lesbian attraction. My father had been an alcoholic. When I was a child he beat me often, and sometimes sexually molested me. His anger scared me—it still does. I learned never to trust men, and to look toward women for love. But my mom was mostly helpless and passive through it all, preoccupied with her own troubles. She never really protected or comforted me. So I spent my life trying to meet my need for love that no one had ever met. That parental combination made me hungry for an intimate, accepting relationship with a woman, a "precious friend" who'd fill the empty space inside.

¶5 Counseling taught me that the pain and disappointment of my family upbringing produced my struggles with lesbian fantasy. I've learned to understand why I am the way I am. These realizations about my past have helped me to make better choices in the present. My counselor helped me to learn that only God can fill the void inside me and quench my deep thirst for an accepting relationship.

¶6 God has been at work in me. Jesus was "tempted in all ways as we are, yet without sin," and I've learned more and more to come to him, and that he will "never leave me nor forsake me." I've become accountable to my husband and a couple of female friends at church, not just to my therapist. I've learned to identify the situations when I'm tempted to old patterns of fantasy, and to resist more effectively. Praise him that I am changing!

INTERPRETING AMELIA

Reading Amelia's story, we find evidence of God's good work in her life. He is setting her free from sin, providing strength to overcome temptation, and helping her grow in holiness and joy. Praise Christ! The final paragraph, ¶6, sounds like normal progressive sanctification. It is a good thing that she no longer struggles alone, but reaches out to both God and the body of Christ. It is good that her conscience is active and accurate, reminding her of her guilt before God. It is good that she depends on the God of gracious promises and has a plan to face temptation. It is good that she has aimed at actual change, and seems to be changing by Word and Spirit.

But we hear other interpretive voices mingled into the story, particularly in ¶4 and ¶5, which express distinctives of her counselor's orientation. The counselor mapped an interpretive grid onto Amelia's life, enabling her to realize the "reasons" why she did what she did. Counseling taught Amelia to credit her father's violence and mother's lack of nurture as the *cause* of lesbian desires. It further taught her that these desires arose from an inner emptiness. After teaching that the human heart is essentially passive, empty, and needy, the counselor also teaches a "good news" that Jesus meets those psychological needs.

How should we evaluate this interpretation? When we look at both Scripture and lives as they are lived, it is clear that painful life experiences *never* determine why people think and behave the way they do. Temptations and trials do not pattern our sins or make our hearts empty. Instead, the past offers a context where the active, willful heart reveals and expresses itself.

A FAULTY VIEW OF HISTORY

James 1 offers a compact summary of this biblical perspective. "Various trials" beset us all (James 1:2). Amelia's childhood sufferings certainly qualify. But the tendency to fall for specific temptations arises from within us. It is not inserted into us by experience, as if suffering, the Devil, or God were producing our sins. Amelia's "own lust" carried her away and enticed her (1:14). In God's redemptive working, her sufferings and sins can lead to growth in wisdom, as truth becomes fruitful in his children (1:2-5, 17-18). It is possible to read Amelia's story as this biblical kind of story, if one excises the deterministic view of the past and the passive, empty self that infuse ¶4 and ¶5. Unfortunately, these distinctives of her counseling sound a false note.

In reality, the particular facts of Amelia's personal history could lie behind any number of radically different lifestyles. This is because experience does not ultimately compel the heart's choices and habits. The *same* family history might belong to someone with (1) lesbian desires, like Amelia; (2) a heterosexually immoral lifestyle; (3) an anti-social withdrawal into a fearful, hermit's existence; (4) a life of escapist indulgence in temporary feel-goods (food, sex, athletics, TV, drugs, computer games); (5) boyfriends or a husband significantly like one's father, thus making a bad marriage; or (6) a committed, loving marriage to a godly, loving man. The consequences of personal history are infinitely malleable. History explains anything, everything . . . and nothing.

Consider each of those six scenarios briefly. The first outcome was assumed in the counseling Amelia received: "My vile father and absent mother made me mistrust men and long for lesbian love." That sounds plausible on an initial reading. But a second scenario, an Amelia given to heterosexual promiscuity, is equally plausible: "My non-nurturing mother contributed to my distrust of women as ineffectual and distant, while the sexualizing and abuse from my father fueled my hunger for intimate relationships with men. I'm attracted to the very activities and men that hurt me." And a third scenario makes equal sense! "Because of my family background, I find it's just safer not to relate to people at all." An anti-social Amelia experienced such rotten relationships that it seemed better to retreat into protective isolation.

The self-indulgent fourth Amelia is similarly asocial, but here the drug of choice is pleasure, not fearful avoidance: "My family created a lot of pain and unhappiness, but when I drink all the pain goes away and I feel good." In the fifth scenario, an Amelia falls for the same type of man over and over, hoping against hope to redeem the bum and rewrite her life's script: "Even before we married, I knew my husband had a temper, but I figured he would grow out of it. He didn't.

I feel like my life is a broken record." Finally, in the sixth scenario, the crucible of ungodliness taught an Amelia to love and value godliness in others: "From life experience I saw clearly what was wrong in my own family's relationships, and how God's ways were redemptive and good. By grace, I was looking for something different, and when I got to know my husband-to-be I knew exactly what it was that God had given me."

In each case, a counselor prone to view history as determinative could "find" a causal link from past experience to present lifestyle! Six very different "Amelias"—and these six life stories are not made up—might each believe that she now understood why she is the way she is. If the same set of experiences can lead to such wildly different responses, then those experiences explain and cause nothing predictable about the human response. Knowledge of a person's history may be important for many reasons (compassion, understanding, knowledge of characteristic temptations), but it never determines the heart's inclinations.

We only know that heartache and temptation occurred. But why does the heart respond to evil with evil, and not good? Why one form of evil, and not another? History cannot tell us. Only the active-worshiping-heart-responsible-before-God finally explains and causes any particular way of life. Amelia has come to believe that she understands her past history. But psychodynamic myth has mingled a significant illusion with elements of Christian truth. To say that her lesbian struggles were caused by unhappy childhood circumstances fails to bow before the unfathomable riddle of sin. Sin is its own final reason. Any theory that claims to explain sin actually falls prey to sin's intellectual effects, and wriggles away from both theological truth and psychological reality. Sin is the deepest explanation, not just one more problem begging for "deeper" reasons.

THE FAULTY VIEW OF THE HEART

A second, closely related problem threads through Amelia's story: she has been taught that her heart is a repository of unmet needs, a passive receptacle determined by painful life experience. Awareness of the "active heart" taught in the Bible seems absent from her story and counseling.[2] Instead, it is said, her inner emptiness and neediness for love, once misdirected toward fantasy women, now needs to be redirected toward Jesus. A loveless childhood produced the void, even as it determined the object of perverse desire that would fill it. Amelia's psychotherapist derived his model of counseling primarily from Larry Crabb's *Inside Out*.[3] The core motivation theory—the heart as essentially empty, needy, disappointed in love—derives its structure from secular psychodynamic psychology, and runs counter to the Bible and reality.

Diagnoses and explanations are always signs pointing toward proposed solutions. The "good news" taught by Amelia's therapist was logical: Jesus fills inner voids. He sought to get Amelia to change the object toward which her desire for acceptance looked, but did not seek to change the dominance of the desire itself. If Amelia's "need" to feel loved is an unchangeable given (passive heart), then change only involves turning from disappointing parents and "special friends" to a Jesus who *will* meet her deepest need. But if, in fact, Amelia loves human affection more than she loves God (active heart), change involves turning from idolatrous craving to the Jesus who died for sinners, who lives to remake us into lovers of God and neighbor, and who will return bringing glory and joy.

Amelia's psychotherapy mingled these two myths into her self-understanding: a faulty view of personal history and a faulty view of the heart. In addition, her counselor also failed to address two other problems that lie on the surface of her story.

The Heart's Instinctive Choices

Amelia's repeated assertion that lesbian attraction was something she "never consciously chose" is significant. She reiterates that she was the unwitting recipient of lesbian desires. The therapist's notion of a passive, history-determined heart was persuasively mapped onto this experience—and blinded both parties to the fact that Amelia's experience needs to be reinterpreted biblically, not taken at face value.

A common misunderstanding of the nature of sin seems to have reinforced the psychological theory. Amelia (and presumably, her therapist), thinks like Pelagius, not like Augustine and the Bible. Under the Pelagian construct, we are only responsible for conscious acts of our will. If "I consciously decided to be a lesbian," then it would count as responsible choice and therefore sin. But if "the decision was made for me," then an external cause is responsible for her deep-seated and mysterious problem.

In truth, our core sin patterns rarely arise only from our conscious decisions. Which of us ever initially *decided* to be proud, people pleasing, or perverse in our sexual longings? We do not need Nike to tell us to "just do it." Sinners sin instinctively. That Amelia can remember no conscious moment of choosing lesbian lust is no particular surprise. Some people can remember a fork-in-the-road moment; others can't. In most significant sin patterns, we witness a combination of specific choices and seeming "just-thereness." As Amelia's self-knowledge deepens, what now sounds like "Who me?" and "Why me?" will become "Yes, me. And praise God for his grace." But her counselor did not help her grow in true self-understanding before the face of God.

THE HEART'S FEAR OF MAN

The other unaddressed problem in Amelia's story is the common theme beneath her secrecy, preoccupation with acceptance, occasions of temptation, fantasies of intimacy, and relief at her counselor's gentle response. The tendency to orient our lives around the opinions and approval of others is termed the "fear of man" in the Bible. This typical pattern of our sinful hearts does not appear to have been identified. The counselor's passive heart theory blinded him from seeing an "unmet need for love" as, in fact, the active heart's fear of man. Fear of man (and its partners, pride and unbelief) is one of the core dislocations of our idolatrous hearts. It frequently—invariably?!—cohabits with homosexuality . . . and with heterosexual sin and other sins. Like the love of money, the fear of man is a root of every sort of evil. It is a deeper and truer way to explain what motivates Amelia than either the need for love or historical determinism.

The Bible's view of human nature is subtle and searching. For example, Amelia's happiness and sense of relief—"This person accepts me!"—is in part the natural joy of a candid friendship. But it can also express the heart's defection from God. A man-fearer feels happy when the idol is stroked. Amelia's bondage to human acceptance is a far more significant "psychodynamic" than speculation about the cause of her desires.[4]

Amelia seems to be a sincere believer, wanting to put secret sin to death. My criticisms are not about her or the genuine work of a faithful God. But it is sad that one-and-a-half years of counseling engendered two significant strands of false consciousness and two significant gaps in self-understanding. It appears that her counselor nourished her with a mixture of Bible truths, half-truths, and fictions. The Holy Spirit animated the biblical truths and bore fruit in her life anyway, to the praise of God's glorious grace. That he works despite each of our failings as counselors is always to his credit. But that is no reason for counselors and counseled alike not to put aside the half-truths and blind spots mediated by the Therapeutic. My intention is not to quibble with what the living God has *really* done in Amelia's life. But I do voice disagreement with the interpretive map others placed over her life experience.

Amelia is an ambiguously cured soul. Her story captures the Therapeutic in action, when it mingles with Christianity into a syncretistic psychotherapy. This is what the ministry of the Word competes with. The Therapeutic is more than ideas to critique. It misdiagnoses and misdisciples the hearts of Amelias. God's sheep need better and more wholesome nourishment. Ministry of the Word must reach Amelias. Yes, we need skills to do broad philosophical and cultural apologetics, but we also need skills to reach into the details of people's lives. The cultural apologetic paints broad strokes in the background, but both preaching and counseling must keep personal apologetics in the foreground. They must reach Amelia—and her counselor. May Christ make each of us increasingly clear and unambiguous as we grow up in his image!

13 WHAT DO YOU FEEL?

We live in a society where the words "I feel" have become the basis of much decision making and much popular counsel.

- "I've lost all feelings of love for my husband" . . . therefore, the marriage is hopeless.
- "I just don't feel like reading the Bible" . . . so I don't do it.
- "I feel that God is an ogre, just like my own father was" . . . so tell God you are angry at him.
- "Tell me what you feel" . . . then we'll really know each other.
- "Get in touch with your feelings" . . . for feelings are the magic key to personal integrity.
- "Follow your feelings" . . . for feelings are the authoritative guide to personal fulfillment.

How do you feel about this morass of feelings? The words "I feel" have become an expression used for anything and everything people may experience, think, or want. We need to penetrate the smokescreen of language to discern what people truly mean when they use feeling language. Then we can look at the way the Bible speaks about feelings, as well as the way it redeems the domains that are spoken about as feelings. Lastly, we will consider several ways the counseling process is informed by attention to what people feel.

UNDERSTANDING THE LANGUAGE OF FEELINGS

Some uses of feeling language are simple. If I cut my finger while slicing a tomato, then I *feel* pain. That sentence is clear. But many other uses of "I feel" are vague or even self-deceptive. Consider this only slightly exaggerated paragraph:

"When I *feel* hurt because I *feel* my husband has wronged me, then I don't *feel* like going to talk to him. Instead, I *feel* like leaving because I *feel* he won't listen anyway. I *feel* justified in the anger I *feel*. I don't *feel* the Bible applies to our particular conflicts."

Have you ever heard a person talk this way? "I feel" creates a potent and fuzzy cloud of legitimacy around a dozen dubious statements. It's tough to argue with feelings. But take a closer look at them. What do you find when you unpack the meanings within the feelings? There are, in fact, four different uses of the word "feeling" in the previous paragraph.

"I Feel" Describes Sense Perceptions

Cut your finger, and you feel pain. You have experienced an external, physical event. People also experience other kinds of things. You experience internal events. For example, "I feel tense" when my muscles knot and my stomach churns. You experience interpersonal events. For example, words can be like stabs of a sword or like rotten food (Prov. 12:18; Eph. 4:29). When such words strike you or enter your system, you will feel pain or misery. Feeling, in this simplest use, is a synonym for sensation, for things we perceive happening to us.

But even this use of the word has its complications. Consider the sentence, "I feel hurt because I feel my husband has wronged me." Did he wrong her, so that her hurt is justified? Or did he run afoul of her expectations, and hence she interpreted his actions as sword thrusts? Or was it some of both? She will "feel hurt" in any case. Wise biblical counseling cannot take even perceived sensations at face value. Things become even trickier with the other common uses of "I feel."

"I Feel" Expresses Emotions

This is an extension of the first use of feeling. We do experience our emotions: "I feel angry or anxious, depressed, happy, affectionate, fearful, guilty, thankful, excited." But here the word becomes even fuzzier. For example, to say "I feel angry" does bring out one important part of what is going on. But it hides other significant parts of anger. Anger, like all emotions, is something you do *as a whole person*. Anger involves *active things* such as thoughts, attitudes, expectations, words, and deeds, as well as the more passively sensed "feeling" of being angry.

Much current pop psychology says, "Anger just is. It's simply a valid feeling. It's neither right nor wrong. You have no reason to avoid facing it. Therefore, let's talk about your anger." That might sound helpful on the surface. This explanation can get people who deny their anger to face the truth about their emotional experience. But it draws people out by getting them to believe the illusion that they are basically okay.

Wisdom nurtures personal honesty by truth, not illusion: "Anger is a common human response to a perceived wrong. It is even part of being made in the image of a moral God. Anger can be either right or wrong. You must face it. Let's talk about your anger." Anger, in fact, is complicated, not simple. Biblically, anger may be either justified or unjustified, either wrongly or rightly expressed. It is much more than an emotion. Human anger is potentially righteous but is usually laced with sin.

The need for an objective, moral evaluation is obscured when anger is viewed simply as a feeling. If anger is a feeling that happens to me, then it is intrinsically legitimate. "Just as when I cut my finger I feel hurt, so when you offend me I feel angry. I need only to get in touch with my anger and then express it in socially appropriate ways." But when anger is evaluated by God (e.g., James 1:19–20; 3:2–4:12) that simple equation breaks down. I acknowledge anger in order to examine it in God's light. In all likelihood I will learn about my self-righteousness, my god playing, my demands. I will be brought to my need for God's grace in Jesus Christ. I will change the way I express anger. I will cut the very causes of warmaking out of my heart. I will learn to become a peacemaker.

"I Feel" Expresses Thoughts, Beliefs, and Attitudes

"I feel that my husband wronged me. I feel he won't listen. I feel justified. I don't feel that the Bible applies." This use of "I feel" is very problematic. We learn a lot about the speaker but very little about what is true or what she ought to do. To speak of opinions and beliefs as feelings obscures far more than it reveals. Thoughts are represented as intrinsically valid if they are "felt," that is, experienced with a sense of inner conviction. Many people live as if their "feel thats" were authoritative convictions. This usage ("I feel that") must be rephrased to bring out the implicit or explicit content.

Opinions and beliefs are meant to be evaluated in the light of truth. What did happen? What do you think and believe? How do you judge people or your situation? Finally, is what you think true and righteous, or false and sinful? Instead of posing these sorts of questions, "I feel that . . ." ducks conscious evaluation of my ideas and judgments. What I feel just *is*. True-for-me replaces truth. The Bible has devastating things to say about leaning on your own understanding, about being wise in your own eyes, about the way that seems right to a man, and about people who delight in airing their opinions (see Prov. 3:5; 3:7; 14:12; 18:2). While the feeling of being cut with a paring knife is authoritative, the "feeling that something just is" is highly debatable.

"I Feel" Conveys Desires

"I don't feel like going to talk to him. I feel like leaving." This use of feeling is also fuzzy and problematic. It loads implicit authority into our impulses, desires, intentions, choices, expectations, and fears. Far from being givens to obey, these are meant to be examined biblically. The words "I feel like" often obscure our responsibility for our desires. People act as if their "feel likes" were authoritative impulses! Deceptive desires determine choices.

What we want to get may be perfectly legitimate: "I feel like pizza and Pepsi, not cauliflower and milk." Such desires are often not problematic. (Though not always! Relationships have been destroyed when even minor preferences become life-ruling demands.) What we want to do may be perfectly legitimate: "I do feel like going to talk to my husband and solving this." But the Bible teaches us that our "feel likes" are frequently desires of the flesh. Most of our "felt needs" are idolatrous desires. They are meant to be killed by the Spirit, not indulged. Such is the way of life, freedom, wisdom, and joy in Christ!

These third and fourth uses of "feeling," beliefs and desires, get at the heart of disoriented human motivation. In fact, the mindset of the flesh, with its false beliefs and ruling desires, creates the misconceptions and emotional swamps that complicate the first two more straightforward uses of the word "feeling."

BIBLICAL COUNSELORS AND FEELINGS

"Feelings." What a difficult word to pin down when it is used to communicate four very different things: experience, emotions, thinking, and desires! How do you use the words, "I feel"? How do your counselees? Can you think your way through the traps that the language of feeling presents to you? Do feelings typically reveal authoritative perceptions, emotions, opinions, and impulses which can be taken as givens? Or do they reveal facets of human life meant to be evaluated biblically? Do they typically reveal the real me, who is meant to be actualized and asserted? Or do they reveal the human drift from God and toward self, the flesh, autonomy, and subjectivity?

For more than twenty years biblical counseling has said that to be "feeling-oriented" is the central motivational problem in people. This has often been misinterpreted by critics and would-be biblical counselors who have failed to wrestle with the complexities and depths of the biblical view of people.

When Jay Adams first said that to be feeling-oriented is the central motivational problem in people, he meant this: sinful people are driven by lies and lusts. This has often been caricatured as if biblical counselors were necessarily hostile or neglectful toward people's emotions and experience.

But a biblical analysis of motivation does not mean being against emotions. It does not mean ignoring experience. Wise counselors care to know what a person is experiencing situationally or emotionally. They care to know what a person feels is true or feels like doing. Does thinking clearly about fuzzy things mean being against those things? May it never be. Does careful analysis imply that honest feelings should be swept under the rug? May it never be. People should not stuff what they honestly "feel." How can you address what you are unaware of? God traffics in reality, not pretense and avoidance. How can you be heard and helped if you will not honestly acknowledge what is going on? Biblical truth penetrates your experience, emotions, beliefs, and desires. God meets you where you are.

The notion that people are feeling-oriented is not a simplistic notion, for it explains the complexities of tangled lives. A biblical understanding of "feelings" lets us look behind the often deceptive language of daily life. In your Bible concordance you will not find many references to "feel" or "feeling." But the freight these words now carry is discussed throughout your Bible. We can pierce the confusion, seeing what makes people tick. We can invite people to intelligent change in the light of biblical truth and the power of the Holy Spirit.

The Bible cuts to the root of the problem of "feelings." The Word of the Knower of hearts "judges the thoughts and intentions of the heart" (Heb. 4:12). In modern feeling language, we could say that the Bible exposes and judges the *feel thats* and *feel likes* that determine how people in darkness live. Every man did what was right in his own eyes—i.e., what he felt. And what a wonderful alternative we have been given: the truth of our Lord and Savior Jesus Christ to bring both mercy and power to change!

REDEEMING HUMAN EXPERIENCE

As we have seen, in potential counseling situations the ambiguous words "I feel" are commonly used in four distinct ways. The phrase speaks of experience, emotions, thoughts, or desires. Serious problems arise because the word is typically loaded with authority: "If I feel it, then it's inherently true, right, and valid." Clear biblical thinking pierces the fog of ambiguity and authority that wraps itself around "feelings." As minds and hearts are renewed by the Spirit's life-giving truth, everything about us is touched.

What can be said positively about those arenas which the contemporary language of "feeling" has captured? What does renewal in the image of God look like in those arenas? Experience, emotion, belief, and desire are in the sphere of our inward transformation by the Holy Spirit's power and truth. "Feeling" is usually not the best word to use for such diverse riches. Many other words are more vivid and accurate. Consider the following.

Your Experience
You are made by God to experience pleasure and pain. Read Psalm 107. Notice how the experiences of blessings and hardships are vividly told. On the one hand you hear of people who experience hunger, thirst, fainting, misery, despair, fear, and sorrow. Hardships

drive you to God for help and refuge. On the other hand you hear of people in blessed circumstances who experience thankfulness, joy, satisfaction, quenched thirst, safety, and peace. Blessings beckon you to God for rejoicing.

Of course, life experience registers in our body and soul. We feel things. We would be stones if we didn't! Christian experience in a fallen world never entails freedom from pain or absence of pleasure. God's promises are an appeal to the experience of blessing. "How blessed is the [person . . . whose] delight is in the law of the LORD, [for] he will be like a tree firmly planted by streams of water, which yields its fruit in its season, and its leaf does not wither; and in whatever he does he prospers" (Ps. 1:1–3). His warnings are an appeal to the experience of misery: For those who hate God, "their worm will not die and their fire will not be quenched; and they will be an abhorrence to all mankind" (Isa. 66:24).

We've all been reminded that hardship is a valid experience in the Christian life. Betrayal, poverty, sickness, accusation, bereavement, and isolation are hard. Temptations are hard. The battle with our own natural selves is hard. All these things we experience as trouble.

But let's think a minute about the legitimate pleasures. For example, how about marriage and sex? In a culture of rampant immorality, interpersonal hostility, abuse, and divorce, it is understandable that marriage and sex acquire threatening or squalid connotations. But the Bible equates the "voice of joy and gladness" with the "voice of the bridegroom and bride" (read Jer. 33:11). The sheer sensual pleasures of obedience in Proverbs 5:15–19 and the Song of Solomon almost can't be printed here! Read an uncensored version of Proverbs 5:19. God's holy law here commands that erotic love be full of ravishing delights. So much for the idea that keeping God's commandments is a drudging, legalistic affair!

Consider also the pleasures of food and drink. The Holy Spirit renews people to enjoy food with thankfulness, eating and drinking with wisdom and pleasure. But our culture infects people deeply. It creates obsessed, guilty, anxious, or matter-of-fact food consumers, rather than glad feasters. Our culture produces faddists, gluttons, or ascetics. Food has taken on various sinister overtones: a savior, a cause of fat, a source of various poisons, fuel for the machine. Will you delight to eat and drink at the marriage feast of the Lamb? Even now, can your experience be retooled to feel grateful pleasure in food, in marriage, and in many other good things? The Bible says a resounding YES (1 Tim. 4:3–6).

Your Emotions

The gamut of emotions may be godly. God is both the angriest and the most tender person in the Bible. Jesus is both the most sorrowful and the most exultant. Are you becoming like this God and this Christ? Even the redeemed groan, for our Lord was a man of sorrows, acquainted with grief. This life is lived in a vale of tears and in the shadow of death. But there is also inexpressible and glorious joy. Sheer joy is the characteristic emotion of true intimacy with God and with people. This life has delights and foretastes of the real life that is to come.

There is hatred of evil in those who come to love the light. When Moses shattered the tablets of stone in anger, he mirrored the anger that the holy Lord expressed only minutes or hours before. There is also guilt to be felt, reshaped, and resensitized by true standards. There is gratitude to be felt, for our Lord is merciful.

The Psalms have always been favorites of God's people because they express honest human experience and emotion in a context of faith. In the Psalms you meet God where you are. The cry of need and the song of joy are each appropriate in image-bearers of the glory of God.

Your Beliefs

With all his heart, soul, mind, and might, the sinful man "feels" his lies to be true. Crucial beliefs and opinions are deep-seated. What we "really believe" is not casually discarded or exchanged. Lies and distortions are stubborn, plausible, deceitful, and ingrained. We are usually persuaded that our "feel thats" are true.

The same is true on the renewed side of the ledger. New people in Christ learn to wholeheartedly believe that truth is true. Occasionally the language of feeling may be appropriate to express renewed thinking. One of the Spirit's chief works is to create the heartfelt conviction that God's promises are true. Generally, however, "I feel" is a poor substitute for many better words. It highlights the subjective in a realm where truth, lies, and opinions ought to be examined objectively.

What is true can be believed with subjective passion. Biblical objectivity is not barren and abstract. Knowledge of truth contains life, commitment, and force. Biblical faith is far more than bare cognition, self-talk, positive thinking, a worldview, or intellectual assent to doctrines. The Christian who knows clearly loves strongly. Believes robustly. Thinks passionately. We not only think that Jesus is the Vine. We *really* think it and so abide in him with joy and hope (John 15).

Your Desires

With all his heart, soul, mind, and might, the sinful man "feels" his lusts to be good. The Bible tells us that sinners yearn for money, pleasure, security, significance, health, food, self-righteousness, worth, power, knowledge, happiness . . . every sort of blessing squandered at the Fall. New people in Christ also desire intensely. But the objects of our desire are all transformed. God is never made the errand boy of our wandering desires for good things.

The Bible says that God's children should seek, long, and thirst for God himself (Ps. 42; Luke 11:9–13). We should want righteousness and obedience to our King (Matt. 5:6; 6:33). We should long for the resurrection life that Jesus will reveal (Rom. 8:18–25; Rev. 22:20). Pop theologies baptize the longings of sinful hearts: health and wealth, significance and security, self-esteem, power to get what you want. But the Holy Spirit is in the business of changing what you want. Should you *want* what you ask for in the Lord's Prayer? Yes and Amen!

There are riches to be mined from the ground now trampled and mired by the modern jargon of "feelings." Enter and dig! The Bible teaches that as you learn a simple and pure devotion to Christ, you will find your experience, emotions, beliefs, and desires braided into a single unified strand. You will bear fruit in good works prepared beforehand by the One who is recreating you in his image.

THE LANGUAGE OF FEELINGS IN WISE COUNSELING

We have explored the realities behind the popular language of "feelings." In order to sharpen critical thinking, we looked specifically at how people use and misuse those ambiguous words, "I feel." We have explored how the Bible illumines and redeems the things that "feelings" describe. In giving us the mind of Christ, the Bible gives us a world of delights and sufferings. We have seen that challenging our culture and the human heart over the authority of feelings does not imply that we deny, ignore, or deprecate what people feel. Our goal is to bring light and life into fuzzy and darkened realms of human life. What are some practical implications for how we talk with each other? What does all this imply for how we talk to other people and how we talk about ourselves?

Human beings instinctively oscillate between two sinful extremes. In the "objective" mode we typically deny feelings and so avoid the realities of the interior life. Much of the time people are pragmatic, unreflective, driven by external pressures or by unstated demands, fears, and goals. In the "subjective" mode, on the other hand, we typically indulge feelings and so make feelings supreme. "Getting in touch with" denied feelings is the world's way of addressing one problem by creating another.

The Holy Spirit and the Word of God set us free to live in a third way. This third way neither denies personal honesty nor equates truth with such honesty. You must pay attention to feelings (all four meanings)! You must not live or counsel as if feelings are the supreme reality.

What does this mean practically? Two key questions guide us. First, how do you get to know a person well? Second, how do you speak wisely to people?

How Do You Get to Know Someone?

What does it mean to know a person? How do you come to know yourself or someone else? In part, seek to know what people feel (while not neglecting what people do, think, and so forth). Learn to pay attention to experience and emotions. These are crucial components of who people are. They are signals that register what is happening to them and within them.

For example, the "feeling" of being stretched too thin, of being overwhelmed or stressed, is important. It cues you to ask important questions. Are there cares to be cast on God? Are your priorities wrong? Are you forgetting the God who is in control, who gives rest, who calls you only to doable tasks? Are you doing or expecting too much? Are you simply facing plain old hardship, suffering, or temptation? Have you procrastinated? Should you ask for help? Some or all of the above? Your experience of pressure catches your attention.

The feeling of being overwhelmed often drives people to God, to self-evaluation, to seeking help. It also often sets people up for reacting via workaholism, suicide, anger, depression, drugs, or other escapisms. Is the feeling normative? No. It has a cause you need to discover and a "way of escape" you need to find because "God is faithful." Is the feeling important? It sure is. It is the point of entry, where words of truth and deeds of love will often make contact with a person.

Experience and emotion typically indicate what is going on in our relationships with God and neighbor. Let me give two brief examples. Anxiety, which so overwhelms a panicky person, can become a friend—a cue that you are living as if there were no sovereign God in the universe. Anger, which can destroy relationships, can motivate you to tackle problems constructively and make peace. Are anger and anxiety givens, simply to be acknowledged and expressed? No, they have a cause. They can be transformed in ways honoring to God. Are they important? Yes, they are the raw materials out of which godliness can be produced.

Wise living involves alertness to experience and emotion. The goal of such self-awareness is not introspective self-preoccupation. Such awareness is rather a matter of integrity and honesty. It is meant to lead you to those twin radical "extrospections": faith and love.

Two of the most helpful kinds of questions to ask yourself or another are:

1. What joys, highlights, delights, purposes, or glad anticipations fill you as you think of the past, present, or future?

2. What sorrows, burdens, guilt, frustrations, hardships, preoccupations, or fears press upon you as you think of the past, present, or future?

These are "feeling-toned" questions that invite people to become honest. Even the much abused (and, on the other side, much maligned) question, "What do you feel?" has its place as an open-ended way to enter another's life. Wise counselors, parents, and friends will not treat the answers given as sacred and unquestionable. But questions such as these gain valuable knowledge and express loving concern. They ask, "Who are you and what is your world?" The inquirer sticks around for the answer.

Such questions also set the stage for more specific love, counsel, encouragement, confrontation, and intercession or praise to God. They are starting points, not stopping points. They can open a door into a person's behavior, belief system, value system, and the like. Much of the data-gathering homework biblical counselors traditionally have given finds its starting point in people's emotions and experience. For example, it is logical for a struggling counselee to keep a record of incidents producing anxiety, stress, anger, unhappiness, lust, or whatever other problem is the current focus. Emotion and experience are often the proverbial "red light on the dashboard" that cues both counselor and counselee to significant issues.

How Do You Speak to People?

How will you give wise feedback to people? Wise, biblical counsel teaches about and reaches into every realm that people typically distort by using the language of feeling.

For example, on many occasions biblical counsel will encourage the right sort of experience and emotion. Many people do not know that it is legitimate to experience hardship, pain, and temptation when someone attacks them. Many people think the ideal Christian is either an unfeeling stoic or someone with a continual smile for Jesus. But look at Jesus himself in the Garden of Gethsemane. Pick a few psalms at random. Count how many times Joseph weeps. Listen to Paul in Philippians. He writes about a wellspring of joy and then in virtually the same paragraph says that if his friend had died he would have had "sorrow upon sorrow." There are some surprising fruits on the tree of righteousness that biblical counseling seeks to produce through the Holy Spirit. Are Romans 8 "groanings" a legitimate goal of wisdom and godliness? Of course!

From a different angle, aware of the pitfalls, a counselor might want to use the words "I feel" on certain occasions. For example, in illustrating how experience and emotion differ from (and often derive from!) belief and desire, a first-person story could help a "feeling-oriented" counselee sort through his or her confusion. "When I am slandered, I feel pain. I typically feel and react in anger, discouragement, and fear. If I believe that I must be respected, liked, or agreed with, then my reaction—and even my experience—will be intensified and prolonged. As I repent of the lies and lusts that control my reaction to slander, then I am freed to forgive and to confront the situation constructively." The story carries truth about "feelings" and helps counselees become more accurate.

In another situation, the words "I feel" might be a good way to communicate a certain tentativeness. In the physical realm the sentence, "I feel like my leg might be broken," communicates a combination of experience and conjecture. In counseling it might be proper to say, "I feel (I wonder? intuit? have a gut sense? suspect?) that there's something more going on here." Perhaps this is a useful way to mention the "halo data" we get from body language or tone of voice. Perhaps it is a way to broach the intuition that "something's not quite right here but I can't put my finger on it." "I feel" rather nicely captures a blend of thoughts, experience, and emotion here and communicates an open-minded uncertainty. It is not a word for certainty but for a tentative idea to be checked out.

The other popular uses of the word "feeling," for beliefs and desires, demand a rapid translation for counseling to proceed in the Bible's light rather than in the confusion of the flesh and secular psychology. Certainly part of the process of gently leading a counselee will involve incorporating some of his or her language. It would be entirely appropriate to say, "You feel like doing . . . ?" or "You feel that . . . ?" in order to clarify that I have understood the person. But that would be the prelude to a biblical reinterpretation of the counselee's desires and beliefs.

Whether you are asking questions, giving tangible help, or giving biblical counsel, there is a place, a time, a way, and a purpose to communicate about feelings. Will you get it straight in a world that would make you bent? Will you be wise in a world that would make you foolish? The language of feelings is the vernacular of personhood in twenty-first-century America. Wise counselors must carefully consider how the language of truth intersects with the language of confusion.

"The entry of Thy words gives light" (Ps.119:130).

14 | LOVE SPEAKS MANY LANGUAGES FLUENTLY

Recently a friend asked me a question that I think is of wider interest. He wrote, "I wonder what to make of the ideas presented in Gary Chapman's book about 'the five love languages.'[1] Some of it seems to make sense. It accurately describes some of the differences between my wife and me. I'm an actions-speak-louder-than-words person; she's wired for honest sharing and quality time. Our conflicts frequently boil down to collisions between our very different expectations. And we've learned that part of loving each other is giving what actually blesses the other. But something about the book doesn't sound right to me. It seems like a glorified form of 'You scratch my back and I'll scratch yours.'"

This man's response to *The Five Love Languages* captures in a nutshell the helpful strengths and the underlying weaknesses of this and similar books. On the positive side, the book rings true when it describes how people typically come wired. For example:

- Love is expressed in many different forms. To describe these as "languages" vividly captures this variety and hints at potential difficulties in communication. It's a great metaphor.
- People experience being loved in many different ways. Oftentimes, care will either communicate or misfire, depending on whether the language "spoken" comes in the language of the "hearer."
- People tend to demonstrate love to another in the same way they want to receive it, whether or not they're speaking that other person's language.
- When people don't get what they want or give what the other wants, it tends to breed anger and estrangement.

In addition to these accurate descriptions of life lived, some of the advice that Chapman offers is constructive:

- Learn the other's language in order to love more thoughtfully. Because love considers the interests of another person, it makes sense to consider well what brings blessing to *this* human being.
- Take the initiative and persist in loving, whether or not the other person changes. True love is self-giving, not self-seeking.

So, as my friend indicated, when he loves his wife well, the two of them sit down regularly and simply talk for an hour or two. He lets her in on his joys and struggles, and seeks to draw her out. The relationship thrives when they connect to each other. When she loves him well, she carries her share of the chores and responsibilities. She looks for ways to take things off his shoulders. The relationship thrives when they help each other.

"Love languages" describe different strokes for different folks. My friend feels loved (and tends to express love) by Chapman's "Love Language #4: Acts of Service": helping, providing, protecting, and other ways that actions speak louder than words. His wife, on the other hand, feels loved (and tends to show love) by Chapman's "Love Language #2: Quality Time": honest sharing to generate mutual understanding and an atmosphere of trust. The other three love languages discussed in *The Five Love Languages* (hereafter 5LL) also each have their fluent native speakers: affirming words (#1), gift-giving (#3), and physical affection (#5). It's helpful to know this about each other. To act on it sweetens relationships.

What phenomena is Chapman looking at, understood theologically? Such differences express the outworking of God's creation and providence. God makes people with wide variations of temperament, personality, interest, and motivation. He arranges and governs wide variations in life experience, opportunities, socialization, and enculturation. Furthermore, the Lord of all the earth often seems to put people together in marriage who are wired differently. As a result, either we grow to complement each other by learning to give intelligent love, or we incinerate the marriage on the battlefield of insistently different demands.

Golden Rule Improvisations

5LL also accurately describes how we tend to misfire in attempting to love others. We tend to do for others exactly the same things that we want them to do for us, without actually considering their interests. For example, one year on my dad's birthday, my brother and I gave him a kit to build an elaborate scale model of the U.S.S. Constitution, complete with microscopic details right down to the rigging and paint. My dad loved to hike, camp, swim, and sail, but he was never known to sit down and do a craft project. Guess who was into building models? We loved Dad, but not very well.

Obviously, the most basic violations of the Golden Rule occur when we simply mistreat others, doing malicious things we'd hate to have done to us. But perhaps the most common misunderstanding of the Golden Rule is that even in attempting to love others we do what *we* would want. It's a less heinous form of self-centeredness, more clumsy and ignorant than hateful. Such clumsiness and ignorance is the problem that *5LL*, at its best, actually addresses. Chapman taps into a deep instinct in human nature. If you give people what makes them feel given to, they will tend to give back. If you pay attention to what rings the bells of your spouse (or parents, roommates, kids, boss, and coworkers), then you'll treat them better. They'll probably treat you better, too. At the same time, if you ask them for what you want in an open, less demanding, less oblique way, then they'll probably do better at giving you what you want. On the flip side, spouses (and parents, teachers, managers, salesmen, pastors, and other counselors) who don't pay any attention at all to what makes others happy will mistreat others and create alienation.

Let's say I'm in the market for a minivan. If car salesman X sells me a lemon at a rip-off price, I'll intensely dislike him. Because he has done *evil*, I'll seek legal recourse, pursue reparations, and report him to the Better Business Bureau. If salesman Y tries to sell me a sports car when I'm really looking for a minivan, I'll merely dislike him. Because he's *clueless*, I'm not likely to do business with him or to recommend him to friends. But if salesman Z sells me the minivan I want at a fair price, I'll like him. Because he gave me what I was looking for, I'll tell my friends. He fulfilled my desire for a minivan, and I fulfilled his desire for a commission, and so we get along great. *5LL* aims to turn clueless people into helpful people. But it doesn't address shysters like Mr. X. It also doesn't address customers who want to buy a new minivan every week.

What is Chapman working with here? Unwittingly, he exalts the observation that even tax collectors, Gentiles, and sinners love those who love them (Matt. 5:46–47; Luke 6:32–34) into his guiding principle for human relationships. This is the dynamo that makes his entire model go. This is the instinct that he appeals to in his readers. If I scratch your back, you'll tend to scratch mine. If you're happy to see me, I'll tend to be happy to see you, too. So, 5LL teaches you how to become aware of what others want, and then tells you to give that to them. This is the principle behind *How to Win Friends and Influence People* and *The 30-second Manager*. It's the dynamic at work in hundreds of other books on "relational skills," or "attending skills," or "salesmanship," or "how to find the love you want." Identify the felt need and meet it, and, odds are, your relationships will go pretty well.

NOT FAR ENOUGH

Those who pay attention often win affection. That's not necessarily bad, as far as it goes. But it doesn't go very far, and it goes bad easily, and it misses so many other really important things that are going on at the same time. When the crowd was hungry, Jesus fed them and they loved him. (But when he bid to change their agenda by dealing with their bread obsession, they grumbled.) When Martha and Mary lost their brother, Jesus gave Lazarus back to them. (But before he gave them what they wanted, he worked to change what they really wanted and needed.) When Jesus healed the crippled woman and rebuked the religious leaders, the leaders were incensed and humiliated. No affirming words or acts of service for them, and they didn't like it a bit. When the shrewd servant cut his master's creditors a break, they loved him and welcomed him in. (Then Jesus changed the subject and upped the ante: Will heaven welcome you in?)

We might say that Chapman offers a bit of practical, moral wisdom about how "you, being evil, can learn how to give good gifts to your children and spouse" (tweaking Luke 11:13). Up to a point, *5LL* can be informative, correcting ignorance about how people differ from each other, and making you more aware of patterns of expectation that you and others bring to the table. The exhortations to take the initiative in giving to others could make the world a better place: "Many couples . . . say that choosing to love and expressing it in the primary love language of their spouse has made a drastic difference in their marriage. . . . It creates a climate where the couple can deal with the rest of life in a much more productive manner" (pp. 173–74).

So far, so good. I have little doubt that the testimonials about happier marriages are honest. Common grace, even among tax collectors, does do some genuine good in this world. It raises human relationships above the level of naked self-interest, adversarial manipulation, and bullying. Dog-eat-dog marriages become happier when couples learn how to generate some win-win dynamics. If I am to love another wisely, I will attend to what communicates care and concern to *this* particular person.

Love languages are part of the story of human relations. But speaking love languages is surely not the whole story. In fact, it is practical, immoral wisdom—manipulation or pandering or both—when it becomes the whole story. Part of considering the interests of others is to do them tangible good. But to *really* love them, you usually need to help them see their itch as idolatrous, and to awaken in them a far more serious itch! That's basic Christianity. *5LL* will never teach you to love at this deeper, more life-and-death level. Chapman's reasons for giving appropriate love to others, his explanation of what speaking another's love language does, his ultimate goal in marriage, and his evaluation of the significance of love languages are deplorable.

False Premises

The core premises of *5LL* are simply false. They pander to the very problem that most needs solving. Chapman writes:

Could it be that deep inside hurting couples exists an invisible "emotional love tank" with its gauge on empty? Could the misbehavior, withdrawal, harsh words, and critical spirit occur because of that empty tank? If we could find a way to fill it, could the marriage

be reborn? Could that tank be the key that makes marriage work?
(p. 23)

Read those sentences again slowly. No doubt, people often feel extreme hurt and bitterness when they are not loved. People commit
adultery and avoid, argue, and judge when they perceive their spouses
as failing them. But think hard about this. If your spouse or parent or
friends loved you better, would your problems be fundamentally
solved? Does having an empty love tank cause you to mistreat others?
Do you return evil for evil because evil is done to you? If love tanks
could only get filled all around, if others could just speak your language and if you could just speak theirs, would that really produce the
kingdom of perfect relationships? If you could only give others
enough of the right thing, would they love you in return? Is the principle that "Gentiles love those who love them" really the key principle for producing marital success and happiness? The answer to each
question in this paragraph is a profound No.

The *5LL* model fails Human Nature 101. Like all secular interpretations of human psychology (even when lightly Christianized), it
makes some good observations and offers some half-decent advice (of
the sort that self-effort can sometimes follow). But it doesn't really understand human psychology. That basic misunderstanding has systematic misleading effects. Fallenness brings not only ignorance
about how best to love others, it brings a perverse unwillingness and
inability to love. It ingrains the perception that our lusts are in fact
needs, empty places inside where others have disappointed us. The
empty emotional tank construct is congenial to our fallen instincts,
not transformative. It leaves what we instinctively want as an unquestionable good that must be fulfilled. It not only leaves fundamental
self-interest unchallenged, it plays to self-interest. Chapman gives tax
collectors, Gentiles, and sinners something they can do on their own
that might work to make them happier. The case studies end with,
"My love tank has never felt so full and I've never been happier." It
sounds more like opiates for the masses than the revolution needed to
bring in the kingdom of solid joys and lasting treasures. Chapman's
model is premised on a give-to-get economy: "I will give to fill your
love tank. But in the back of my mind I'm always considering whether
and when I'll get my own tank filled."

A FALSE ECONOMY OF LOVE

On the one hand, the model creates an economy of love that is highly sentimentalized. For example, why does a person commit adultery? "Thousands of husbands and wives have been there—emotionally empty, wanting to do the right thing, not wanting to hurt anyone, but being pushed by their emotional needs to seek love outside the marriage" (p. 131). This portrays the poor adulterer as a victim, as well-intended, needy, and disappointed by others' inability to love him the right way. The adulterer's self-pity and self-righteousness are neatly preserved by the empty love tank notion. There is no call to really face yourself, to fear the Lord, and to come to repentance. There is no need for a substitute to take the death sentence for capital crimes you have committed. There is no need for living water and resurrection because you are dead in sins and because you worship lusts under the alias "emotional needs."

On the other hand, this model creates an economy of love that is cruel and seductive. For example, why do children act up and act out?

> If the emotional need is not met, they may violate acceptable standards, expressing anger toward parents who did not meet their needs, and seeking love in inappropriate places. . . . Most misbehavior in children and teenagers can be traced to empty love tanks . . . . The growing number of adolescents who run away from home and clash with the law indicate that many parents who may have sincerely tried to express their love to their children have been speaking the wrong love language. (pp. 163, 169, 175)

Notice again the sentimentality about both parties: you meant well, and your kids are simply running on empty. None of you have actually done anything that might cause a blow to your self-esteem or might necessitate Christ's bloodshed on your behalf.

Notice also the cruelty: your ignorance caused Johnny's problem by draining his emotional tank. Parent, if you could only have filled his tank, and connected better to him. . . . Such a logic is bitter. But notice also that it is still extremely seductive, because of the same causal dynamic. Your ability to redeem the situation lies at hand. If Johnny does evil things because you failed to fill his tank, then the possibility of his restoration also lies in your power. Just start speaking his language. Of course, no one can guarantee the outcome, but we can come pretty close: "If all goes well and their emotional needs are met, children develop into responsible adults" (p. 163). That is a psychologist's dream, not a Christian's hope.[2]

The same cruelly seductive principle applies to reaching an adulterous or hostile spouse. Dedicate yourself to filling the other's tank — for example, by compliments and sexual availability (pp. 147–59). There is "a good possibility" that the misbehaving spouse will reciprocate "because we tend to respond positively to the person who is meeting [our deepest emotional need]" (p. 153). Even God's call to "love your enemies," to which Chapman refers throughout this section, is bent to his "Gentiles love those who love them" paradigm, not to the Bible's call to something qualitatively different. Chapman motivates a bitter wife to love her bitter husband for six months by a vision for gradually filling his love tank so that he might eventually reciprocate and fill her tank. Where Jesus says, "Expect nothing in return" (Luke 6:35) and tests what we are living for by how we handle evil, this woman acts in the hope of fulfilling her dreams.

5LL does slightly alter the "You scratch my back, I'll scratch yours" calculus. It is a "glorified version," taking a small step in the right direction by reversing the order. "I scratch your back (and then it's likely you'll scratch mine)." Chapman's full working philosophy might be summarized this way: "I'll find out where you itch, and I'll scratch your back, so you feel better. Along the way, I'll let you know my itches in a non-demanding manner. You'll feel good about me because your itches are being scratched, so eventually you'll probably scratch my back, too." Chapman softens the demand and encourages unilateral initiative, but everything is still hitched to fundamental self-interest. 5LL replaces naked self-interest with civilized self-interest. "I give, hoping to get" is a step above "I only give if I've gotten," but it's not all that different. The music of relational give-and-take still plays in the key of ME, though the arrangement is different.

OUR LOVE LANGUAGES REALITY

I happened to be reading Anne Lamott's book on writing, *Bird by Bird*, the same week I read 5LL.[3] Lamott is one of the Lord's more uncivilized saints—the kind of odd believer who makes one feel amazed at God's goodness and a little queasy at the same time! She sees many things with searing clarity, and she never pulls a punch. I got thinking, what might be Anne Lamott's love language? Interestingly, she happens to discuss in passing each of the five things that Chapman labels "love languages." But none of them are her real language.

Make no mistake, Anne Lamott likes words of affirmation and good book reviews (LL #1), but then she talks about how they can be "cocaine for the ego." She likes quality time with people who are her friends (LL #2), but what comes out when you really know people is often ambiguous or even hellish. She likes thoughtful gifts, the bouquet at the door or a casserole when she's been too busy (LL #3), but such small favors brighten an abyss of infinite need for the world to be made right. She likes it when others help her, or when she helps others as a teacher or as part of a nursing home ministry (LL #4), but at the end of the day she's still alone with what she must do to live her life with integrity. She likes physical affection (LL #5), but she knows great ambivalence because touch so often proves perverse.

Lamott's writing aims to honestly depict dark, raw forces spinning down the vortex of the human condition. I'd say she really wants one thing, that her primary love language is this: "Oh our God and only Savior, have mercy on us. Remove the sin and misery that cling so closely. Destroy evil and perversity from within us. Destroy pain and death that come upon us. Lord, have mercy on us." She has an empty redemption tank. Her love language plays hardball, not whiffleball.

Gary Chapman's world seems so sunny and easy in comparison. The problems of life seem so fixable. His advice is so doable. A bit of education and a bit of self-effort are all that's needed for life to sing. The marriages in his book don't need Jesus' blood, sweat, and tears. The people don't need help and power from outside themselves in order even to stumble in the right direction. They don't need Jesus to come back, because the current fixing is adequate. Now it probably wouldn't hurt Anne Lamott to lighten up a bit now and then. She lives far out on the ragged edge. But 5LL is just too easy. It could profit from a big dose of hard-edged realism and glorious salvation.

Chapman treats desires as givens, as "love languages" to be spoken in order to fill "love tanks" that become empty. He never deals with the fact that people can desire evil. Immorality, violence, stubborn willfulness, heavy drinking, obsession with career or looks or money or house or reputation—do these come from empty places inside basically good people? I don't think so. Such things arise from active evil inside us. Chapman never deals with the fact that even desires for good things can be evil desires in God's analysis. Our "love languages" are a curious mix of creation and fall.

For example, I thrive on intimate conversation, on honest knowing and being known in a context of loving, mutual concern. I like to understand and be understood: LL #2. It's part of why I love counseling and the opportunity to really know people in a constructive context. It points to a great way that friends bless me, and we get along fine. But it also describes a monster inside that would swallow the universe. A love language (or a lust language) instinctively tends to look at all reality through the lens of "my needs." I've found that one acid test of my heart is how I handle being misunderstood, caricatured, dissed—*not* how I handle being accurately known and loved! It's when someone doesn't speak my "love language" that I find out what I'm made of, and by God's grace begin to change what I live for. Desires for good things easily become imperial demands that would enslave the very people who might try to speak my language—or yours. The lust that perverts such languages sets up an unholy law, by which to command and judge the performance of others in the eyes of an unholy king.[4]

Chapman's couples know no repentance and no forgiveness for what they long for and live for. *5LL* amplifies the pulse beating deep within fallen hearts; it does not change the music. It gives no intrinsic reason to worship Christ crucified, to live with a grateful heart, to repent of only loving those who love me, that I might learn to really love enemies for Christ's sake.

In a lengthy case study of an adulterer, Chapman simply describes a man who got burned out and feels bad when his mistress stops giving him what he wants. When his tank runs on empty again, he returns to counseling, and he and his wife set about learning to speak each other's love languages to fill each other's tanks (pp. 129–36). She meets the needs the mistress failed to meet. He loves that, and gives to her, too. Everything is restored.

This particular story is appalling. There's no nicer way to say it. Chapman prettifies our lusts, rather than naming them for what they are in God's eyes. If we name them for what they really are, the Lord of life will forgive us. He will rewire us by grace and the expulsive power of new affections, so that we might speak a new language fluently.

The closest 5LL comes to our need for the Gospel is a paragraph on page 174: "The ability to love, especially when your spouse is not loving you, may seem impossible for some. Such love may require us to draw upon our spiritual resources." *May* seem impossible? For *some*? *May* require us to draw on spiritual resources? This coddles us and insults God.

CHRIST'S LOVE LANGUAGE

Jesus puts things in a different light. Your ability to really love your enemies, to be perfect as your heavenly Father is perfect, and to do good even to the ungrateful or wicked absolutely requires the intervention of the Godhead. It required that Christ suffer and die because of your natural enmity to God. It requires the Holy Spirit's power to give you a wholly new life. It requires the Father's patient hand to prune and grow you in a way of life that is otherwise impossible—even inconceivable. It requires nothing less than radical repentance, living faith, and renewal of your whole heart that you might begin to learn how to really love. Such a faith working through love is the product of a good news worth living and dying for.

Chapman's couples live in a world whose problems they caused and whose problems they can fix (maybe with a little help, if necessary). Jesus' couples live in a far more desperate world. The couples in Jesus' case studies learn to repent of their innate love languages and love tanks. They acknowledge their need of divine help from outside. They slowly learn to give others truly good gifts. And yes, they generously speak the love languages of others. Just as Jesus fed bread to the hungry in John 6, so my friend will sit down and talk intimately with his wife. Redemption is not less than what Chapman tells people to do. But it is so much more, and it does everything for such different reasons. Jesus' couples do lots of other things in addition to seeking to love accurately. They seek forgiveness and forgive. They call things what they are. They aim to redemptively remake what others live for, even as God is remaking them. They live for God, not for getting what they want. Jesus offered himself as the bread of life, when all that the hungry crowd wanted was more pita bread to fill their empty bread tank! After that one small gesture in the direction of the Gospel on page 174, Chapman returns to his drumbeat of love languages.

The love of Christ speaks a "love language"—mercy to hellishly self-centered people—that no person can hear or understand unless God gives ears to hear. It is a language we cannot speak to others unless God makes us fluent in an essentially foreign language. We might say that the itch itself (an ear for God's language) has to be created, because we live in such a stupor of self-centered itchiness. The love language model does not highlight those exquisite forms of love that do not "speak your language."

You and I need to learn a new language if we are to become fit to live with each other and with God. The greatest love ever shown does not speak the instinctively self-centered language of the recipients of such love. In fundamental ways, the love of Christ speaks *contrary* to your "love language" and "felt needs." Does anyone naturally say to God, "I need you to rule me so I'm no longer ruled by what I want"? Does anyone naturally say, "For Your name's sake, O LORD, pardon my iniquity for it is great" (Ps. 25:11)? Does anyone naturally say, "My greatest need is for mercy, and then for the wisdom to give mercy. I long for redemption. May your kingdom come. Deliver us from evil"?

God's grace aims to destroy the lordship of the five love languages, even while teaching us to speak the countless love languages with greater fluency. Consider what Chapman's five so often sound like in real life.

- Affirming words? I feel loved when the crowd cheers, and when you offer me flattering compliments, like the "Mirror, mirror on the wall, who's the fairest of them all?"
- Quality time? I feel loved when you drop everything to focus on me, are completely understanding, give me unconditional love, agree with all my opinions, and never disagree with me, question me, or interrupt me.
- Gifts? I feel loved when you are my Sugar Daddy, giving me money, buying me lots of nice stuff, taking me on exotic vacations, and pampering me.

- Acts of service? I feel loved when you do exactly what I want, and don't make any demands on me, and say, "Your wish is my command."
- Physical touch? I feel loved when you go along with my kinky sexual fantasies and when you make me feel like the most special person in the world.

Notice how each of the five love languages often speaks with a dark and greedy growl.

Notice the black hole of insatiable demand when love languages call the shots, when the emotional love tank rules with an iron will or a self-indulgent smirk or a pouty tantrum.

We usually recognize when other people's "love languages" grow overtly perverse (Chapman never discusses this problem). We rarely recognize when our own language gets edgy. And we have a very hard time recognizing that the love languages are perverse even when they rule "reasonably." They were never intended to rule.

At the end of the day, a book such as 5LL makes some interesting observations. It can point out some details you might not have noticed. You ought to pay attention to the varied languages of human experience, your own included. It offers a few helpful tips that might help you love someone better. That's good. But you'd better not buy the reasoning. 5LL speaks essentially "unwholesome words" (Eph. 4:29) when it comes to identifying and addressing the real needs of the human condition. How can all this be? How can perceptive observations, wide case experience, and some good advice be wedded to an utterly perverse underlying dynamic? How can someone who knows people and wants to help them get the actual dynamic of our souls so wrong?

5LL is not unusual in this regard, but commonplace. The *kind* of thing that this book does is replicated in every Psychology 101 textbook, in each of the personality theories, and in all the self-help books on the shelves of Barnes & Noble, not to mention those in many Christian bookstores. A torrent of observations is systematically shunted into the wrong categories; bits of half-decent advice head boldly in the wrong direction. The same kind of thing is replicated in any conversation where the actual human condition is neither faced nor addressed, whether we call it counseling or therapy or a good talk or shooting the breeze. When the analysis of what is wrong does not lead directly to our need for the person and work of the Messiah, then that analysis is shallow. The solution necessarily becomes some version of "'Peace, peace,' when there is no peace."

Where do you turn if you are blinded with pain and rage, with fear and despair, with disappointment and desire? What do you do if you are plunged into escapist fantasies and waking nightmare, if you are driven by sordid passions and patterns of self-destruction? What help is there for you amid all the hells that attend broken and breaking relationships? Will it help you to aim for the standards by which tax collectors, Gentiles, and sinners attempt to make life work? Is it enough to try to make others feel good about themselves in hopes that they'll make you feel good about yourself?

Christ will take any one of us—blind and flailing beasts, tax collectors, Gentiles, sinners, feuding spouses, the whole lot, even nice people—and will freely make us over into children of the Father. Those for whom he died, he lives to remake.

Yes, love others generously and accurately. I pray that your love will abound still more and more in real knowledge and all discernment. Intelligent love is a gift of God, a fruit of the Holy Spirit.

Yes, take unilateral initiative, and don't quit. Love your enemies. Unreciprocated love expresses the image of your Father.

But aim for a lot more, too, and do everything for very different reasons. "The love of Christ controls us, having concluded this, that one died for all, therefore all died; and He died for all, so that they who live might no longer live for themselves, but for Him who died and rose again on their behalf" (2 Cor. 5:14). Grow fluent in the love of Christ, the love language that no one naturally speaks or hears, but everyone needs.

15 BIOLOGICAL PSYCHIATRY

For about ten years, through the mid-1990s, wherever you turned in the counseling world you heard that problems in living were caused by painful experiences of being used, misused, and abused by others. Unpleasant emotions and destructive behavior were based on a sense of woundedness and emptiness from bad relationships. Melody Beattie's *Codependent No More* (1987) and John Bradshaw's *Homecoming* (1990) were huge sellers. In the evangelical world, inpatient, for-profit psychiatric services such as Minirth-Meier Clinic, Rapha, and New Life Treatment Center prospered by offering essentially the same theory. Evangelical psychologists and psychiatrists wrote bestsellers espousing the theory that emotional pain and emptiness play the primal, determinative role in our souls: e.g., Larry Crabb's *Inside Out* (1987) and Robert Hemfelt, Frank Minirth, and Paul Meier's *Love Is a Choice* (1989).[1]

Childhood experience was where the action was. Because our families were dysfunctional, we acted out the script of born loser and unhappy victim—until we could find intrapsychic healing and emotional filling. "*Why* do I think bad, feel bad, and act bad? Because I was abused. My father made me do it. Give me healing relationships and help me think healing thoughts about myself." Those were the glory days of "nurture," and thus the glory days of psychotherapy and support groups. If you were submerged within the social organism, then hanging around better people would make you better.

Then the world changed.

FROM NURTURE TO NATURE

That needy and hurting inner self, so marred by tragic experience, faded into the background. Along about the mid-1990s, everyone discovered that our genes, hormones, and brains caused problems in living. Our bodies, not our families, were dysfunctional. Imaging technologies—PET scans and the like—let us peer into the brain to watch the neurons fire, tracing the patterns and identifying the sites where emotional states and behavioral choices occur. The Human Genome Project generated one cover story after another about the genetic underpinnings for common sins. In *It's Nobody's Fault* (1997), Harold Koplewicz said that difficult children suffer a neurotransmitter shortage, and there's nothing wrong with them as people or with the way they were brought up. In *Listening to Prozac* (1993), Peter Kramer said that we have entered the era of "cosmetic psychopharmacology." We can now tinker chemically with the brains of people who are depressed, anxious, diffident, or aggressive: "Prozac can turn pessimists into optimists, turn loners into extroverts."[2] Brain chemistry and genetics become the *significant* cause of your personality, your proclivities, and your problems: a sunny or a melancholy temperament; tendencies toward violence, drunkenness, overeating, laziness, distractibility, or shyness; choices for homosexuality or promiscuity. The *significant* cause is always the most interesting cause, and the one you want to address to really change things. Or it's unchangeably hardwired, and therefore the behavior should be accepted as normal and amoral.

Because our bodies are dysfunctional, we are puppets that dance on neural strings to tunes programmed by our genes—and the right drug can smooth things out when the dancing gets spastic. "*Why* do I think bad, feel bad, and act bad? I'm miswired. My physiology made me do it. Give me healing medications to calm me down or lift me up so I can feel and function better." We are now living in the glory days of "nature," and thus the glory days of biological psychiatry. If you are a machine with malfunctioning parts, a mere organism, then whatever makes the parts work better will make you better.

Of course I've oversimplified our historical context to make a point. Things are never quite so tidy: Minirth-Meier Clinics prescribed Prozac, too, for all their wounded codependents. Fad theories may have their fifteen minutes of fame before fading from view, but they usually take a very long time to totally disappear. The concept of psychological needs and woundedness is still with us and won't vanish soon. But, have no doubt, the world did change in the mid-1990s. The *action* is now in your body. It's what you got from Mom and Dad, not what they did to you. The *excitement* is about brain functions, not family dysfunctions. The *cutting edge* is in hard science medical research and psychiatry, not squishy soft, feel-your-pain psychologies.

Psychiatry is back. Since the 1960s, psychiatrists had continually retreated from treating everyday life. In the face of numerous new psychotherapy professions, psychiatrists had stopped talking to people, and had set up shop in their biological-medical heartland. But now biology is suddenly hot. Psychiatry has broken forth, a *blitzkrieg* sweeping away all opposition. The insurance companies love it because drugs seem more like "medicine," seem to be cheaper than talk, and promise more predictable results. Psychotherapy professionals are on the defensive, fretting over how to survive under "managed care," vaguely disreputable intellectually, with the golden days of the late 1980s gone.

Psychology in Disarray

As biopsychiatry now plays from a position of intellectual strength, the psychologies are playing from weakness. They have been in cognitive disarray for decades, but are now paying the price. As theories continued to proliferate, the possibility of a Grand Unified Theory of human nature became a pipe dream from the first half of the twentieth century. There is no hope that a Freud or Adler, a Maslow or Skinner, a Kohut or Satir might actually be *right*. No one expects that a new millennium genius will appear with a flair for both innovation and the grand synthesis. No one expects anyone to come up with the *true* psychology. So "eclecticism" is no longer a dirty word. Once it stood for lack of intellectual rigor, a pragmatic making-do. Now, in an age of theoretical skepticism, it becomes the only honest course of thought and action: so therapists are "multimodal" and theoreticians pursue a "principled eclecticism."

Microtheories and microstudies are the only things that can be offered: "grief reactions in Hispanic lesbians in their thirties" bear no theoretical relationship to "joy reactions in state champion teenage football players in Massachusetts." There is no unifying perspective. The Many devours even the possibility of the One. Postmodernism and multiculturalism pound the final nail in the coffin: since everything is only a matter of your interpretation or mine, then everything reduces to power relations. So psychotherapy professions legitimate themselves only because they have the clout to be licensed and reimbursed, not because they possess demonstrable truth, goodness, or efficacy. "Psychology" singular is in fundamental trouble, because no one believes there is any such thing. There are only psychologies left.

PSYCHIATRY'S GRAND UNIFIED THEORY

But what is true of the psychologies and psychotherapies is not true of psychiatry. The only viable candidate for a Grand Unified Theory in the whole people-helping area is not strictly a "psychology" at all, but biopsychiatry. Your "psyche" becomes a byproduct of your body. Medicine is poised to claim the human personality. Sigmund Freud, a physiologist by training, dreamed of the day when the drama of human life could be comprehended biologically and cured medically. He spun his myths amid the inability of medical science to climb in behind consciousness, behavior, desire, conscience, emotion, and the rest. But Freud believed that someday science would get into the *brain* that operates within and through the id, ego, and superego. The conscious and unconscious mind would one day be explained by the brain.

Many people now think they can put their hands on the pot of gold at the end of that rainbow. The dream of materialistic reductionism seems tantalizingly close to coming true. These days, biological psychology is the only plausible claimant (besides biblical faith) to a Grand Unified Theory of human functioning. It was idiocy and social suicide to say that everyone was a victim of abuse. It's too unpleasant to say that we are sinners against the God and Father of Jesus Christ the only Redeemer. People want to say that we are essentially bodies, because then we can fix what ails us. This is the proverbial

800-pound gorilla that sits wherever it wants, threatening to squash *both* psychology/psychotherapy and Christianity.

For years biblical counselors have challenged the *psychologizing* of human life, arguing that human beings are fundamentally and thoroughly relational—"covenantal," to put it technically; living *coram Deo*, to put it in the language of our fathers in the faith. The grand synthesis of *all* the facts about people is . . . Christianity. Psychologized people seek to explain and fix life through some interpretation of human life that excludes God, sin, Christ, sanctification, and the rest of truth. But it is time to update our language a bit. Currently, the *biopsychologizing* of human life is having a huge effect, both in the culture and the church. We minister to an increasing number of biopsychologized people who think about themselves, their spouses, or their children as *bodies* run amok.

An article from *The Economist* put matters well: "Much of the new knowledge from genetics, molecular biology, and the neurosciences is esoteric. But its cultural impact is already running ahead of the science. People see themselves not as wholes with a moral center, but as the result of the combined action of parts for which they have little responsibility."[3] The knowledge base may be overstated or underdeveloped as yet, but the ethos is clear: logically, you are not a YOU when it comes to any responsibility for what's wrong with you, but only a machine whose parts aren't working.[4] Practice also tends to run far ahead of knowledge: what isn't working can be replaced, rewired, upgraded, or oiled, even if we don't totally understand the underlying mechanisms yet.

The church typically lags a bit behind the culture's way of thinking. But the ethos and practice of biopsychiatry are deeply affecting the church already. If it's broken, or even just not working optimally, it can be fixed from the outside by a drug: better living through chemistry. In your ministry and in your church you are probably already facing the ethos and the practices. Many people in both pew and pulpit are on mind-, mood-, and behavior-altering drugs. We all increasingly face the ideas and knowledge claims, too. The cover story in *Time* magazine informs the everyday queries and choices of Christian people. Eventually such ideas make it into the educational system as the received wisdom of the culture with which to disciple the next generation.

TWO ARGUMENTS IN REBUTTAL

This chapter can only go a short distance toward addressing the problem I have described in broad strokes. I'll offer two brief arguments in answering this challenge to the Faith. The first is a "presuppositional" argument, the second a "historical evidences" argument. The first is by far the most important, but I will only state it, as it has been said many times before by many other people. The second is only an auxiliary argument, but it offers the peculiar comforts of a big picture perspective—when built upon the first argument.

First, what God has said about human nature, our problems, and the only Redeemer is true. His truth is reliable. What the Bible says about people will never be destroyed by any neurological or genetic finding. The Bible is an anvil that has worn out a thousand hammers. Neurology and genetics are finding *lots* of interesting facts. New findings will enable doctors to cure a few diseases, which is a genuine good. More power to them, and we will all be the beneficiaries. But biopsychiatry cannot explain, nor will it ever explain, what we actually are. All people *are* in the image of God and depend on God body and soul. The ability even to figure out the human genome or design a PET scan is God-given. Furthermore, all people *are* morally insane with sin, living as if we were gods, even while God restrains sin's logical outworking. That's why the implications, applications, and hopes of neurobiologists' findings combine the good with the terrifying and perverse.

Biopsychiatrists and microbiological researchers interpret their findings and determine the implications through a grid that is bent with sin. At the price of curing the few, biopsychiatrists will mislead the many. *They* do not act as their own theory ought to predict, as machines or mere organisms. They act like people made in the image of God and misdirected by sinfulness. Let God be found true and every man a liar. And they can be redeemed, personally as well as intellectually and practically. God's children *are* in Jesus, and learn to love Jesus, changing gradually from insanity to wisdom. That is the presuppositional argument. The Bible's presuppositions are not contrary to the facts of neurobiology, any more than they are contrary to the facts of suffering, socialization, war, sexuality, emotions, or history. Christianity is the grand "synthesis," the unifying "theory," the truth.

That leads to my second argument against the biopsychologizing of human existence: "This, too, will pass." It is helpful to get a bit of historical perspective. Recognize that we are in the midst of the *third* major biopsychiatric wave over the past 140 years. In each case a new bit of knowledge or a new efficacy was extrapolated into vast hopes for solving the ills of humankind. In each previous case, biopsychiatry did a little bit of good and left a lot of disillusionment.

The first wave lasted from after the Civil War until about 1910. New neurological knowledge—e.g., localizing certain brain functions because of the effects of head wounds received in the war—was generalized into attempts to define and treat problems in living medically. "Neurasthenia" or "weak nerves" became the catch-all explanation for commonplace anxiety, depression, aimless living, irritability, and addiction to vices. Various modes of strengthening nerves were employed: rest, diet, walks in fresh country air, working on a farm, avoiding stress, drugs.

From a somewhat different angle, Ivan Pavlov's physiological psychology in the 1890s was a primitive attempt to reduce human existence to a mosaic of neuro-electrical activity in the cortex. His experiments also offered a crude demonstration that behavior and glandular function could sometimes be manipulated. Pavlov's mentor, Sechenov, had defined his materialist philosophy with the following programmatic statement that the student took to heart: "The brain secretes thought." That is an astonishing metaphor, and demonstrates the force and logic of the biologizing worldview.

This first biopsychological fad faded as its significant efficacies proved to be limited or little more than common sense. Its failure to cure the human condition became all too obvious, and something more attractive and comprehensive came along. Freudian psychology swept in, bringing the first "talking cure" or psychotherapy, with behaviorism and behavioral therapy following shortly thereafter. This first wave hasn't completely disappeared, however. One still occasionally meets an elderly person who mentions that so-and-so suffers from "weak nerves," an echo of that 1880s euphemism for the sins of anxiety and grumbling.

The second biological wave, during the 1940s and 1950s, was constructed on the efficacy of three newly discovered medical treatments for disturbed people: electro-convulsive therapy and lobotomy in the 1940s, and the phenothiazine family of drugs in the 1950s. By using shock therapy, destroying brain cells, or administering thought-stabilizing medication, doctors could tinker with the body's electrical system, localized brain functions, and chemistry. Mood, behavior, and thought processes were all affected. But this biopsychiatric wave receded as vast hopes were dashed by intractable realities. Some symptoms were alleviated, but people weren't *really* changed . . . and the side effects were dreadful. With a rush of new psychotherapies in the 1960s—family systems, reality therapy, group therapy, etc.—biopsychiatry was buried from public view. ECT and the phenothiazines linger on, but no one attaches vast hopes to them any more. They are in the dreary, use-when-nothing-else-works part of the psychiatric arsenal.

The third wave is now upon us. It glitters with the same bright hopes as its predecessors, though of course it appears much more sophisticated. (Similarly, phenothiazines seemed very sophisticated in comparison with "rest cure" and lobotomy.) Again, the new knowledge is generated by striking new abilities to localize brain functions: now MRIs teach us, not the sequelae of bullet wounds. The new drugs don't have the disturbing and visible side effects that used to leave patients dry-mouthed, rigid, and dopey. No one pushes an ice pick in through the eye socket anymore and twists it around in the cerebral cortex (the way lobotomies were done). The brain may not be a gland secreting thought, but it *is* an electrochemical organ that produces thought, emotion, and behavior.

We now hear of genetic structures, brain chemistry, and drugs designed to influence very specific neurotransmitter sites and functions. Again, there is some real and fascinating knowledge here. But it is the same *kind* of knowledge as the previous fads, shaped and blown out of proportion by similar myths. The perennial hope is that we will understand and cure what ails us by localizing brain function, greasing the neuroelectrical system, and buoying up our chemistry.

Biopsychiatry will cure a few things, for which we should praise the God of common grace. But in the long run, unwanted and unforeseen side effects will combine with vast disillusionment. The gains will never live up to the promises. And the lives of countless people, whose normal life problems are now being medicated, will not be qualitatively changed and redirected. Only intelligent repentance, living faith, and tangible obedience turn the world upside down. In current euphemisms, we say so-and-so "has" ADD, or "suffers from" anorexia-bulimia, or "is" bipolar. Without in any way minimizing the realities to which such labels are attached, we must say that such supposed diagnostic entities have the same substantiality as "weak nerves."

The Next Wave

This third wave will also pass, though it does seem to have the potential for a decent shelf life because it has good science mixed in with fad and myth. But because there *is* more to human life, no biopsychology can ever satisfy as either explanation or cure. Some new theory will capture the popular fancy—probably a talking cure, a psychology, a meaning system. My guess is that it will be either something "spiritual" or something "social." In the twentieth-century West (and continuing to the present), interest in Eastern and occult religions also came in waves like biopsychiatry, waxing and then waning. A sophisticated and learned neo-Jung might upgrade the sloppy experientialism of New Age and the sentimentality of Gaia into a spiritualized psychology. But we are also about due for a new behavioral theory and therapy, some tough-minded social psychology that pours its intellectual and practical energies into sociocultural conditioning: education, media, recreation, entertainment, family, community, and politics will be where the action is. I'm no prophet, but I am confident—both by presupposition and by historical evidences—that if we wait a few years or decades the cutting edge will no longer be biology, just as it is no longer childhood trauma or how your self-talk affects your self-esteem.

But the fad is currently in full force. The Human Genome Project has some wonderfully savvy publicists on staff who feed us all a stream of tantalizing knowledge bits charged with fantastic implications. I recently read an article saying that we might be able to reverse the aging process and live forever! It was exhilarating stuff, accompanied by the appropriate hand-wringing about ethical implications.

I can't argue with the bits of science cited, but here's what history reminds us. When the gene mapping is complete, when the folks on

Prozac still can't get along with their spouses, when the fountain of youth still does not arrive in a bottle, when money and achievement fail to satisfy, and when your clone grows up to hate you . . . sinners will yet find Christ to be the one we need. Just maybe that next new theory will be something wonderful. Perhaps that next wave of "spirituality" and "sociality" could be Christianity come into its own! That's worth pouring our energies toward! By the grace of God, perhaps he will enable us to bend the course of history to a vigorous revival of Christian life, thought, and practice!

Just maybe that new spirituality and new community will be the body of Jesus Christ growing up into the fullness of the knowledge of Christ. Then, by the grace of the Lord, burned-out codependents, disillusioned Prozac habitués, and people who just realized they'll die anyway will grab at the hem of your clothes saying, "We want to know the Lord. We are tired of fads and disappointed hopes, tired of trying to reduce life to one thing or other that cuts God out of the equation. We need real mercy and tangible hope. We want what you have."

Only the Faith is able to make the grand synthesis, to make all of life hang together: physical existence, social relations, thinking, suffering, emotions, economics . . . as well as "religious" ideas, practice, and experience, both individual and corporate. Biopsychiatry? After discovering some marvels, doing a little bit of good and a lot of harm, and absorbing a lot of time, attention, money, and energy, this too will pass. But the kingdom of God will come to pass and will not pass away.

A CHALLENGE

From the starting point thirty-five years ago, biblical counselors took a position on the relationship between biopsychiatric problems and moral-spiritual problems that has stood up well over time. Probably the most common rule of thumb is "See a doctor for your body. See your pastor, other pastoral counselors, and wise friends for your heart, soul, mind, might, manner of life, and the way to handle sufferings." Jay Adams often urged pastors to work "back-to-back" with M.D.s. He had those he counseled get a physical check-up first to rule out identifiable biological problems. But he also noted that the rule of thumb was only that. It did not answer all ambiguities: "the dividing line between problems caused by organic factors and non-organic factors is often fuzzy."[5] And it failed to describe how counseling ministry always plays a role in addressing the biological: the Christian counselor's work "constantly involves the organic dimension" because sufferers need counsel and prayer along with whatever other forms of aid apply (James 5:13–20).[6] Doctors who have participated in the first thirty-five years of biblical counseling have operated on the common sense assumption that good diagnosis can generally distinguish the truly and decidedly physiological problems from the moral-spiritual problems, whether the latter appear openly or come veiled in psychosomatic symptoms. There has always been a humility about the intricacies of this psychosomatic-whole-with-a-moral-center whom God has made. And there has always been a well-founded confidence that ministry can always give hope and direction, whether the biological problems are medically soluble or whether they remain ambiguous, insoluble, and terminal.

But what if medical doctors and medical research come to say that our emotions, behaviors, and cognitions *are* identifiably biological phenomena in their very essence? that all, or the most significant, problems in living reduce to biology? that your body determines your heart, soul, mind, and might? that a drug can really fix this or that thing that Christians call "sin"? No longer will you be able to say "Go get a medical checkup to find out if there's a physiological cause for this anxiety, this depression, or this distorted thinking." There *will* be such a cause, by definition, in every case. A purported physiological cause for everything will mean a medical treatment for everything, a designer drug to do whatever is needed to make you feel and function in tip-top shape. There won't even be "psychosomatic" problems any more, because the emotional, motivational, behavioral, relational, and cognitive problems registering in physical symptoms will be identified as having a physical cause! They will be *somato*-psychosomatic, so why bother with the intervening variable?

Biblical counselors writing about these issues have always left room for a "gray area" between the physiological and moral-spiritual. Jay Adams described organic causes, moral causes, and areas of ambiguous "other" or "combinations from both" in the causation of bizarre, "schizophrenic" patterns of thinking and behavior. Thus counseling (always indicated) and medical treatment (sometimes called for) were combined flexibly and in various proportions.[7]

Adams and others have always opposed promiscuous use of medications, and left a certain carefully guarded place for medication to help with biologically-grounded problems. Adams affirmed the strategic use of antidepressants: "The physician might uncover some of the infrequent cases of chemically-caused depression and in very serious cases may help the pastor to engage in meaningful counseling by temporarily administering antidepressants."[8] Ed Welch distinguishes those problems that may have a biological component tangled in with moral factors (e.g., some hyperactive kids and some depressions) from those things that are not biologically determined (e.g., heavy drinking and homosexuality).[9]

But what happens when biopsychiatry comes and says, "Eureka! We have identified the gene for schizophrenia and bipolar. We have localized the part of the brain that produces obsessive-compulsive disorder. We have found the neurotransmitter that affects all depressive moods, and we have designed a drug that lifts all bleak moods into a realistic good cheer. We have found the genes both for homosexuality (it is a normal genetic variation) and for alcoholism (we can test for it prenatally and alter it with gene therapy)"?

In such a situation, we who seek to counsel biblically need to say more. And we need to say it carefully, clearly, boldly, and persistently. When medicine seemed to mind its business in the old way, the rule of thumb worked. But when medicine takes some bits of new knowledge and operates in the imperial mode, we need a more discriminating diagnosis and prescription if we are to profit from the common grace goods in medicine, and are to resist being colonialized.

We have work to do. We need to develop our practical theology more fully in order to address the current controversies and to provide guidance for the people of God who will be beset, often confused, and sometimes misled. In many ways, it was "easier" to resist the codependency-dysfunctional family model of the late-1980s or the "Rogers with a dash of Freud" of the 1950s and 1960s. Those were just bad psychologies that fell when measured against the good psychology that the Faith learns from the Bible: the dynamics of human nature, the meaning of sufferings of all sorts, etc.

But biopsychiatry is *medicine,* against which the Faith looks and sounds like just one more "psychology" to be bulldozed away by all-triumphant biological reductionism. When we protest, "But we can *counsel* angry and anxious people to repent and to learn faith and love," we will *sound like* we are asserting something along the lines of "Cast out that demon of cancer" or "Just believe in Jesus, and throw your eyeglasses away." When anger and anxiety are seen as treatable bodily ailments, we will sound like bizarre spiritualizers—even to people in the pews and in other pulpits. We have work to do to protect and build up the body of Christ.

Conclusion

Toward Simplicity

I would not give a fig for the simplicity this side of complexity,
but I would give my life for the simplicity on the other side of complexity.
—Oliver Wendell Holmes

On the near side of complexity is simplistic;
on the far side of complexity is simple.
—Addison Leitch

One of my friends teases me by saying, "You never met a nuance you didn't love." He's right. When writing a sentence I can hardly get from the capital letter to the period without tossing in a nuance—or three nuances—or a half dozen nuances and one seeming contradiction in the light of which the initial point makes wonderful sense, if only we haven't all drowned in the torrent! My friend is embarrassingly right. I do love the variety and variability, the richness and depth, the various perspectives on the same thing.

It's part of why I love counseling. You get to know and love real people. They're never, ever the same: complexity. And, yet, it is uncanny how much we're all so, so alike: simple. It's part of why I love literature and history. A good novelist has an eye and ear for the distinctives of person and place. A good poet feels and finds words for the particularities of experience. A good historian touches and tells the textures of life lived. And we, who never knew those people who lived there back then, we who never had those exact experiences, we see, feel, and touch something of our common humanity.

Jesus spoke exceedingly simple words. When he said, "You serve either God or mammon," he exposed every possible variant on the abuse of money and possessions. He addressed oil sheiks and subsistence farmers, welfare mothers and suburban lawyers. Simple words slice all the way through, to the bottom of each human soul. *You* serve either God or mammon, whoever you are, and however many different ways you do it. A simplicity lays bare evils without number: anxiety or presumption, inferiority or superiority, theft or manipulation, miserliness or indulgence. Jesus' words reveal simple beauties: contentment and gratitude and generosity. Jesus makes us stop to see ourselves in the MRI of God's gaze. But notice, his words don't *eliminate* the necessity for further thought and observation. Rather, they *enable* further thought and observation. In fact, they *mandate* further work, exploring the nuances. How does this culture, that person, in this situation serve or mis-serve? God's gaze teaches you to see; it doesn't tell you not to look. This simplicity teaches us how Jesus sees into and through complexities, varieties, and idiosyncrasies.

Jesus said, "I am the way, the truth, and the life; no one comes to the Father but by me." Simple. In twenty-five words or less, he captures the hopes and fears, the joys and tears, of the whole human race. He snags both the true and the false hopes, in whatever configuration or combination. His words call to each person in every time and place. Come to the Father of life. He exposes every illusory way, every pretender to truth, every promise of life that actually chokes out life. Yet all the details still remain to be noticed and described. All the particulars still need discovering. The simple on the far side of complexity will illuminate, embrace, and change every single one.

The things Jesus speaks convict us of our sin so that we see that we all need his intimate mercy—in the same way, in our own ways. This is the simplicity on the other side of six billion complexities. This simplicity understands and redeems real complexities; it does not erase them, ignore them, or homogenize them. On the far side of all cultural variants and each individual idiosyncrasy are the profoundly simple truths.

Of course, Jesus' words can be *used* simplistically. We can turn heart-searching and life-altering truth into a cookie cutter, pat answer, formula, and quick fix. We can turn a vista gazing at all life into a closet that shuts it out. We can turn marching orders and an open door into reasons to stay home and bar the entrance. That is our problem. We can live on "this side," the near side, of the complexities of the human condition.

And it *is* our problem. We so often and so easily do this. Like a child set down before a grand piano, we mechanically pick out "Mary had a little lamb" with one grubby finger, missing or slurring notes, thinking, "*This* is what playing the piano is all about. This is the Word of God. This is the Gospel. This is the way, the truth, and the life. This is repentance, faith, and obedience. This is the faith delivered once for all to the saints." And in the name of wonderful things, we blunder along ignorant, myopic, and obtuse. In a word, simplistic. The truth on the near side of complexity isn't worth a fig. It doesn't do the jobs that need doing.

We have a big job ahead. To put it a bit more technically, doing practical theology is hard. It's hard to *live your life well*: Practical Theology 101. Hard as it is to be "religious" about religion, it is harder to be simply human: to rejoice always, to pray without ceasing, to give thanks in all circumstances, to treat others with patience and kindness, mercy and generosity. It is hard to remember that God is simply wonderful and worthy, independent of our pains and pleasures. It is hard to remember to cast every care on your Father who cares. It's hard to be needy in Christ's direction whenever you sin and whatever you suffer. It is hard to remember to give thanks for every good thing that ever happens, to thank the Giver who simply *is* good. It is hard to be truly human. I hope that the electrifying joy of Ephesians, the sound comfort of Psalms 10 and 131, and the deeply inviting reasoning of Luke 12 will enter the inner workings of each of our hearts. It is my hope that living faith will bear fruit in intelligent, diligent love.

And it is hard to *think well*: Practical Theology 201. I hope that you have been stimulated and clarified by thinking through defense mechanisms, love languages, unconditional love, feelings, desires, and the rest. It is my deeper hope that you have also learned a way of thinking about people that keeps God in view. Because the next year, the next decade, or the next person you talk with will present you with a new and different spin on life that plausibly excises God. The problems keep changing. The lie is always mutating, like the flu. Last year's vaccine doesn't work any more. Every person and circumstance is different, so the truth will always need to be adapted afresh. It's hard not to be conformed to this world, because the world you face is elastic. Like the sea god Proteus, the lie changes shape at will, like restless waves.

Seeing with New Eyes has aimed to glimpse some of the riches of PT 101 and PT 201. But there are many more wonders for us to consider. We've spoken of God's gaze and intentions. To see more truly (to really see what is) is then to love more wisely (to do what really needs doing). A future book will explore practice and action, those ways of serving others and joining with others that we call "ministry" and "church."

It is hard to *do ministry well:* Practical Theology 301. We can summarize many of Paul's prayers in two longings: to know God better and to love people more intelligently. Both "better" and "more intelligently" demand that we hammer things out into the particulars. What does wise love look like? How do we converse with others in ways that make the right kind of difference? How do we understand the knotty problems of life, so that we can offer people real help? We all know what wise, mutual, life-changing counseling means: "Speaking the truth in love we grow up . . . speak only constructive, timely words that give grace to those who hear . . . encourage one another daily" (Eph. 4:15, 29; Heb. 3:12–13, author's paraphrase). But *how* do we do something that is so easy to say and so hard to do?

It is hard to *do church well:* Practical Theology 401. Church so easily becomes . . . well, becomes "church" (you fill in whatever ruts are most familiar). But if Jesus is full of grace and truth, then it must be possible to form communities more full of grace and truth. By hook or by crook, by blood, sweat, and tears, we can at least row the boat in the right direction. The old saying was *ora et labora:* pray and work. Many elements go into building a community that glorifies God heart, soul, mind, and might. We won't say it all, but we will camp on several things of central importance. The flourishing of wise, mutual, life-changing counseling is one proof that everything else about church is accomplishing what it's supposed to.

A third book planned on these themes of the faith's psychology and the psychological faiths, will aim to define the call of Christian faith in the context of the therapeutic culture in which we live. Some people in the Old Testament were once commended because they "understood the times, with knowledge of what Israel should do" (1 Chron. 12:32). Wisdom is always living wisdom, conditioned by the times in which people live. Christian truth is *eternal* truth, but it is never timeless truth. It is always *timely* truth, addressed to specific people facing specific problems. It is not an assemblage of disembodied propositions, abstract principles, nameless and placeless verities. Almost every page of Scripture contains the names of specific people, places, and circumstances. That's for a reason. Jesus Christ, who is the same yesterday, today, and forever, is forever meeting us, whoever we are right where we are. PT 101 brings Scripture to life. PT 201 reinterprets all of life through God's gaze. PT 301 wrestles out how to speak the truth in love. PT 401 hammers out the shape of communities of faith. And PT 501 reminds us that all these attempts to live Christianly happen in the context of our historical moment.

It is hard to *understand our calling well:* Practical Theology 501. The third book will consider our times, the various models of counseling that compete with Christian counseling worthy of the name Christ.

There are jobs to do. Throughout these books, I will always use the term "biblical counseling" with two different meanings in my mind. These different meanings exist in tension. On the one hand, "biblical counseling" is a *goal* to live and die for. On the other hand, "biblical counseling" is a *current achievement*, partial and imperfect like all human achievements. Imagine a vista of far off snowy mountains, radiant in the morning sun, inconceivably massive: the Jungfrau, Pike's Peak, Mt. Everest, Kilamanjaro, Mauna Loa. In the foreground are the plains or the foothills on which we toil toward the high mountains. When I get eloquent about biblical counseling, I have in view the far off snowy mountains: our goal. Restoring Christ to counseling and counseling to the church is a direction, a task, a trajectory. When I say what *I* think biblical counseling is, or voice a criticism of biblical counseling, I'm plodding across the plains and up the foothills of our current attainment. We surely have notable deficits in the maturity of our understanding of Scripture, in the breadth and depth of our practical theological understanding, in the skill and effectiveness of our love, in the viability of our current institutional structures and ministry roles. There is always a gap between aspiration and achievement. We may be simplistic, mishandling certain complexities, when we need to become simple enough to enter and handle every complexity with wise love.

But it really matters to aim in the right direction. If we are leaping toward the snowy mountains, or running, maybe walking, even plodding, or limping, even if we are barely creeping along, in fact, even if we are only facing in the right direction, momentarily stuck, but at least with good intentions, it makes all the difference in the world. We, the people of Christ, will get there. Someday. All together. Better to be fighting just to face in the right direction than to run fast in the wrong direction. God will one day fulfill every good intention prompted by faith (2 Thess. 1:11).

These essays are not systematic or comprehensive. But I hope you have discerned already (and will discern) that something both systematic and comprehensive threads through the whole. There is an underlying unity. This sampler is not random and disconnected. I have sought to put in place a few signposts to the place of wonders. The far off snowy mountains are real. God's people will one day speak the truth, the whole truth, and nothing but the truth, in perfect love, and nothing but love. We can climb in that direction now. The gaze and intentions of the real Christ can in fact shape the interactions between real people in the real world. Grasp that reality: living faith working out into intelligent and purposeful love. Hope for that. Aim for it. Cultivate it. Pray in that direction. Counsel in that direction. Preach in that direction. Live in that direction.

This is the purpose of all that God has done in Christ. He who promises is faithful, and he will do it.

Notes

Introduction: The Gaze of God

1. C. S. Lewis, "Is Theology Poetry?" *They Asked for a Paper* (London: Geoffrey Bles, 1962), 165.

2. Until 1992, this journal was called the *Journal of Pastoral Practice*. Chapters 11 and 13 in this collection appeared under that name.

3. Dietrich Bonhoeffer, "Confession and Communion," in *Life Together* (New York: Harper & Row, 1954), 118–19.

Chapter 1: Counsel Ephesians

1. Historical theology, the "church history" piece of the theological curriculum, also makes an important auxiliary contribution to practical theology. We follow behind many interpreters and misinterpreters, many practitioners and mispractitioners of this letter over the course of almost two millennia.

2. As an aside, Ephesians resonates with each of the Ten Commandments, though only the fifth is directly quoted. The language of the coveting command is specifically reiterated in 5:3, 5, and more broadly applied in discussions of lust-*epithymia* in 2:3 and 4:22. The false testimony command threads through a wide-ranging treatment of harmful and constructive speech (Eph. 4:25–27, 29–32). Positive implications of the theft command are developed in 4:28. The adultery command is broadened to include general immorality and filthy-mindedness (5:3–5). The murder command is also broadened, with several pointed comments about anger and the gracious alternatives (4:26–27, 31–32).

The Sabbath command appears remotely, in the call for kindness to servants, and perhaps in the seating of Christ as rest from his re-creation labor. The command not to take the name of the Lord in vain appears in broad strokes in the call not to return to a futile life (4:17–24; 5:5–11), and perhaps in its narrower aspect in 5:3. The idolatry command is given its wide, metaphorical application in 5:5, where it merges with the desire-drivenness of the tenth command. The command to have no God but the

259

holy Lord obviously runs through the entire letter. Furthermore, the two great commandments that summarize the will of God—love the Lord God and love neighbor—permeate the entire book, appearing with particular directness in 6:24 and 5:1–2.

3. Controversy can be a good thing, too. In God's providence, it stimulates the elaboration and living application of truth. In the long run, controversy purifies the faith and practice of the church. The Bible abounds with controversy. Some sort of tension, debate, confusion, threat, division, or need stood behind every New Testament letter. We can't and shouldn't avoid all controversies. I hope that the body of Christ will grow stronger and wiser in the process of hammering out more particular differences. Speaking the truth in love, we grow up in all things into Christ.

CHAPTER 2: WHO IS GOD?

1. Granted, we are not the literal "you" for whom Paul actually prayed and from whom he sought prayer. But throughout the letter we ought to have no trouble hearing ourselves addressed wherever you, your, we, us, and our are mentioned.

2. Patrick O'Brian, *The Far Side of the World* (New York: W. W. Norton, 1984), 201–3.

3. Of course, the vast majority of counselors—all secular and many Christian—err in the opposite direction. They assert the human ingredient stripped both of Scripture and of living, verbalized faith in the present Redeemer.

4. There are times to use indirect or even ambiguous words, of course, just as there are times simply to be quiet or to say, "There's nothing more to say." But the direct battle for the souls of men ought to mean that those things, too, are strategic choices coming from wisdom, not simply unexamined habits.

5. There are times to hold back the full message temporarily for strategic reasons, but that ought to be a conscious choice.

CHAPTER 3: GODLY ROLES AND RELATIONSHIPS: EPHESIANS 5:21–6:9

1. Ephesians does teach one distinction among people within the common calling. God has given certain people as gifts to the rest in doing the ministry of his Word (Eph. 4:11). Their task is to equip everyone else within the body, so that all of us will do the work of ministry (4:12–13), learn to avoid the world's lies (4:14), do our part with our words and gifts (4:15–16), and change our thinking, motives, and lifestyle (4:17–6:9), participating in Christ's victory over darkness (6:10–20).

2. Note that the church is likened to the *wife* of Christ—imperfect, in need of cleansing and transformation by the word of grace. The word "bride" does not appear in Ephesians, though theological shorthand often uses that word to describe the church's wifely relationship to Jesus. Wife is not only literal, but better, because Paul stresses the ongoing *process* of a one flesh relationship with someone who has failings. We are not yet the radiant bride, adorned in all her glory. The Holy Spirit al-

ludes to the future, bridal glory of the wife in 5:27. One might well say that the glories of the wedding ceremony occur *after* the give-and-take of living as husband and wife with Christ! In Revelation 21:2 the *bride* is finally revealed perfected, in all her adornment. Christ's wife gets better looking with age—cleansed from every spot and wrinkle (5:27)—and the wedding celebration comes at the end of that part of the story!

3. The language of beauty, glory, radiance, and adornment is particularly appropriate regarding these issues. Eph. 5:27, 1 Peter 3:1–5, and Titus 2:10 use language of adornment and glorious beauty to comment on the results of rightly ordering domestic relationships. God's glory shines in us with remarkable brilliance when we get these difficult things right. The opposite is shame and dishonor to God. (See Titus 2:5 and 1 Peter 2:12 and the stains and dishevelment of the Wife in Ephesians 5:27.)

4. Just as God's directives to "kings and subjects" legitimately extend to other governmental arrangements, so the Bible's commands to "masters and slaves" apply in principle to the very different economic relationships of our corporate economy.

5. Sometimes in the Bible's discussion of these things, the semantic field broadens to embrace the common call as well as the particular focus. For example, the call to "honor" another is usually applied to those who stand under another: child, slave, flock, and citizen (Eph. 6:2; 1 Tim. 6:1; 1 Tim. 5:17; Rom. 13:7). But honor should be shown to one's wife as if she were a precious, cherished, and fragile vase; to widows who have earned their gray hairs of wisdom; to one another in the body of Christ; and to all human beings, because the opposite attitude would be disrespect (1 Peter 3:7; 1 Tim. 5:3; Rom. 12:10; 1 Peter 2:17). Similarly, the call to live as a servant of another is naturally applied to slaves and to children (Eph. 6:7; 1 Tim. 6:2; Phil. 2:22), but then it is also generalized to everyone: "serve one another in love" (Gal. 5:13).

6. The "egalitarian" point of view drifts in this direction.

7. Mothers are included in the "father" role of Eph. 6:4. They are mentioned twice in the previous verses (6:1–3), where "parents" and "father and mother" receive their children's obedience and honor. Why are only "fathers" pointedly addressed in 6:4? Some teach that fathers are particularly tempted to provoke or discourage children through harshness and domineering (thus the negative commands of 6:4 and Col. 3:21). Others suggest that fathers are uniquely tempted to neglect their responsibility to get involved and nurture their children (thus the positive command of 6:4).

There may be a grain of truth in these observations. However, mothers are tempted to identical sins. I suggest that Paul is not making an implied statement about temptations supposed to characterize fathers alone. Rather he uses "fathers" to highlight the *pattern* that runs through this entire section. God is the *Father* who abounds in Psalm 103 tenderness, generosity, wisdom, and mercy; we are all *children* who have received all his benefits. God's children who are also "fathers" (i.e., both fathers and mothers) have particular responsibilities to image the Father by loving and guiding rather than domineering or neglecting. Both tenderness and teaching are ways both mothers and fathers image God the Father. (See Ps. 103, Isa. 49:15; 1 Thess. 2:7–8; 2:11, and Prov. 31:26.)

8. The "traditionalist" point of view tends to drift in this direction.

9. Ephesians 5:21—"submitting to one another in the fear of Christ"—does not wash out the particular distinctions that 5:22–6:9 teaches, contrary to some opinions. Paul's logic in 5:21 is not unambiguous, but the net effect is the same whichever way the verse is interpreted. On the one hand, if Eph. 5:21 expresses the common call, then it is analogous to Gal. 5:13. The Spirit uses servant and submission language to establish the general attitude that saturates all relationships of grace (see note 5 above). The call sets up, rather than eliminates, the particular emphasis either on submission or on loving nurture in what follows. Husbands and wives will express their dedication to the Lord and each other in different ways. Note how "submit" and "fear" are pointedly repeated as characteristics for wives as Paul develops the analogy of church and Christ (and note the parallelism within all role relationships).

On the other hand, the force of 5:21 may be something more like shorthand for, "Rightly order your domestic relationships," as a segue into the first party that Paul will discuss. As an introductory and transitional statement it uses one part of a more complex thought to stand for the whole. The entire thought would be something like this: "Submitting to one another in the fear of Christ [and loving one another like Christ loved you and gave himself, in each case emphasize what is appropriate to your particular role relationships]." The tight syntactical link between 5:21 and 5:22 is often obscured both in discussions and in Bible versions: the verb from 5:21 serves in 5:22.

If Paul had chosen to open each pair of relationships the opposite way, beginning with husbands, he might have said in 5:21, "Loving one another, as Christ loved the church, husbands [should love] your own wives. . . ." Then when he switched to wives (the equivalent of 5:25), he would have said, "Wives, as the church submits to Christ, so also the wives [submit] to their husbands in everything." Whether 5:21 is a heading for all six role relationships (common calling), or a transition that predominantly applies to the three relationships of subordination (particular focus), the net effect is the same as we receive the total thought world of our Lord regarding these matters.

CHAPTER 4: PEACE, BE STILL: PSALM 131

1. Isaiah wrote, "The wicked are like the tossing sea, for it cannot be quiet, and its waters toss up refuse and mud. 'There is no peace,' says my God, 'for the wicked'" (57:20–21).

2. Interestingly, the name we most often use, "Christian," is used only three times in the Bible. It is a more impersonal name someone else might use to label you (Acts 11:26; Acts 26:28; 1 Peter 4:16). But these other names are intended to resonate more with your internal sense of identity-in-relationship.

3. In a wondrous image, Shakespeare's Bassanio speaks of all the deceptive show that arises because "hearts are all as false as stairs of sand" (*The Merchant of Venice*, III:2).

Chapter 5: Why Me? Comfort from Psalm 10

1. The translation that appears is largely from the New American Standard Bible (1995). I have made several minor alterations, breaking compound sentences into shorter sentences, and changing "mischief" to "trouble" in verses 7 and 14. The only substantial change is in the second half of verse 2, discussed in note 3 below.

2. This difficult sentence either means "the wicked *burn after* the afflicted" or "the wicked *burn* the afflicted." The first case describes the hostility and passion of harmful people. The second case describes the sufferer's hurt and fear. Either is consistent with the rest of Scripture. I will take it in the first sense, following this translation.

3. This is the one place I have departed from the NASB, which has "Let them [the wicked] be caught in the plots which they have devised." The Hebrew could either be further description of the wicked (as I have taken it) or a request to God that they reap what they sowed. Either is consistent with the rest of Scripture. A call for the wicked to reap what they sow occurs later in the psalm and will be discussed in Section III.

4. In many psalms that lament suffering and cry for deliverance, the sufferer also confesses his own sins: 25, 38, 40, 69, 143.

5. Paul does not ignore the suffering of the innocent victim who loves God. He discusses this at length in Rom. 8, quoting Ps. 44, another psalm of affliction, in 8:36. He embeds our sufferings in God's larger purposes.

6. "Mighty ones" might allude to the claws and fangs of the lion as it rips, kills, and feeds on its prey.

7. This psalm is not for those whose sense of "brokenness" primarily arises from their own thwarted lusts. It is for those who are truly "poor in spirit" and need God.

8. In Helen's case, the church did a wonderful job. But sufferers can still find hope and God's particular grace when normal social supports have been destroyed, as did Corrie ten Boom in *The Hiding Place*.

9. "Fire and brimstone" have fallen into disrepute in part because they are often only one-third understood. Yes, God delivers a *dreadful warning to the ungodly*. But destruction of evil is also the Lord's *loving rescue of his own people*, which generates hope amid affliction. This is not inconsistent with loving and forgiving our enemies, and praying for their repentance; to do anything else would usurp God's right to judge (see Rom. 12:14–21). Judgment is also presented as God's *demonstration of his own glory and righteousness*, prompting wonder and rejoicing in those who love him. We will someday marvel at the God who brings full and final relief. (See the fire and brimstone of Gen. 19:24; Ps. 11:6; Ezek. 38:22; Rev. 14:10; 20:10; cf. 2 Thess. 1:3–10 and 2 Peter 2:6–10.)

10. Cited in Charles Spurgeon's *Treasury of David* regarding this verse.

CHAPTER 6: DON'T WORRY: LUKE 12:22–34

1. Many biblical quotations in this chapter are the author's paraphrase.

PART 2: REINTERPRETING LIFE

1. Baal worship, armed resistance to Babylon, and religious circumcision are no longer live questions (the themes endure, however). But some old debates never leave us. The voices transcribed in Proverbs still sound forth today: seducers unto criminal, immoral, or self-serving behavior. And the stoic philosophers of Acts 17:18 have been recast into a modern counseling idiom by cognitive-behavioral psychology.

CHAPTER 8: I AM MOTIVATED WHEN I FEEL DESIRE

1. A fear is simply desire turned on its head: "I *don't want.*"
2. Abraham Maslow, *Toward a Psychology of Being,* 2d ed. (New York: Van Nostrand Reinhold, 1968), 22.
3. Ibid., 22–23.
4. See the chapter, "X-ray Questions," for many other doorways into the engine room of our motivations.
5. The Old Testament typically focuses on idolatry as the way people go astray. This doesn't mean that the Old Testament is externalistic. Visible idolatry simply registers, for all to see, the failure to love the Lord God with heart, soul, mind, and might; it registers an internal defection. There are places where the problem of idolatry is turned into a metaphor for the most basic internalized sin (see Ezek. 14), and visible idolatry always expressed a defection of heart from God. There are places where the human heart is described as insane (Eccl. 9:3), evil (Gen. 6:5), full of cravings and lies (Num. 11–25), uncircumcised, hard, blind, and so forth. The New Testament also equates sinful desires with idolatry, metaphorically, on several occasions (see Col. 3:5; Eph. 5:5). Idolatry can summarize every false, life-controlling master (1 John 5:21).
6. We often hear warnings against externalistic religion. But internalistic religion creates equally serious problems. Christians often seek some experience or feeling, some sense of total brokenness, some comprehensive inward transformation—and miss that biblical change is practical and progressive, inside and out.
7. Col. 3:5; 2 Peter 2:10.
8. John Calvin, *Institutes of the Christian Religion,* translated by Ford Lewis Battles (Philadelphia: Westminster Press), 604.
9. Eph. 4:22.
10. Gen. 6:5; Ps.19:12; Eccl. 9:3; Jer. 17:9; Eph. 4:17–22; 1 Tim. 1:13; 2 Peter 2:10–22.

11. John Calvin, *Institutes*, 65, 108.

12. Eph. 4:22 (cf. 4:17–19, which reinforces the notion of a characteristic lifestyle); 1 Peter 1:14.

13. Gal. 5:16–25; Rom. 6:16–18; 8:12–16; Ps. 23:3.

14. The following passages get a start on this question. For each passage ask, "What does this person *really* want, long for, pursue, delight in?" Pss. 42:1–2; 63:1–8; 73:25–28; 80;. 90:8–17; Prov. 2:1–6; 3:13–18; 8:11; Isa. 26:8–9; Matt. 5:6; 6:9–13, 6:19–33; 13:45–46; Luke 11:9–13; Rom. 5:1–11; 8:18–25; 9:1–3; 2 Cor. 5:8–9; Phil. 1:18–25; 3:8–11; 3:20–21; 2 Tim. 2:22; 3:12; 1 Peter 1:13; 2:2; Rev. 22:20.

Chapter 11: Human Defensiveness: The Third Way

1. Herbert Butterfield, *The Origins of Modern Science* (New York: Basic Books, 1981), 1.

2. Antoine Lavoisier, *The Elements of Chemistry*, trans. in *Great Books of the Western World*, vol. 45 (Chicago: Encyclopedia Brittanica, 1952), 1.

3. Friedrich Nietzsche, *Beyond Good and Evil*, trans. Helen Zimmern (London: T. N. Foulis, 1914), 86.

4. T. S. Eliot, "Burnt Norton" in *Four Quartets* (New York: Harcourt, Brace & World, 1971), 14.

5. J. G. Machen, *Christianity and Liberalism* (Grand Rapids: Eerdmans, 1923) 47f.

6. Albert Bandura, *Social Learning Theory* (Englewood Cliffs, N.J.: Prentice-Hall, 1973), 158.

7. Eph. 2:1–3 is an exceedingly rich summary passage that includes all of these. Rom. 6:11–22; Gal. 5:16–24; Rom. 12:2; 2 Tim. 2:26 describe each in turn, as well as the option: "slavery" to righteousness, to the desires of the Spirit, to God's will, a "slavery" which is freedom.

Chapter 12: The Ambiguously Cured Soul

1. An earlier version of this discussion appears as one section in my chapter, "A Flourishing of Fresh Wisdoms" by Johnson, Gary, and Fowler White, eds., *Whatever Happened to the Reformation?* (Phillipsburg, N.J.: P&R, 2001), 205–28.

2. See Edward T. Welch, *When People Are Big and God Is Small* (Phillipsburg, N.J.: P&R, 1997); David Powlison, "Crucial Issues in Contemporary Biblical Counseling" (in Powlison, ed., *Counsel the Word*, Glenside, Pa.: CCEF, 1997); Powlison, "How Shall We Cure Troubled Souls?" in John Armstrong, ed., *The Coming Evangelical Crisis* (Chicago: Moody, 1996); Powlison, "Idols of the Heart and 'Vanity Fair' "(*Journal of Biblical Counseling*, 13:2, 1995). See also numerous other articles in the *Journal of Biblical Counseling*.

3. Larry Crabb, *Inside Out* (Colorado Springs: NavPress, 1988).

4. Edward T. Welch, *When People are Big and God is Small* (Phillipsburg, N.J.: P&R, 1997) provides a rich and biblical discussion of both problem and solution.

CHAPTER 14: LOVE SPEAKS MANY LANGUAGES FLUENTLY

1. Gary Chapman, *The Five Love Languages: How to Express Heartfelt Commitment to Your Mate* (Chicago: Northfield, 1995). Chapman and several coauthors have written follow-up books addressing children and teens more particularly. Other popular books in the same genre include Willard Harley's *His Needs, Her Needs* ("Become aware of each other's emotional needs, and learn to meet them. . . . The ten emotional needs are admiration, affection, conversation, domestic support, family commitment, financial support, honesty and openness, physical attractiveness, recreational companionship, and sexual fulfillment"); and John Gray's *Men Are from Mars, Women Are from Venus* ("Men and women give the kind of love they need and not what the opposite sex needs. Men primarily need a kind of love that is trusting, accepting, and appreciative. Women primarily need a kind of love that is caring, understanding, and respectful.").

2. Notice, I'm not saying that a parent should not "speak Johnny's language" as part of attempting to love him well. I'm questioning Chapman's interpretation of what such intelligent love means and what it does.

3. Anne Lamott, *Bird by Bird* (New York: Alfred A. Knopf, 1995). She tells the story of her faith in *Traveling Mercies* (New York: Alfred A. Knopf, 2000).

4. Again, remember that we are criticizing the premises, explanatory dynamic, and goals of 5LL, not the call to treat others with thoughtful generosity.

CHAPTER 15: BIOLOGICAL PSYCHIATRY

1. *Inside Out* is different from *Love Is a Choice* in ways that reflect favorably on Crabb. But both teach that the underlying mechanism of the soul is the same needy, wounded, longing, empty heart that has been relationally victimized and deprived.

2. Peter Kramer, *Listening to Prozac: A Psychiatrist Explores Antidepressant Drugs and the Remaking of the Self* (New York: Viking Press, 1993).

3. Alun Anderson, "Are you a machine of many parts?" *The World in 1999* (London: *The Economist*, 1999), 109–10.

4. It is perhaps not surprising that people usually think of themselves as machines only when things are not going well. Most people, scientists included, still take credit for their achievements, abilities, successful choices, and opinions, just as they did when dysfunctional families were the rage.

5. Jay Adams, *The Christian Counselor's Manual* (Phillipsburg, N.J.: P&R, 1973), 439.

6. See Jay Adams, *Competent to Counsel* (Phillipsburg, N.J.: P&R, 1970), 37–40; Jay Adams, *Ready to Restore* (Phillipsburg, N.J.: P&R, 1981), 32; Jay Adams,

The Christian Counselor's Manual (Phillipsburg, N.J.: P&R, 1973), 437–43. The discussion in *CCM* well captures subtleties and ambiguities in the relationship between moral and organic problems, and thus between M.D.s and pastors.

7. Jay Adams, "The Christian Approach to Schizophrenia," *Journal of Biblical Counseling*, 14:1 (Fall 1995), 27–33; reprinted in David Powlison, ed., *Counsel the Word* (Glenside, Pa.: CCEF, 1997), 52–57.

8. Jay Adams, "Depression," *The Encyclopedia of Christianity*, vol. 3 (Marshallton, Del.: The National Foundation for Christian Education, 1972), 362–63.

9. Edward T. Welch, *Blame It on the Brain?* (Phillipsburg, N.J.: P&R, 1999).

Index of Scripture

David Powlison is the editor of the *Journal of Biblical Counseling* and a member of the faculty and counseling staff at the Christian Counseling and Educational Foundation in Glenside, Pennsylvania. He also teaches at Westminster Theological Seminary.

Powlison grew up in Hawaii and graduated from Harvard University. He became a Christian while working in a psychiatric hospital, through the ministry of his college friend, Bob Kramer, to whom this book is dedicated. Powlison earned an M.Div from Westminster Theological Seminary, and an M.A. and Ph.D. from the University of Pennsylvania.

Powlison is the author of *Power Encounters: Reclaiming Spiritual Warfare; Competent to Counsel? The History of a Conservative Protestant Anti-Psychiatry Movement*; and numerous articles. He has written many booklets in the Resources for Changing Lives booklet series, and edited *Counsel the Word*.

Powlison is a board member and Fellow of the National Association of Nouthetic Counselors.

Powlison and his wife live in Glenside, Pennsylvania. They have three children.

RESOURCES FOR CHANGING LIVES

Addictions—A Banquet in the Grave: Finding Hope in the Power of the Gospel. Edward T. Welch shows how addictions result from a worship disorder—idolatry—and how they are overcome by the power of the gospel. 978-0-87552-606-5

Age of Opportunity: A Biblical Guide to Parenting Teens, 2d ed. Paul David Tripp uncovers the heart issues affecting parents' relationship with their teenagers. 978-0-87552-605-8

Blame It on the Brain? Distinguishing Chemical Imbalances, Brain Disorders, and Disobedience. Edward T. Welch compares the roles of the brain and the heart in problems such as alcoholism, depression, ADD, and homosexuality. 978-0-87552-602-7

Instruments in the Redeemer's Hands: People in Need of Change Helping People in Need of Change. Paul David Tripp demonstrates how God uses his people, who need change themselves, as tools of change in the lives of others. 978-0-87552-607-2

Seeing with New Eyes: Counseling and the Human Condition through the Lens of Scripture. David Powlison embraces, probes, and unravels counseling and the problems of daily life with a biblical perspective. 978-0-87552-608-9

Step by Step: Divine Guidance for Ordinary Christians. James C. Petty sifts through approaches to knowing God's will and illustrates how to make biblically wise decisions. 978-0-87552-603-4

War of Words: Getting to the Heart of Your Communication Struggles. Paul David Tripp takes us beyond superficial solutions in the struggle to control our tongues. 978-0-87552-604-1

When People Are Big and God Is Small: Overcoming Peer Pressure, Codependency, and the Fear of Man. Edward T. Welch exposes the spiritual dimensions of pride, defensiveness, people-pleasing, needing approval, "self-esteem," etc. 978-0-87552-600-3

Booklet Series: *A.D.D.; Anger; Angry at God?; Depression; Domestic Abuse; Forgiveness; God's Love; Guidance; Homosexuality; "Just One More"; Marriage; Motives; Pornography; Pre-Engagement; Priorities; Sexual Sin; Suffering; Suicide; Teens and Sex; Thankfulness; Why Me?*

FOR FURTHER INFORMATION

Speaking engagements with authors in this series may be arranged by calling The Christian Counseling and Educational Foundation at (215) 884-7676.

Videotapes and audio cassettes by authors in this series may be ordered through Resources for Changing Lives at (800) 318-2186.

For a complete catalog of titles from P&R Publishing, call (800) 631-0094.

OTHER TITLES OF INTEREST:

Addictions—A Banquet in the Grave: Finding Hope in the Power of the Gospel (978-0-87552-606-5) by Edward T. Welch

Growing Up Christian (978-0-87552-611-9) by Karl Graustein with Mark Jacobsen

Idols of the Heart: Learning to Long for God Alone (978-0-87552-198-5) by Elyse Fitzpatrick

Instruments in the Redeemer's Hands: People in Need of Change Helping People in Need of Change (978-0-87552-607-2) by Paul David Tripp

Pleasing People: How Not to be an "Approval Junkie" (978-1-59638-055-4) by Lou Priolo

When People Are Big and God Is Small: Overcoming Peer Pressure, Codependency, and the Fear of Man (978-0-87552-600-3) by Edward T. Welch

For more information on these and other titles, please visit our website:

WWW.PRPBOOKS.COM